LITTLE DANCER

T0347696

LITTLE DANCER

Melanie Leschallas

unbound

First published in 2022

Unbound
Level 1, Devonshire House, One Mayfair Place, London W1J 8AJ
www.unbound.com
All rights reserved

Text design by PDQ Digital Media Solutions Ltd.

A CIP record for this book is available from the British Library

ISBN 978-1-80018-120-5 (paperback)
ISBN 978-1-80018-121-2 (ebook)

Printed in Great Britain by Clays Ltd, Elcograf S.p.A

1 3 5 7 9 8 6 4 2

For Craig, Max and Rosa

PART ONE

'The vicious muzzle of this little girl hardly in puberty, flower of the gutter, is unforgettable'

Revue de Paris, 1881

PROLOGUE

Tuesday, 23 May 1871
Montmartre, Paris

Halfway up Rue Lepic, on the eastern side where the narrow cobbled street snakes sharply to the right before climbing steeply up to the heights of Montmartre, there's a small, tumbledown house jammed between two much larger ones, like an afterthought. Serge van Goethem, a Belgian tailor, lives here with his wife and two daughters.

Gigi van Goethem has not slept. She lay on her bed in her underclothes once the monstrous sound from the *mitrailleuse*, that infernal newfangled volley gun, down on Place Blanche finally stopped at around three or four in the morning, and nearly dropped off. But then her neighbour, Emma Béranger, rapped on the door to share a cup of wine and whisper the latest news between sips. The order is that nobody must leave their house until further notice. Batignolles has fallen, Clichy too. Only the eastern districts are holding strong. Thirty thousand Versaillais are approaching from the west. Dabrowski is dead. Emma must have seen the look on Gigi's face because when they'd drained the cup Emma put her arm around Gigi and assured her that there was still hope, that neither of their husbands' names appeared on the latest list of fallen citizens.

It's over, Gigi had muttered to herself as she peered through a broken blind and watched Emma run across the street back to the bakery. *It's over.*

Later that day Marie van Goethem is sitting under the kitchen table watching her mother make soup for her father and the other Communards who should surely be here very soon. Her mother looks strange. Her body is slumped forward over the cooking pot and one of her hands is braced on the draining board as if she's in pain. It makes Marie's empty stomach sink to see the bow of Gigi's apron wonky and half undone, the damp strands of red hair snaking down her long pale neck. Usually, her hair is piled up and perfectly pinned with three pearl-tipped hairclips. There used to be five but the other two went to the pawn shop a month or so ago.

'Marie, will you please stop bloody dreaming. Be a good citizen for Papa, *ma petite*. Come and help me chop these vegetables. I'll let you have the sharp knife.'

'Why can't Antoinette do it?'

'She's with Emma and Paul over at the bakery. And anyway you need to start learning how to cook.'

Marie feels too heavy to move. 'In a moment, Maman.'

Steam blooms up from the pot. A whiff of stewed vegetables mingles with burning oil from the lamp on the mantelpiece and some other smell she can't quite place.

It's so quiet. Usually, at this hour, there would be the low rumble of carts going to the market, hammering starting up from the building works at the top of the Butte de Montmartre, the smug trit-trot of scrubbed horses taking barouches to their masters on Boulevard de Clichy. This silence unnerves her.

'When will Papa be home?'

No answer. Marie's copy of *Fantine* is propped up on her knee. Her father gave it to her as an early sixth birthday present a week ago. Before he went off to fight, he used to plonk her on his knee and read her a few paragraphs every night. Marie can't read yet, but she has been learning to form letters at the new school set up by the Commune. Marie traces the inlaid gold letters on the spine of the book with her finger, breathes in the smell of leather mingled with Papa's pipe smoke and prays that he comes home soon. The floor is hard and cold but there's nowhere else to sit, apart from Papa's chair and it would be wrong to sit there. All the other chairs have been taken to the barricade at the Porte de Montmartre along with Gigi's beloved mahogany dresser. The dresser belonged to Gigi's grandmother and has always been too big and too ornate for every apartment and house they've lived in, too *bourgeois*. At least that's what Serge, Marie's father, muttered as he and three comrades carted it out last week.

Marie hugs her knees to her chest, lays her head on *Fantine* and watches the light filtering in through broken shutters, making patterns on the wall where the dresser used to be. Oh well, soon it will all be over. She will go with her father to collect Gigi's dresser from the barricade. The shops will open up like spring flowers and the world will be full of light again. Papa's chair is still there by the unlit fire and soon he will come home and fill it. Perhaps if she imagines him sitting there hard enough, she can make it happen. Marie longs for him to burst in sighing and exclaiming at the injustice of the world. He'll throw his hat on the table, kick off his boots, rub his eyes, collapse into the chair, lay his dear head in the worn halo near the top,

3

his fingers worrying at the holes in the winged back right there where he used to stash his tailor's needles. She'll wait until he lights his pipe then jump onto his lap and try to spot some words she knows while he reads to her.

A yelp wakes her. Her own yelp. The gunfire has started again.

'Don't worry, little one,' says Gigi. 'That's way over at Porte Maillot. Papa says that barricade is almost as strong as ours.'

Yesterday Madame Béranger from the boulangerie bustled in with half a loaf of bread and kept shaking her head and whispering to Gigi about barricades falling all over the city and 'firing squads'.

'What's a firing squad?' Marie asks from under the table.

'You and your incessant questions.' There's hardness in Gigi's voice now. 'I'm losing patience now, Marie. Marie! This is your last warning. Get your bony fucking arse off the floor and do something useful for once.'

Marie hates it when Gigi shouts. Time to get up. She kisses *Fantine* and leaves the volume under the table for safekeeping, stretches her arms above her head, yawns loudly to show she's not scared and starts chopping next to her mother. A carrot darts out from under the knife and Marie flinches, thinking her mother will shout at her again. But Gigi just stares blankly into the pot as she stirs and seems not to notice. It's hard to see in the slices of sunlight that come through the barricaded window.

Marie finishes her second potato and notices that her hands are shaking. She whimpers despite herself as the gunfire gets closer. Gigi freezes mid-stir. Marie drops her knife and hugs her from behind.

She knows she must be brave – it's what Papa loves most about her. But it's so noisy now, the flimsy walls of the house

4

shudder with every burst of fighting. One of the planks nailed to the window comes loose. A baby in a neighbouring house starts wailing.

'I'm scared.' The treacherous words come out of her despite her best efforts.

Gigi pretends not to notice. She turns around and stoops to pick Marie up.

'When did you get so big?'

Gigi's smile is straining at the seams, her voice too high. Like she's acting. Marie hooks her bare legs around her mother's waist and throws her head back. Gigi laughs and spins her around. They are both delirious with tiredness and hunger and waiting. Marie loves to see Gigi laugh like that, like before. Marie notices how wilted her mother looks and plants noisy kisses on her forehead and her freckled cheeks. If she's a good citizen, if she loves Gigi enough, gives her kisses and makes her laugh, everything will be normal.

'Je t'adore, Maman.'

'Oh, Marie, I love you too. You passionate little ruffian. I love you too.'

There are white ripples from old salt stains and new damp patches under her mother's arms that turn the worn fabric of her dress darker and make her smell earthy. The song of a blackbird on the cherry tree outside the back window breaks through the growing din all around. The looping tune festoons the bursts of artillery fire. Those cherries must be almost ripe by now, Marie thinks to herself as she slides down from her mother's waist.

'Won't you sing me "Le Temps des Cerises", Maman?'

'No, not now, my love. Maybe later.'

'I'm hungry.'

'You are always hungry.' Gigi narrows her amber eyes at

Marie. They glitter like a cat's eyes in the semi-darkness. 'Not long now, Marie. Not long now. When the army are pushed back and the Republic is saved, we will have mountains of cherries and chops on silver platters fresh from the Palais Royal. And absolutely no soup!'

'Absolutely no soup!' Marie chants above the din.

'That's it. Be brave. Think of – think of Louise Michel.'

Marie draws herself to attention and starts chopping again. She thinks of the great Louise, leader of the Women's Union and commander of this section of the Garde Nationale. Most people are scared of *la Louve Rouge*, the Red She-Wolf. Papa says that she can howl pain and anarchy from the Pantheon to the Arc de Triomphe. Only yesterday, Louise was talking by the fire with her father, kicking off her boots and warming her feet while she told the story of how she and Nathalie Lemel had defended Place Blanche at the head of a company of women. Even Papa had nothing to say to top that. Louise Michel declared that soon women will be able to do everything that men can, and nobody will bat an eyelid at a general with a chignon. Marie had heard her say exactly the same thing to torrents of applause and a few jeers at Place Vendôme a few weeks ago. But it was good to hear it again.

Marie drops the potatoes into the pan. That's when things start to speed up. The column of grey light that runs from the door to the table is broken now, flickering. Footsteps, lots of them, trudging, splishing in the mud, running, dragging up the hill, a river flowing the wrong way. The door jumps. Somebody must be leaning against it. Panting, a cigarette stubbed out, the smell of cigar smoke. Ragged shouts.

Marie goes over to the window, tries to see between the boards.

'Where's Papa? Where's Papa? I want him to come home. Make him come home, Maman, make him…'

'Hush, little one. Hush!' Gigi leaves the stove, wipes her hands on her apron and joins her. Marie can hear Gigi breathing heavily behind her.

'Is Papa – is he going to die?' Marie bites back the words, but they creep out of her throat anyway. Like deserters.

'No, no, of course not. Go and sit under the table again, Marie.'

'No, I don't want to.'

Gigi holds Marie's shoulders from behind, lets out a sharp sigh.

'Then stand still. They mustn't see us.'

'Ow! You're hurting me.'

'And button your fucking mouth.'

The footsteps outside are all joined up now, thundering upwards. There must be hundreds of people. Through the boards, glints of metal, ragged voices, coughing and shouting. 'Get in line, get in line. To arms!'

'No, no. It can't be true.' Gigi is peering through a hole in the boards. There's a shuffling of feet, a few shouts. And then silence falls like a guillotine.

'What's happening?' Marie looks back at her mother, tugs at her skirts for an answer. But Gigi has her eyes closed now and is making the sign of the cross over and over again.

'Are we praying?' Marie whispers.

'Yes, *ma petite*. We are praying,' her mother hisses.

'What shall I pray for?'

'Anything. Anything.'

'Fire!' comes the command from outside.

A deafening burst of gunfire. Marie blocks her ears with her hands, but she can still hear the screaming and wailing which follows the gunfire, starting low and growing higher and higher. Like a hundred cats fighting. No, not cats.

'What's that?' she asks, swallowing back tears and trying to look through the boards.

'Nothing. Get away from the window!' Gigi coughs at the dust coming through the boards and drags her back to Papa's chair. Marie hangs onto the back of it. Gigi is shaking. Marie has never seen her mother shake and she doesn't like it. She clings onto her mother's skirts.

'What's wrong, Maman? What's wrong?' But her mother won't look at her. 'Maman!' Marie hears her own voice breaking but Gigi is far, far away and she can't reach her.

A knock. The coded knock of the Garde Nationale: two double knocks, the galloping rhythm of the first two words of '*La Marseillaise*': *Allons, enfants…*

Louise Michel's sharp skinny silhouette in the doorway. A cloud of dust coming in with her. Behind Louise a clump of blue uniforms, no sign of Papa. And on the other side of the road, a wall splashed in red with a pile of clothes at the bottom of it. No, not clothes – bodies. Marie opens her mouth to speak but no sound comes out. Louise steps forward to block her vision.

'Gigi. Marie.'

It's impossible to see Louise's face in the sudden glare from the open door. But her voice is strangely soft. Not the voice familiar from the revolutionary speeches Louise gives from ramshackle stages all over Paris.

'Where is he? Where is Serge?'

Gigi darts forward and clutches at Louise's lapels. Her voice is trembling. Louise removes Gigi's hands very slowly and holds them in her own. She draws herself up even taller than she actually is and steers Gigi back towards the fire, holds her big bony hands up to silence her. How docile Maman is, Marie thinks. It hurts to see her like that.

'*Avancez!*' Louise barks.

A few blue uniforms shuffle in behind Louise, their hats by their sides, carrying a body wrapped in a muddy red flag, the face covered in a freshly pressed white handkerchief edged in the most delicate lace. It is startling in the middle of all that darkness and dirt. The men lift the body onto the table and then squat against the wall. Marie wants to dart under the table and collect *Fantine*, but she doesn't dare. At the back of the group is a tall pale man, clean-shaven with dark pomaded hair. A gentleman. She recognises him from somewhere. What on earth is he doing here? Nothing makes sense anymore. She looks back at the body. Some soldiers brought a body in yesterday too, on the way up to the cemetery. It was horrible. She thinks how hard they will have to scrub to get the blood off the table again, how disgusting the smell will be.

A limb rolls and slides from under the flag. Monsieur Béranger, the baker, pushes it back in gently, as if he were folding butter into a croissant before putting it into the oven. Marie stares at the body. The hand nearest her is dangling off the edge of the table – light hairs on the fingers, two white ridges on the ring finger, thumbnail neatly trimmed. The back of her neck prickles, her gut clenches, the room starts to sway. She hangs onto her mother to stop herself falling.

'Papa! No! Papa!' She reaches for her father's hand. 'It's Papa! Maman, it's Papa! Get up, Papa! Get up!' She hears her own voice as if she is watching the scene from across a river.

'Hold her, Gigi. Gigi!' Louise commands.

'Get up, Papa. Get up! Please get up.'

9

Gigi yanks Marie back and folds her head into her skirts. They stink of potatoes and sweat. Why isn't anybody moving? Marie pushes against Maman's grip and manages to look back at the body, reaches out her hand to Papa, but her mother won't let her move. 'Let me go!' She bites the hand Gigi has put over her mouth. What are they all doing? She must pull him up, wipe the blood off him, give him some soup.

'He died a hero,' Louise says. 'We were driven back across Pont Neuf. There was nowhere to hide. It was nobody's fault. He—'

A loud explosion drowns out her voice.

'We must go, comrades, we must go!' Monsieur Béranger has opened the door and is peering out. The street is a mess of blood and screaming. 'The artillery are coming. I have to go home. Have mercy, let me go home. Please let me go home.' He is coughing and crying now, jamming his knuckles into his blackened eye sockets. Another soldier cuffs him and he stumbles.

'Coward! You bloody coward of a useless baker!' The other soldier pulls the door shut.

'Silence!' Louise slams her hand on the door and the men stop fighting and stand to attention. 'Those who want to stay and hold the Porte de Montmartre may stay. Those who wish to go home, that is your decision.'

Louise turns her gaze back to Marie and her mother.

'Gigi, we must take him now.'

What does Louise mean? Take him where? Marie looks to her mother. She will know. She will sort this out. But Gigi is floppy and staring like a rag doll, her hands by her sides. Marie is free to move but her feet are not hers anymore. She looks from her mother to the body and back again. She waits for her mother to do something, to act, to make things right. She is there but she is not there. She cannot read what she sees. It is like letters falling off a page. Everything becoming blank.

Louise is shaking Gigi's shoulders. She does not respond. 'We cannot wait, Gigi. Do you hear? You must pay your last respects. He will be buried with dignity; you needn't worry about that. I will make sure it happens. Listen, Gigi. We have to go. The firing squads are coming. There are five thousand dead already. Do you want to pay your last respects?'

A loud wailing, starting low and rising above the din. Marie realises it is coming from her mother. She didn't know Gigi could make such a horrible sound. It corks her own breath in her throat.

'Damn you, Louise Michel. Damn you and the bloody Commune. This is all your fault. Turning my husband's head with your deluded fucking ideas. You always go too far, Louise. Swanning about in that ridiculous greatcoat like Napoleon the fucking third, with your beak in the air whipping up trouble, leaving us poor fucking mortals to pick up the bloody mess you've left behind.' Gigi's voice is like artillery fire, growing ever louder.

'We were all fine before you came along. I hate you, I fucking hate—'

'Compose yourself, Gigi, you will get us all killed.'

Louise slaps Gigi's face. Marie cannot be sure if she is dreaming; details of the scene come and go in her mind. The look in her mother's eyes, the sound of Louise's slap, the soup bubbling over in the corner. And her father lying on the table in the middle of the room.

'You must scrub your hands, the table, everything. Do you hear? If they find gunpowder, if they smell it on you, on Marie, you will both be shot. Do you hear? Do it! If not for yourself, then do it for your daughters!' Words, things, faces, all mixed up and moving too fast in Marie's mind. She's drowning, her heart beating in her ears; she tries to grab her mother's hand, but the fingers are limp.

She feels Louise's bony fingers tilting her chin. 'Courage, *ma petite*. Courage!' Her face fills Marie's vision. She tries to anchor herself in that face. Louise looks like an old woman – the fine lines on her forehead deep with dust, the whites of her eyes webbed in red, cheeks sallow as a cheap candle. But when she smiles, even now, there is a flicker of something like hope from her coal-black eyes. 'You must march on for your father, Marie. March for him!' Louise's voice cracks and she coughs and turns to Gigi. 'Hold out your hands, comrade.' Louise repeats her order more loudly and rifles in her pocket, pinning her mother with her gaze. Her mother cups her palms as if she is receiving her first communion wafer. Two rings gleam in her hand now. One gold, one silver. The rings are so bright, like something out of a fairy tale.

Marie is curled up on her father's knee by the fire. 'One for the family, one for the Commune.' She intones his words while she spins his rings around his finger.

'That's right, Marie. That's right.'

The soldiers are getting up now, spitting and cursing. She blinks the dust out of her eyes. Her father's body seems to float up from the table and slide out the door. The pale gentleman stands next to the body, like a ghost. He puts a big hand up as if to say sorry or *adieu*. She sees herself running to catch her father's hand, to hold his big square face between her hands one last time, but realises that she has not moved. Then her mother's fist closes around the rings and she disappears. Everything disappears.

CHAPTER ONE

April 1878

'You will go to the opera tomorrow, Marie. You will dance and you will learn to flirt and stand naked in front of any artist who asks.'

Gigi slams down the iron. The table shudders above Marie's head. She's squashed in under it, reading *Fantine* for the hundredth time.

'And if you can get some rich man to set you up in an apartment on Boulevard Haussmann, like that slut Amélie Reine, we will all come and live with you and put our feet up.'

Stand naked! Gigi must be joking. Marie knows why she is angry – Amélie is an old friend from her mother's days as a cabaret singer, an old friend who has since done well for herself. And it hurts. Marie has always known when her mother is hurting.

'I don't want to go and dance at the opera with Antoinette. I want to stay here with you.' Marie strokes her finger along the cracked spine of her father's old volume of *Fantine*, traces the number 'I' at the bottom of it and wonders if she'll ever get to see any of the other volumes.

'"Don't want" doesn't come into it, Marie. You're nearly

thirteen years old now. I'd already been working for three years by the time I was your age.'

Gigi sprinkles a bit of water from the cracked blue glass jug by her side and noses the iron into a corner of the eighteenth and last pillowcase of the day. She winces at a sharp pain in her shoulder. If her body gives up on her now, they are all sunk.

Gigi lays the iron aside, goes over to the open door, raises her face to the sun. It would be better to have more business and not to have time to take a break. But she might as well make the most of it while she can. She puts her palms on her hips and leans back. Gigi lets herself close her eyes for a moment and imagine she's stretching like this back on the riverbank at Aix-en-Provence where she used to work with her mother.

'One day I'll take you to Aix-en-Provence, Marie, show you where I used to work. You'd love it. Washing clothes out in the open air… there was always plenty of time to chat. It's so hot in the summer down there, Marie. Much hotter than here. When the head laundress wasn't there, we used to splash about in the river while the washing dried on the grass. Ha! My friend Violette and I, we laughed all the time. We spent most of the time messing about, but somehow, we got away with it. I wonder what happened to her?'

Marie thinks that her mother must be hypnotised by the bright low sunlight because she has never heard such openness from her. She must grab this rare chance to find out more. The few details she's heard about Gigi's life are engraved on her memory.

'Is Aix-en-Provence where you lived with Grandma – when you were a little girl? In that grand house with the stone lions outside.'

'Yes, Marie. What a memory you have! But this was later, after everything fell apart.'

Marie feels her mother start to drift off. She must hold her in the story with a question.

'What was Grandma like?'

'Well... She was very beautiful. Very unhappy too. She hated having to work at the laundry, considered herself above such things. Not really her fault. She was born into another class, wasn't given to practical things, I suppose. Ha! Bit like you when I come to think of it, *ma petite*!'

Gigi looks round at Marie and winks.

'Your grandpa died when I was ten years old. Turned out he had a secret gambling habit. He'd run up huge debts by the time he died. We had to sell everything. So that was the end of the grand house and the fucking lions.'

Gigi shakes her head at men in general. She can hardly believe now that she ever lived in a house with windows that never rattled, unbroken shutters and doors that closed without you having to ram them shut. She can still smell the expensive lemon-scented floor polish, feel her toes wriggling in the violet satin slippers her father bought her for her tenth birthday, picture the intricate rose pattern on the family china. Gigi yawns and stretches her arms above her head.

Marie notices how red and scaly her mother's elbows are, looks at her own arms to check hers haven't gone the same way. She notices the scab on Gigi's forearm, winces when she remembers how Gigi dropped the hot iron on herself after a visit from their bastard of a landlord, then stormed out and didn't come back for three hours. Marie had been scared Gigi might have been run over by a carriage – or knifed in a backstreet. Or arrested.

15

Marie gazes at her mother, wills her to say something about Papa, decides to try and pin her down with another question.

'How did you meet Papa?'

Just saying the word out loud, acknowledging her father ever existed, feels like a betrayal somehow, makes Marie's throat dry up. Gigi looks back and tuts as if some stranger has poked her in the back.

'For God's sake, Marie. Why this, how that! It's so long ago. I – I can't remember much about it…'

Gigi lets out a long, guttering sigh. The evening sun shines into the steamy vapour pouring out of the house and makes an opalescent halo around her head. Marie holds her breath. Two workmen in overalls covered in white dust walk past on their way back from the building works at the new church next to St Pierre. Marie narrows her eyes at them. Almost everybody in Montmartre hates the huge white basilica being built on the site where many of their relatives lost their lives just seven years ago.

When Gigi does speak it comes out in a torrent.

'We met at the wedding party of Serge's cousin – it was at a bar in the Mazarin quarter. I sang in the evening sometimes to make extra money. Usually, I sang to myself while everybody ignored me, but that evening there was this man standing at the back on his own, kept staring at me the whole time and smiling to himself. He came up to me when I'd finished, told me I was the most beautiful girl he'd ever seen with the "voice of a fierce angel". He still had a strong Belgian accent then. I fell for him immediately. He said I was wasted in a bourgeois little town like Aix…'

Gigi's voice trails off. She picks at the scab on her arm. 'Your father always had a way with words.'

'Then what happened?'

16

The sun starts to sink into the houses up towards St Pierre church. Gigi lets out another long, heavy sigh; it sounds like an iron being laid slowly on hot wet linen.

'He pursued me that whole summer. He used to take me and Violette out boating on the river on Sundays and after work on Wednesdays he'd bring us a picnic to eat by the river. It tasted like heaven. He read me poetry. And philosophy, of course... which I hated even then. I liked it best when he told me stories of Paris, how I could become a famous singer and never have to scrub another man's shirt again, apart from his of course. He had big plans to set up his own clothing manufacturers here, using the most modern machines that existed. He fancied himself as some sort of Jean Valjean, said he'd treat all his employees with respect and kindness, pay them fair wages, support them when they were sick like my mother. He spoke with such passion, Marie. I'd never heard anyone speak like that before. We started going to political meetings together.'

Gigi straightens up now. A cool breeze wafts in and sets the bed linen billowing like sails. '*Nom de dieu*, where is your fucking sister?'

'Tell me the rest, Maman. Please tell me the rest.'

'On midsummer's day, when we were out on a boat in the middle of the river – just the two of us – he got down on bended knee and asked me to marry him, then promptly fell off the boat into the water. I jumped in after him. We laughed until we thought we'd drown.'

To her surprise, Gigi feels tears pressing up from her chest.

'Then Serge lost his job, so it seemed like a good time to leave and follow our dreams, fools that we were.'

Marie hates it that Gigi calls her father Serge instead of Papa, as if he's nothing to do with her.

'Why did Papa lose his job?'

'Why, why, why! Talking to you is like being grilled by the fucking police. Insurrection. That's why Serge lost his job. As usual.' Gigi's voice is harder and tighter now. 'He started a union with some of the other tailors' apprentices and demanded a pay rise. Grandma was appalled when she found out and we had a big row. I should have known then.'

'Known what?' Marie sticks her head out from under the table. Gigi wheels around, claps her hands as if breaking a spell and clasps them around Marie's head.

'Enough, Marie. The past is gone. Water under the bridge. Stop dragging it up all the time. I've told you before, I don't want to talk about it. I don't want to fucking talk about it!'

Gigi realises she's gripping Marie's head too hard. She takes her hands away, strokes her daughter's cheek.

'Sorry, my love, but if you don't stop with all this – this digging into things that don't concern you – you're going to get us all into trouble. Do you understand?'

Gigi turns away and fingers the sheets on the drying rack to see if they are dry. The rack stands right next to the table, on exactly the spot where Papa's chair used to be. Marie knows her mother disapproves but she can't help herself climbing into her hiding place and thinking about Papa. If she gets into the right position, if she kindles enough love in her heart, if she can imagine him clearly enough sitting there cross-legged, one foot swinging, won't he come back? If she scrubs at it hard enough won't this reality dissolve like mud off a sleeve in soapy water? Her father will walk in, all in one piece, and all will be well.

Marie looks out through the open door onto the street, blinks away the flash of a blood-spattered wall, makes herself focus on the blank-eyed workers trudging home up the steep narrow hill. A seamstress pauses, drops her basket on the cobbles, plants a hand on her hip. She arches backwards, gazes up at the narrow river of sky between rooftops. What is she dreaming about? An artist comes next. He is obviously not a Montmartrois, by the way he is gaping around and grinning, as if he is at the Louvre. The artists are everywhere, like rats, scurrying about, bright-eyed, looking for trouble. This one trips on the cobbles next to the seamstress, drops his huge canvas and reddens. The seamstress laughs and he makes a foolish, over-blown bow, picks up her basket in one arm and they stumble on. They'll likely be propped up at the bar at the Moulin de la Galette before sunset. Strange how life just carries on.

Madame Béranger's badly sewn hems hang down by Marie's nose. Marie's stomach is growling. She prays for one little cube of chicken or rabbit. The juice on her teeth, the weight in her stomach at night. The bedlinen comes from the boarding house above Madame Béranger's bakery. They would never have considered dealings with a boarding house until a year ago. But now they have to take what they can get. A wave of laundresses washed in from the provinces, rates are down, and business is thin on the ground.

Marie comes out from under the table and does a little comedic pirouette to make her mother laugh. But Gigi doesn't seem to notice. Her gaze darts about like a pickpocket these days. Marie longs for one of Maman's old slow smiles! One that lasts longer than a moment and makes her warm inside, the smile that used to be always there when she needed it, the smile that she could rely on, that made her feel safe. But it doesn't come.

They take the sheets off the dryer and whip them out flat, pegging the four corners in their fingers. In out, in out. Halves.

Quarters. Into the basket. They step around each other in the courtly dance they know so well until the basket is full.

Antoinette arrives home just after dinner. She strolls in, unlaces her boots very slowly (to annoy her mother) and sits down at the table.

Gigi picks up the boots and puts them neatly by the fire with a sharp sigh. 'We hardly see you these days.' She plonks a bowl of soup in front of Antoinette but doesn't look at her. 'You'd better get that down you and then help your sister prepare for the audition tomorrow.'

'But I was going to meet a friend at the Alcazar.'

'Well, you can't.' Gigi clatters about at the sink, hums and sighs to herself. 'Anyway, I have to go out and see somebody about work.'

Antoinette scrapes her chair against the floor and slurps noisily to show her disgust. 'Does your work involve consorting with the Green Fairy and that disgusting butcher in a bar on Rue de La Goutte d'Or?'

Gigi freezes with her scrubbing brush in the air for a moment then snorts and resumes what she is doing.

Marie prays there won't be another argument, but she can feel her sister angling for one.

'It's freezing in here.' Antoinette shoots a sharp look at Gigi's back.

Gigi throws down her scrubbing brush, turns around and glares at Antoinette. 'Any more complaints?'

Antoinette shrugs and then tries to make more noise eating her soup than her mother is making doing the washing up. Why do they have to compete? Can't Antoinette just let it go for once? They are as stubborn as each other. Antoinette won't look at their mother anymore and she knows it hurts Gigi and makes her angry. Marie watches her sister's face in the candlelight, wills her to keep her thoughts to herself and her temper in check so they can all have a peaceful night.

Antoinette is never still anymore. She moves her chair in and out, taps her foot on the floor. Two frown lines come and go between her fine arched eyebrows as she eats; she chews at a flake of dry skin on her bottom lip between slurps of soup and looks around at everything apart from her mother or sister, as if she is wondering where she is. Was she like that before? It's hard to remember.

'Why are you looking at me like that, Marie?' Antoinette leans in towards her and crosses her eyes. Marie can't help laughing. Her sister always knows how to make her laugh. 'Hey, I like your new hairstyle!'

Marie reaches up and feels knots and bits of hair sticking up from where her head has rubbed against the underside of the table. 'Ha ha. Very funny.' She slaps her sister on the arm and notices veins bulging out there. How thin her sister has become. Is it just because she dances so much and eats so little or is she sick? Will she end up being carted off to hospital and never seen again like Madame Béranger's daughter? No, no. Don't think like that. Antoinette is strong, Marie tells herself. She won't leave you. She won't die.

'Antoinette!' Gigi's straight back is an admonishment in itself.

'Come on, you slum cat. I'll take you upstairs and sort you out.' Antoinette leaves her soup unfinished and throws her dirty spoon on the table. 'Anything to please our dear mother.'

Marie turns back to send a smile to her mother. Gigi wipes her hands on her apron and smooths a couple of grey hairs across her temples. The hurt in Gigi's face at the way Antoinette treats her is awful, the way she swallows and bites her lip, but Antoinette doesn't seem to notice it. Should Marie go to comfort her mother or follow her sister upstairs? She often feels pulled in two directions like this. She looks from one to the other. Maman nods at her as if to say, 'Go on, I'm fine.'

Marie stands in first position in the narrow gap between her bed and the mottled yellow wall with its daisy-shaped patches of mould. She holds onto the brass bedstead as a barre while Antoinette lounges on the bed. The metal is cold in her hand. 'Go on, then! Tell me what to do.'

Antoinette barks out instructions and admires herself in the cracked mirror, takes on various poses. Her wavy auburn hair tumbles over her shoulders like one of the ladies in the pictures her father used to take them to see at the Louvre every Sunday. Marie feels a little stab of jealousy. Why should Antoinette have their mother's hair and dainty nose? She doesn't look like either of her parents, although, when pushed, her mother assures her that she takes after her favourite grandmother who came from Italy, or was it Spain? Her mother is usually so vague about the details of anything in the past, as if it offends her even to be made to think about it. Marie has learnt more about Gigi today than in the last seven years. Maybe her mother is right: all this thinking is not making her feel any better. She forces herself to concentrate on what her body is doing instead.

'You're not even looking, Antoinette! This is first, isn't it? And, what about third?' Gigi and Antoinette probably wouldn't notice if she just packed a bag and left forever.

'Oh, Marie. It doesn't matter. They don't care. As long as you've got two legs and all your teeth, you're in.'

'But you said the auditions are hard.'

'They are for other girls. But not for you. We have what you might call "friends in high places".' Antoinette taps her nose and winks.

'What do you mean? I don't understand.' Marie comes to sit on the bed beside her sister. 'I thought the only friends we had in high places were the ones re-tiling the roof on the Sacré-Coeur.'

'Good joke, Marie. You're learning.' Marie beams in triumph; she is proud of her joke and her sister is hard to impress. 'Now, come and rub camphor on my blisters and I'll get those tangles out of your hair.'

Marie decides it's better not to ask again about how Antoinette and her mother landed her a job at the opera. She knows from experience it will just spoil things between them if she asks any more questions and then they'll end up in one of those horrible silences where she feels even more alone than before.

The next morning, Marie and Antoinette have to drag their mother out of bed as she has been out late again and fallen asleep in her clothes. But everything feels a little better when Marie is out on the streets. The familiar smell of lilacs and boiled celery and fresh sewage, the screeching song of a carpenter's plane. Brick dust scratches at her throat but she doesn't care. Maman coughs loudly and says she is going to be sick. So they prop her up, and stop a moment to watch the carts carrying cubes of white stone, like giant sugar lumps, up to the new basilica. People say they are building it to make up for the 20,000 citizens who were shot or executed in Paris during Bloody Week. Nothing will make up for that, Marie thinks. Nothing. She can still see the pockmarks from army bullets on the walls of nearly every building, most of them hastily covered over with paint. Papa is up there, buried somewhere. Will they move his body and build on top of it? The thought presses into her chest. Are Maman and Antoinette thinking the same thing? Probably not. Her sister is muttering that her mother is making them late and her mother is blinking at the ground. It hurts to think of Papa, but it hurts more not to think of him. It makes her dizzy to think of his body on the table, but the picture comes into her mind anyway, she can't help it. She didn't even see his face. Maybe it wasn't him at all; maybe he is still alive, and he has lost his memory and is living just around the corner. Sometimes Marie sees a blonde beard or hears a familiar laugh and runs to catch up with the person, her heart hammering in her chest. Once she even tapped a man on the shoulder, but when he turned around, he looked nothing like her father and then she felt stupid and promised herself she would never do it again, would try to forget like her mother and sister.

They stop outside the opera house so Antoinette can re-pin her hair. An old man pushes past and tip-taps up the wide marble steps with a jasper-topped cane. What will it be like to stand in the famous marble foyer? She has heard about it from Antoinette, the curving staircases with their scarlet carpets and the tall gilt mirrors.

'Down here, Marie. That's for the toffs, not us little rats.'

She follows Antoinette's laced red boots down a dark alley and in through the back door of the opera house, up long grimy corridors, darker than their house. They step over buckets of sand, coils of thick rope, a stack of coloured glass squares. They brush past giant canvases painted with trees and exotic birds. 'For the seraglio scene,' Antoinette announces. 'Watch out, they're still wet.' Around another corner and up a long wooden

24

staircase. 'Mind that hole!' They are going so fast Marie can't take it all in. Then Antoinette turns a loose brass door handle, and they arrive in a long, dirty room with rust-coloured paint peeling from the ceiling. The walls are lined with cubby-holes, stuffed with shawls and ballet slippers, pink ribbons spilling out like rabbits' intestines. Greyish light dribbles in through a dirty little window at one end, another door with a loose brass handle at the other.

A couple of girls sit on a long bench, tying their shoes. They don't look up but Antoinette elbows Marie, so she mumbles a greeting and makes herself sit down beside them. Her mother sits next to her, and Antoinette squeezes herself in between them, hissing at her mother to get her head out of her hands and sit up straight like a normal mother. The other girls giggle at that and Antoinette blushes. Marie goes over the positions in her mind, tries to stop her heart hammering. Soft, scuttling footsteps break the line of bright light under the door and the girls sit up straight and stop talking. Her mother squeezes her hand, and she notices how sweaty and cold her hand is.

'Marie van Goethem,' the ballet mistress announces in a high, screechy voice. Antoinette calls her the Crow and is always telling Marie stories about her. Her sudden tempers, her expertise with a cane, the way she swoops when you are least expecting it. Marie swallows hard. *Courage, Marie, courage.* A flash of Louise Michel's steely face urging her on. That's better.

The Crow pokes her knees, her back, asks her to hold her arms up in the air and bends over her, pulls her mouth open and looks at her teeth. Marie stands firm – the Communards endured much worse, after all. It would be an insult to them to be squeamish about this. The Crow's breath smells of tobacco and cherries.

25

Better check on Maman to see she is behaving herself, has not fallen asleep. Gigi is looking right at her with such a tender smile that Marie gulps back tears. The smile tightens and disappears when their eyes meet, but it was definitely there, and she'll store it up in her memory for when she really needs it.

'Is this your daughter, madame?' The Crow says the last word as if it were a joke and Marie wants to hit her. Gigi gets up unsteadily and stares the Crow down. Marie can't help feeling a slight thrill at Gigi's old cheek making a return. She has been so worryingly docile recently. Not like herself at all.

'*Oui, madame*,' Gigi snarls.

'Good,' says the Crow, backing off. 'Five sous a day to start. Six after six months. No drinking, swearing, talking or eating in the rehearsal room. Sign at the desk on your way out.'

CHAPTER TWO

May 1878

After a whole month working at the opera, Marie still can't get used to being constantly on show. The whole of May has been stormy and unsettled and this Monday is no different. The 23rd of May. Seven years since Papa died. Seven years. It feels like yesterday and a lifetime all at once.

Marie is stretching at the barre, listening out for her name to be called above the sound of wind rattling the window frames and scuffles of rain on glass. Will Gigi or Antoinette notice what day it is? Of course not, they never do. If they were a normal family, they would lay flowers on a grave somewhere, wouldn't they? But Papa has no grave that she knows of. The thought makes her dizzy and she blinks her eyes, focusses on her foot on the barre, goes over the steps of the dance she must do later. The tide of the past is so strong, it takes so much energy to pull against it and stay in the present, especially today. All this waiting doesn't help, trying to keep warm so that her muscles won't cramp when she has to do fouetté turns across the room or endless battements at the barre. The Crow has no patience with cramp or any other weakness. Now she knows the steps, it's better when she is dancing than standing around trying to ignore the sideways glances of the other girls. Word has obviously got around that her father was a well-known Communard because the other girls cluster in groups, leaving her and Antoinette alone. A relief, to tell the truth.

The rehearsal room is huge and draughty with tall arched windows at the front and peels of butter-coloured paint on the high ceiling which occasionally drop onto the dancers and make the ballet master curse his bosses for being so mean that they spend all the money on the public areas and nothing on the rest.

The ballet master, the Crow, the pianist and the violinist all huddle together at the window end of the rehearsal room and the 'little rats' stay at the other end near the dressing room. Every day begins with a warm-up at the barre, followed by exercises in the middle of the room. The afternoon is taken up with rehearsals for some of the dancers while the others crowd around the barre or in the dressing room and wait to be called. Marie has got used to the rhythm of it now even if she doesn't like it much. Home is not what it used to be, and she realises with a jolt of guilt that she doesn't miss it. At least here there are no memories waiting to flood her mind with every knock at the door, every raised voice, every haunted look that crosses Gigi's face.

But it's not exactly comfortable here at the opera either. She never understood why the dancers of the corps de ballet were called 'little rats'. Now she knows. It's because they are shut up in the dingy, grimy dressing room most of the day with nothing to eat and are called out when they are needed. Most of the girls are very poor and very thin and covered in nits and blisters and bruises. They are never allowed into the foyer or the public areas and only get to see the pristine boxes, green velvet hangings and glittering chandeliers from the stage. As soon as they are finished, they scuttle back into the dressing room and then out through the dark corridors into the backstreets and straight home or to their 'night job'.

For the first few weeks she just did the warm-up at the barre and the exercises in the centre of the room and was told to watch the rehearsals for *La Source*, one of the ballet master's favourite ballets, which is to be staged sometime next year. But this week she is expected to dance in the back row of the seraglio scene. The Crow marched into the dressing room on Friday and announced that Marie had been chosen for the seraglio scene because she was the only one who looked dark enough. Hardly a compliment, but she supposes she is lucky to be chosen. The Crow said she would see how Marie did and let her take part if she was up to scratch. Some of the girls gasped and complained about the new girl being promoted so soon, until the Crow banged her stick on the ground and called for order. Marie was sure that the Crow winked at her then, but maybe it was just a grimace. 'Courage,' Marie mutters to herself, constantly, until she is sick of the word. Louise Michel's face floats into her mind, those bony fingers tilting her chin up. She must do her best to get the part; it means more money and a more secure place in the corps de ballet. But she also knows it will make Antoinette jealous. Antoinette has not been included in the seraglio scene and she is worried about her place; she has not progressed in three years and there are younger girls yapping at her heels. Well, Marie can't spend her whole life trying to keep Antoinette happy, can she?

Marie goes over the steps for the seraglio scene again and again in her mind; the intricate footwork in the first section, the fast-travelling steps in the second. But her mind keeps wandering off. Her mind always wanders off, like a badly trained lapdog.

Marie finds herself fascinated by a wicker chair which stands empty between where the ballet master stands and the piano. There are several similar chairs at the edges of the room. One is always occupied by Blanche Balnar's mother, who slumps in it reading *La Vie Parisienne* all day in a floral-printed dress, always with the same lace collar, perfectly laundered. She must have tens of those collars. Blanche is tipped to be the next lead dancer at the opera and her mother occupies the chair to make sure her career stays on track. She is the one who gossiped about Papa and turned everybody against them. She brings bags of cherries for the musicians and is always fussing with Blanche's hair and ribbons. Marie sends over a silent curse that her cherries are poisoned. The other chairs are shared between the girls who have been there longest. But the chair in the middle is being saved for somebody. Maybe it's the person they know in a high place who helped her get in? Could it be one of Papa's old friends from the Garde Nationale? But how would they get into a high position, unless of course they were one of those secret rich supporters, the *abonnés*, who hang around at meetings in frock coats with their top hats low over their eyes, their fat fucking hands groping any girl who passes by. The back of the chair is bowed with the weight of whoever sits in it and one of the struts at the back is broken. There's a large black book sitting on the seat which she longs to read.

Marie lifts her other leg high to stop her cramp developing and winces as the barre cuts into a blister on her heel. Her ballet slippers are much too small even though she's cut a slit in the back. And the ribbon around her waist is ancient and frayed. Never mind, she tells herself, Blanche Balnar looks like a spoilt poodle with that huge puffy bow above her fat bum. A stupid and well-trained poodle. And ribbons don't matter, it's inner nobility that counts. That's what her father would have said, but it doesn't stop her longing for a nice new ribbon. Antoinette is so mean with her collection of ribbons from her beloved Paul, she won't even lend her one for a day 'in case it gets spoilt'. She's sure Paul would be happy for her to borrow a ribbon – after all he's her friend too, much as Antoinette likes to keep him to herself these days. She'll mention it to Emma Béranger, Paul's mother, next time she goes to the bakery. Ha! That'll show Antoinette.

The ballet master is strutting around now like a demented pigeon, his round belly silhouetted against a rain cloud, short arms flapping in the white suit he always wears. Marie lets out a snigger before she can stop herself. A group of girls at the other end of the barre stare at her and shake their heads. How awful it is to be looked at all the time, like one of those insects pinned on green felt at the Museum of Curiosities. If only she could magic herself there right now. Papa loved that museum. Every Sunday, he'd take her and Antoinette there or to the Louvre. He was a big believer in education for girls, unlike Gigi. Papa wouldn't let them wear ribbons at all even though Antoinette begged him. He said it was bourgeois and degrading. The three of them were probably the most curious sight in the whole museum: a working man in a many-times mended jacket and a threadbare hat with two girls in tow, Marie skipping along with Papa and Antoinette trailing behind sulking.

'Look! Isn't nature miraculous?' Papa always spoke so loudly that gentlemen harrumphed, and ladies snapped their fans and muttered in irritation. That only made him worse. 'Look, Marie! See how perfectly marked that moth is. Who is to say a moth is better or worse than those gaudy butterflies?' Then the ladies would gather their skirts and rustle away.

Sometimes, especially when the bills were stacking up and there weren't many people at meetings, his speeches at the museum carried on for minutes at a time until he emptied the room. Once they were asked to leave, but Papa stood his ground. Afterwards he declared 'a small but significant victory for the common man (or woman)' and took them to have hot chocolate and *appelflaps* at his favourite Belgian bakery – 'but don't tell your mother'. How thrilling it was to be around Papa, up in the high skies above petty concerns about what other people thought and ribbons and paying the rent. She must try to be more like Papa. When she was with him, she felt scared and excited but safe at the same time. She used to tug at Papa's sleeve and tell him to stop, but really, she hoped he wouldn't. And he never did. The more people tried to hush him, the louder he spoke. Papa was there and nothing bad could ever happen. She wonders if she will ever feel like that again. So solid, so alive. Now, every feeling is a threat. Her body jumps at the most ridiculous little things. She is afraid of the beat of her own heart, that it will drum her to danger, to disaster. Better to lie low, to hide and feel nothing, expect nothing, just hold onto what is left of her family, lose herself in the intricate patterns of dance steps.

'Oi, dreamychops! Wake the fuck up. You'll get us both sacked!' Antoinette hisses in her ear.

Marie looks around her and remembers where she is. She names things in her head: barre, dancers, piano. It's something she does when the world stops making sense. When she doesn't recognise where she is, can't make sense of it and needs to somehow slot herself back into it. It happens sometimes. She is sure it is not normal and she has never told anyone about it.

All the other girls are lined up in the centre of the room, several of them giggling behind their hands. Marie realises her foot is still on the barre from where she was stretching. She blushes and lifts her foot off. It tingles with pins and needles as she hobbles to her place in the back row. Her heart starts to gallop. The ballet master is tapping his cane on the floor, huffing and puffing, calling her name. She raises her chin and copies the starting position from the other girls. The pianist raises his hands, flicks out the tails of his coat. 'Five, six, seven.' *Relevé, chassé.* Or is it *chassé, relevé*? She fixes her eyes on the wicker chair to steady herself. But there is somebody in the chair. It's hard to make out anything in the glare of the huge windows behind, but it looks like a gentleman in a frock coat. Is he really there? There is something about him that makes her stomach lurch. She blinks to check that he is not a ghost. No, just a middle-aged man. Somehow, he looks vaguely familiar, something about the way he holds himself. Taller than most, legs spread as if he will be here a while, and this has all been arranged just for him. Of course. Nothing sinister. Just another *abonné*, one of the rich men who pay a yearly subscription and come to ogle the girls. But the pull in her stomach is so strong. Hunger must be making her dizzy. She wills herself to concentrate, to stop daydreaming. Then the first few bars of the music come to slap her awake. Luckily her body remembers what to do.

CHAPTER THREE

23 May 1878

'Where's Maman?'

Marie stands in the doorway and squeezes the rain out of her hair, takes off one of her old boots, winces as the leather presses against her blister and pours water into the gutter. A sheet hangs above the ironing board, an angry knot of underclothes spills out of the big wicker basket. No sign of her mother.

'Where've you been?' Antoinette doesn't look up. 'Shut that door, will you?'

Marie feels guilty when she sees her sister, ashamed of having abandoned her to walk home alone, ashamed of having sat on Pont Neuf on her own, staring into the river and missing her father so much that for a moment it seemed easier to drop herself into the water than drag herself back here. Memory is a dangerous place. Maybe that's why Antoinette and her mother never go there.

Antoinette is already in her nightdress and shawl, sitting cross-legged on the floor, darning her chemise in a shivering circle of light from the only remaining downstairs candle. A sudden breeze from the door makes the wick turn red.

'No, I won't sew your boot button back on, so don't ask me.'

Antoinette lays down her sewing with exactly the same gentle prodding movement Papa used when his day's work was finished. Marie's heart softens at that, despite herself.

'You're soaking, Marie. Here, come and take your clothes off. I'll fetch your nightdress and there's a bowl of soup in the pot.'

'Where's Maman?'

'Asleep. Upstairs.'

Marie doesn't like the flatness in Antoinette's voice when she says that. She runs upstairs to Gigi's room, her heart hammering. Spit, spatter; a pool of water widening on the floor from a leak in the ceiling. Marie reaches for the pisspot and slides it under the drip. Gigi can't even be bothered to keep her bedroom dry anymore. Marie sighs and picks up a spluttering candle, holds it up to get a closer look. A half-empty bottle of red wine lies on the floor and sloshes to the side when she steps on a loose floorboard. Gigi is splayed out sideways on her bed, one leg dangling over the edge. The lip rouge she's been eking out and using on special occasions for years since her singing days is smeared over one cheek, auburn hair half over her face. Is Gigi dead?

'Marie. Oh, Marie.' Gigi pushes her hair off her face, pulls Marie to her and starts sobbing. 'He left me. He fucking left me.' When she's finished wailing, she drops off again.

And suddenly Marie is not worried anymore but downright furious. She shakes Gigi's body under the covers, sees her eyes flicker open and shut and open again.

'He didn't deserve you.'

Gigi plants a smelly kiss on her forehead. 'Absolutely fucking right, my love. Fucking lump of a fucking embroiderer. Slinging me over for a milk-faced country cunt!'

Gigi pulls her shoulder strap back up, straightens her skirts, tries to focus her eyes.

'Sorry, my little one… finding me… like this… Won't happen again.' Gigi makes the sign of the cross and shakes her head, wipes away a tear. 'Won't ever happen again.' She jumps off the bed, pulls Marie up after her and spins her around. 'You've got so heavy, you little ruffian.' Her bloodshot eyes gather dying sparks from the candle. 'You're right, *ma petite.* He can embroider my fucking arse.' She has set the bottle of wine spinning and now she picks it up, makes a face at it and throws it in the ash bucket.

'Antoinette! Antoinette!' Gigi shouts, stumbling over the pisspot. 'Get your glad rags on. We're going out.'

If only Marie could just hide in her bed and lose herself in the lives of Fantine and Cosette. But she knows it will be good for her and her real family to go out for once and Gigi's sudden good mood might not last long. She rushes down to Madame Charpentier's with the washing covered by her old shawl. Madame Charpentier takes in the washing with a sharp look that says something she is too tired to work out.

Out on Rue Lepic, her sodden stockings squelch in her boots as she looks up at the defiant curve of Gigi's jaw. Just like Antoinette's and quite unlike her own square one which looks even squarer now Antoinette has cut her hair in a blunt fringe.

Shivering raindrops stud Gigi's high chignon. Antoinette has folded her hair up and stuck her best bonnet on top, at a jaunty angle. Marie is proud of them like that. From a distance they look like real ladies. Antoinette is wearing a new green ribbon Paul Béranger has given her, tied in a plump bow. Maybe now she will let him take her out for once.

They walk in and out of pools of gaslight on oily cobbles, skip over slippery patches of dissolving horse dung. Marie inhales the smell of dying fires and hot iron from the smelting works at St Lazare.

'Maybe we can teach you some tricks tonight, Marie, now you've almost got enough up top for a recognisable cleavage,' says Gigi, squeezing Marie's arm and winking at Antoinette.

Marie's heart sinks.

'Come on, it'll be fun,' Antoinette chimes in.

'It's disgusting, flaunting yourself for men.' As soon as she's said it, she knows she sounds like a prude.

'Get off your high horse, Marie. You're not at a meeting of the Union des Femmes now.'

Marie marches ahead furiously, mortified and determined not to show her fear.

'To the right!' Gigi catches up with her and yanks her from under a sudden shower of urine. Antoinette raises her fist at an old lady with a pisspot high above them. Up here the older citizens of the Butte still break the rules and empty chamber pots out the window on a night like this. Who could blame them? Up ahead, the coloured lights over the arch of the Moulin's entrance flicker and wink.

They pause outside for a moment. Antoinette bends down and rearranges her décolleté.

'Couldn't we have gone to the Martyrs Tavern?'

'Not tonight, Antoinette,' says Gigi. 'This is a special night. Tonight, we start afresh, we begin a new chapter. Or whatever the fucking phrase is.'

Antoinette rolls her eyes. Gigi pretends not to notice. She pinches Marie's cheeks hard: 'A mild flush is attractive on a girl.' Marie grits her teeth and tells herself it'll soon be over. The door opens and a crowd of people babble out.

Inside there is a huge, low-ceilinged room with a long bar

at the far end and off to the side a small wooden stage with stepped benches in front of it. Gas globes hang from the ceiling at different heights like grubby pearls. Damp feathers nod next to slippery black top hats and people stand closely packed, hands tucked in over their bellies to make room for waiters weaving in and out, wheeling huge trays over their heads, delivering steaming white dishes and heavy-bottomed glasses full of strange-coloured liquids. The whole thing smells like sweaty horses with cheap perfume sprayed on top, but Marie can't help being fascinated by it.

Antoinette raises her chin and gestures towards the bar at the other side of the room, like a sergeant giving the signal for the charge. Gigi studies the ladies in their finery; she points out the ones who coo and glitter and keep the attention of the gentlemen and the ones who can't, who try too hard and lean too close and laugh too loudly. Marie just nods and says nothing. What a waste of time.

'That is the art of the coquette,' says Gigi, as if she is lecturing from a high stage. 'Oh, and that is Nathalie de Sancaens.' She rolls her eyes and gestures to the singer on stage, a small blonde woman in a purple dress with extravagant yellow fringing around the low-cut bodice and a red ribbon dancing on her throat as she sings.

'What a racket!' mutters Gigi.

Nathalie de Sancaens' voice rasps through the gas-heavy air, one gloved arm waving as if she is drowning, heavily powdered skin gleaming like old wax in the harsh light of the gas jets at her feet.

'Now. Stand up straight, Marie, that's it. See that lady with the red silk fan, how she holds her head and looks around to show off her neck?' Marie looks over and tries to copy the lady.

'No, not like that! Look, like this. As if you are holding an apple under your chin.' Marie tries again but Gigi shakes her head and Antoinette giggles. 'I give up. What are we going to do with you?'

'Why? Why do I have to act like a tart?' She spits it out to stop herself crying.

'You can't eat *Fantine*, Marie.' Gigi clasps Marie's face in her sweaty hands. 'Victor Hugo might be good as a door stop or a pillow, but he won't teach you how to make a fucking living.'

A blue ceramic bowl piled high with tangerines sits on the scarred zinc counter.

Antoinette fingers one as if it's a precious stone.

'Those are three sous a piece.'

The girl behind the bar is tight-lipped, hands on lumpy hips in front of a huge mirror behind shelves of multicoloured bottles of all shapes and sizes. Marie moves her head away from Gigi, raises her chin and looks around to keep her bitter tears in check. Antoinette picks up a tangerine, cups it in her hand and then picks up two more and starts to juggle. She is obviously trying to break the tension and make them laugh. She hasn't juggled for years.

The girl behind the bar looks panicked now, her face twitching all over.

'I said, those are three sous a piece. So pay for them or put them back.'

'Fine,' Antoinette says, throwing the tangerines higher now. They spin in the air and Marie grabs her arm, but she just shrugs it off and catches all three tangerines in one hand. The look on her face is just like Papa's when he stood up to the doorman at the Museum of Curiosities.

39

'I'll take them. And three glasses of wine. Oh, and three of your finest galettes.'

The bar girl narrows her eyes and looks them up and down. It's obvious she thinks they don't have enough cash. A man further along raps his empty glass on the counter.

'Well,' Gigi chips in, one elbow on the counter, the hole in her old black glove gaping slightly. 'Are you waiting for Christmas or has someone sewn up your fucking mouth?' She is shouting above a high trilling note from the singer.

'Thank you, mademoiselle,' the bar girl says to Antoinette, studiously ignoring Gigi. 'Your galettes are on their way.'

Antoinette gives her mother a victorious wink.

'But how can we pay for all that?' Marie can't help asking as they push through the crowd.

'Oh, Antoinette's been doing some extra work. Modelling.'

'Have you?' Marie narrows her eyes at her sister. Only yesterday she was complaining that she hadn't been asked to model for two years and the Crow had threatened to let her go at the end of the year for missing too many classes. 'Have you really?'

'Yes, of course I have. You don't know everything about me, Marie, even if you think you do.'

'But you said—'

'Now, now, girls. Stop arguing and go and grab that table.'

'Are there any other tricks you can show us?' leers a man in a soft brown cap, with a loose button at the crown. He and his two friends are hunched over a game of dominoes. Antoinette flounces past, knocking over his double six with her elbow, and drags Marie after her. He is still standing there when they find a table at the other side of the bar, shaking a scabby fist at them, the button on his hat jiggling along with him.

'What did you do that for, Antoinette?'

'Oh, Marie. Don't bother with them!'

'But why?'

'No money. Now it's your turn, Marie. See over there. Three o'clock. Gold watch chain. Raise your skirt a little and sit up straight, for fuck's sake. That's it! A bit more. Pretend the Crow is behind you with her stick. See, you're really quite pretty, when you make an effort.'

Marie glares at Antoinette and edges her skirt up a centimetre or two. A waiter appears as if from nowhere, sweeps his loaded tray from high above his pomaded head onto the table with the grace of a prima ballerina and flashes her an empathetic smile.

'Come on, Marie,' Gigi joins in. 'He's looking at you now, I can tell. Don't be a baby. I was out singing in bars at your age. And I can tell you that I soon found out that the song didn't make a blind bit of difference, but the higher I flicked my skirts, the more coins there'd be in the hat that evening. You've got to use everything you've got. And, let's face it, that's not much.'

Marie decides to ignore the slightly slurred speech. She picks up her galette, but her mother snatches it out of her hand.

'Not until you've earned it. Watch me.' Gigi turns to face the room of people, tilts her head left and right so that the light catches her jawbone and highlights the full curve of her mouth. 'Now you do it.'

'Do I have to?'

'Yes,' says Gigi, holding the galette up away from her as if she's training a dog. 'That's it! Now try this.' She flicks up her skirts and idly crosses one red-stockinged ankle over the other. Marie watches with her mouth open. She has never seen her mother flirt so blatantly like this before and it makes her cringe, fascinated and disgusted at the same time. 'Go on then!'

41

Marie looks across at Antoinette who is grinning and enjoying the show, expecting her to fail. Right, she thinks, and takes her skirts, flicking them up so high they could see the tops of her stockings, and looks right at the gentleman with the gold watch chain and pouts like the tarts on Rue Blanche do. To her horror the gentleman gets up and comes over with his friend.

'*Victoire!*' Gigi claps her on the back so hard it makes her cough. Marie grabs the galette and stuffs it into her mouth. Oh, God. Here comes the man; if only he'd go away and bother someone else.

'May I offer you ladies a cigarette?' The gentleman stumbles over his words. There are crumbs on his bushy moustache. Then there is a lot of fumbling and stumbling while he looks in his pockets and lights cigarettes for Gigi and Antoinette.

'Please join us, if you like?' Antoinette is already clearing space and ushering them in. 'Oh dear, it's a bit crowded,' she simpers. The gentleman's friend is wide as an omnibus and his breath smells like the sewers. 'Never mind. Marie will sit on your lap.'

'No, I don't mind standing.' Marie blushes and starts to get up, but her mother is pushing her back down.

'Yes, good idea. I'm sure he won't mind, will you, Monsieur…?'

'Duchamp. Monsieur Duchamp.' He tries to kiss Gigi's hand but misses. His top lip is all slimy under his moustache. 'I would be delighted.' He sits and pats the stretched tweed of his trousers.

What can she do? Marie lowers herself onto the tweed, squeezes her legs under the table. His breath is warm and wet on the back of her neck. He breathes with a soft wheezing sound. I hate you, she thinks, looking at Antoinette and Gigi. I'll never forgive you. Ever. She forces herself to sit still and counts the gas lamps hung like grubby pearls around the room while the others laugh and flirt and talk interminable rubbish. Monsieur Duchamp slips a sweaty hand under the table and starts to knead Marie's thigh as if preparing her for the oven, but Marie finds she can mostly ignore the alarming sensation and prevent his hand rising any higher up her thigh by pressing it upwards and crushing it on the underside of the table.

'What's that?' Antoinette's voice is so harsh and loud after her cooing flirty gush that the gentlemen fall silent, blink and cough in embarrassment. Antoinette seems to have forgotten that the gentlemen exist and is glaring at the green liquid in Gigi's glass.

'Oh, nothing. *Calme-toi!* Just a little drink.' Gigi makes apologetic smiles at the gentlemen, picks up her glass in a shaking hand and throws the rest of the green liquid down her throat. Her elbow slides off the table with a jolt and she knocks into Monsieur Duchamp and rights herself. 'Would you kindly get me another?'

Thank God, now Marie has an excuse to get up and away from Monsieur Duchamp. She squeezes out from the banquette, pulls her skirts down and glares at Monsieur Duchamp, who totters away leaving his friend half asleep against the banquette.

Marie is just about to say she wants to go home when she notices that red patches are appearing on Antoinette's neck and she is looking daggers at Gigi. She realises there's a fight starting but is too tired and angry to know what to do about it or even care. She might have guessed it would end like this.

Antoinette leans over the table and pinches Gigi's arm, and she yelps. 'You promised. You promised you wouldn't touch the stuff. Liar! Ha! I can't believe a bloody thing you say anymore, can I?'

43

'*Calme-toi*, Marie.' Gigi looks into her glass, back hunched. 'No harm done. Just one more. I promise.' Gigi looks so small and sheepish now, it's painful to watch her shrink into herself like a beaten animal and hear the shame in her voice.

Antoinette draws back. 'No! No, Maman! You promised, you bloody promised! We're going right now. Marie, put your coat on. Now!'

Antoinette has her back turned and is already dragging Gigi up and pushing her towards the exit while people tut and stare.

They fall into a heavy silence and walk in single file down the hill. Marie keeps her head down and stews all the way home. She is dying to get into bed and read, but as soon as they get inside Antoinette insists that she has something to show them and starts fiddling around trying to light the stump of a candle.

'What now, Antoinette?' Marie cannot face any more of her sister's games tonight.

'Shut your eyes.'

'Why?'

'Just do it. Now hold out your hands.'

Something round and metallic lands in Marie's palm.

'Open!'

Marie sees a gold watch in her hands.

'Bravo, Marie.'

'What?'

She is confused. The watch is heavy. It takes her a moment to make sense of it. Then she remembers seeing it dangling out of the gentleman's pocket. So that was why Antoinette kept leaning into them and picking crumbs out of his moustache.

'Bravo! You distracted him beautifully. You're a natural!'

'Where did you get that?' Gigi is leaning against the ironing board pulling off her boots. She looks like she is going to be sick.

'That fat gentleman with the bad breath. He "gave" it to me. Least he could do, after I had to listen to him burbling on about his stupid wife and her nerves.'

'You stole it. You fucking stole it, didn't you?' Gigi's voice is tight and shaking now. 'What's wrong with you, Antoinette?'

Marie grabs Gigi's arm. 'Let's talk about it in the morning. We're all tired. Let's go to bed.'

But Gigi pushes her away, her eyes still on Antoinette. 'What the hell is wrong with you?'

'With me? Nothing is wrong with me. Don't pretend you didn't know.'

'Of course I didn't know. Are you mad? What if you got caught? The police are probably on their way now. How would we manage?'

'I was only trying to help.' Antoinette looks scared now and her voice is low and shaky. 'I... I thought you'd be glad.'

'Glad? What, that my daughter is a fucking thief?'

Antoinette keeps her head down. She drums her fingers on her thigh as if she's deciding what to do. Then she throws her head up so quickly that her hair tumbles down onto her shoulders, her hat skitters across the floor.

'Fuck you, Maman! Fuck you! Somebody in this shit-hole of a house has got to occasionally rouse themselves from their alcoholic fucking stupor and pay the fucking rent.'

Marie helps her mother, who is hopping about trying to remove her other boot.

'She didn't mean it, Maman. Come on, let's go to bed.'

'Don't bother talking to her, Marie. She's too fucking drunk to listen.'

Antoinette's voice is getting louder and tighter now. She won't show weakness for long. Neither of them will.

Antoinette's eyes are flashing now, catching scraps of light from the guttering candle. Gigi lurches towards Antoinette.

'How dare you talk to me like that, you bitch!' She takes the watch and throws it on the floor. 'Your father always said you were nothing but trouble.'

'He said that, did he?' Antoinette swallows hard. She looks like she's been punched in the stomach.

Gigi and Antoinette are facing each other now like boxers before the bell rings. Mad shadows dance around the walls from the stuttering candle on the floor. A double rap from next door. The neighbours banging a broom on the wall to tell them to be quiet. Neither of them seem to hear it.

'And do you know what he said about you?' Antoinette swallows again and bites her lip.

'What? What did he say?' Gigi hisses. 'What did he say? Tell me what he said, Antoinette.'

'I heard Papa talking to Béranger the night before he died. He said – he said you were a whore. A lazy, good-for-nothing whore. Those were his exact words.'

The two figures are totally still now. They look unreal. Almost comic, like the shadows in a magic lantern show. All Marie can hear now is a dying lump of coal twitching in the grate and the sound of her mother and sister breathing in long juddering sighs. Their chests rise and fall in exact time with each other. She feels sick and helpless, like when she was stuck inside the night Papa died and heard the gunfire getting closer and closer. That night has never really ended.

Gigi raises her arm and for an awful moment Marie thinks she's going to hit Antoinette. But then her arm drops to her side and her whole body goes limp. All the fight has gone out of her, like a spent firework on Bastille Day, falling from the sky. She

46

puts the watch on the table, picks up all their boots, and places them very slowly in front of the faint glow of the fire and starts to climb the stairs.

'Goodnight, girls.'

Her voice is horribly empty.

'How could you do that?'

Marie can't help herself. She's been lying on her bed staring up at the crack in the skylight for hours trying to calm herself down, so as not to start another fight. She knows Antoinette is awake too. No answer. She props herself up on her elbow.

'Why did you steal that watch?'

'Why did you steal that watch?' Antoinette mocks Marie. 'Who do you think you are, the chief of the fucking police?' Antoinette props herself up on her elbow now to face Marie. 'Come down from your high fucking horse, Marie, and join us mere mortals down in the fucking mud. How do you think anybody survives around here?'

'They work hard and stick together.'

'You're so full of shit, Marie. Nobody with half a brain believes any of that idealistic rubbish anymore.'

In the grubby moonlight coming through the skylight, Marie notices Paul's ribbon half-undone on Antoinette's neck. Antoinette pokes at a hole in the blanket.

'Do you think anybody *wants* to sit on sleazy men's laps batting their fucking hands away from their cunt, listening to them drone on and on about their bloody wives? I do it because I have to. I do it because I have to, Marie.' Antoinette raises her head and looks into Marie's eyes. Her voice is soft now. 'If I didn't, we'd be out on the streets by now. All that stuff Papa taught us, it doesn't work anymore. The Commune is over, Marie. No more concerts in the Tuileries, no more requisitioning of property, no more pulling down statues, no more Union des fucking Femmes. That time is over and there's no way back, Marie. No way back. We women must do what we can, use what we've fucking got while we still can.'

Marie thinks of the conversations she hears at the barre, the bruises on necks and arms every Monday. 'Are you…'

'On the game? Marie! No, course not. I'm not that stupid. Why would I let some rich cunt stick it in me when I can stick my fingers in his silk-lined fucking pockets and redistribute the fucking wealth? I flirt a bit but I draw the line at his fingers or anything else inside me or his mouth on mine. Then I take payment myself without having to ask for it.'

'So it's just your own little business then. Like shoe-shining or fortune-telling. How many times?'

'Only a few times.'

'Liar.'

Antoinette lies on her back and puts her hands behind her head. 'Fine. Two years. Since the bailiffs' first visit. It's not fun, Marie. It's not fucking fun at all, if you must know.' Antoinette's voice trails off; she sounds so sad and alone. Two cats squeal and scrabble on the roof.

'Can I come with you and help one day? You did say I was a natural.'

Antoinette snorts and turns her back. 'I said you were good. But not that good. I don't know. Maybe.'

'Do you know what day it is?'

'Of course I do.'

'Do you think Maman knows?'

'Of course she does. Now, stop asking questions and go to sleep.'

Marie turns onto her back, stares into a blank sky. Papa can't have said those things, can he? There were a lot of rows towards the end, but she was too young to understand what they were about. Marie hopes Gigi is too drunk to remember what was said earlier, but she doubts it. She tries not to remember her mother's face when Antoinette called her a whore. The way the light just died in her mother's eyes and something in her seemed to finally surrender. Like on the night they took Papa's body away. There she goes again, calling up images she doesn't want to see.

She grabs onto the cold brass bedstead above her head to steady herself. But it doesn't help. She almost calls out to Antoinette but stops herself. Instead, she reaches under the bed and picks up *Fantine*, feels the reassuring weight of the volume in her hands, traces the embossed letters with her finger. It's the only thing of her father's she has left. And she had to fight to stop Gigi selling it.

There's not enough light to read, so she curls up with her head on the hard leather volume and waits for sleep to swallow her whole.

CHAPTER FOUR

July 1878

At first light, workers start to swarm from the outer arrondissements into the ateliers, factories, workshops and building sites in the pumping heart of the city. By half past five in the morning there's an army of working men in overalls coming down Rue Lepic. They trudge on heavily with their heads down, as if returning from defeat in battle. A few gentlemen dressed in black, who have obviously been out all night and are returning from brothels and high-class drinking dens, stick out like sore, top-hatted thumbs as they wander drunkenly across the path of the marching multitude, disrupting the flow and receiving curses in return. A stonemason in a torn jacket stops to lean on a wall under the sign for the Moulin de la Galette, swigs on a bottle of spirits, slides down the wall and falls asleep. The battalions thin out and dry up completely two hours later. Then there's the sound of shutters opening all down Rue Lepic. It's time for working women – having emptied their pisspots, swept their floors, cleared up after their men, clothed their children, put up their hair, and painted on a smile – to step out into the full glare of the waking city.

*

'Marie! Hey, dreamychops! Marie! We're going to be late!' Two months since the disastrous night out and the weather has turned hot and humid. Marie is finding it hard to wake up and the nightmares don't help. Antoinette elbows her and she is back again. They are outside the house, blinking into the morning sun as it slices through the narrow gap between rooftops.

'Go ahead to Madame Béranger's and get the bread. I'll catch you up when Maman's head clears.'

Marie is happy to be at the boulangerie. The bright sound of the bell when she goes in seems to magic her into another world. The smell of Madame Béranger's heavenly bread makes her delirious with hunger. She must remember that Madame Béranger is actually not Madame Béranger any longer. After her husband was executed, the authorities threatened to close the shop down, so she married a man who used to be in the army to keep them quiet. It was a great scandal and many of their neighbours have boycotted the bakery, but her mother insists Emma Béranger did the right thing, and they must support her. Paul and Antoinette have been sweethearts forever. Maybe Antoinette sent her ahead because she doesn't want Paul to see her with Gigi in such a state. Antoinette is very proud like that. There's Paul in the back room, bending down to put a tray in the oven. He catches her eye and smiles and then gets a clip around the ear from his bully of a stepfather.

Marie tries not to look at the stepfather. After all, he could have been there when Papa died. He might have been in one of the firing squads. The glint of a musket, his eye narrowing as it is now when he shouts at Paul. No – mustn't think about things like that. Besides, nobody will ever know because nobody talks about it. The back of her neck feels like there are ants crawling inside her skin. She tries so hard to push the image away but there is no escaping the pictures that rise up and seep into her body like a stain. Papa's big toe, the nail bruised where his left boot had shrunk in the rain. The blue and purple standing out against his blood-leached skin, all lit up in flickers of torchlight and screaming. Fragments of him come to her like scraps washed up on the tide. Gigi made her swear to never mention it, to just lock all those memories away in a big casket in her head. But she can't. She can control her words but not her thoughts. If only she could make him whole, know the full story of what happened all the way to the end, then maybe she could bury him, in her mind at least. There is nowhere she can visit, nowhere to put a bunch of flowers or sit with him and gather herself. He is just fragments of memory in her mind. Driftwood.

Paul gives a feeble wave while his stepfather isn't looking and she manages a smile in return. Dear Paul, he is so kind and sweet. He has always had a soft spot for Antoinette, even though she is rude to him and never thanks him for all the hair ribbons he buys her, all the times he sneaks out to meet her and risks a beating from his stepfather. 'Well, I never. It's Marie, isn't it?' The woman in front of her in the queue has turned round and is staring at her with merry brown eyes, outlined in kohl. She smells of lilies and her hair is dotted with tiny diamond pins. A mauve parasol hangs off her arm, matching her silk dress and slippers. She looks totally out of place in the boulangerie. Her smile is so warm, her eyes so kind that Marie can't help smiling back. 'Oh, you do have a look of your papa. You really do.' The woman purrs and strokes her powdered chin with a gloved hand.

'Yes, I am Marie.' She straightens herself up and swallows hard. Suddenly, she is wide awake. A thrill runs through her. This woman knew Papa and mentions him casually as if it's the most natural thing in the world. And she spoke about him as if he was in the next room! To hear anyone talk about him with warmth makes him seem real again and that somehow makes her feel more real too. She can't help staring at this beautiful lady, the fine lace at her sleeves; her father would have loved that lace. Marie can't remember ever having seen this creature in her life before. She holds her breath, waits for the woman to say more about her father, anything. But the lady just keeps staring at her with such kind eyes that she bites her lip to stop the tears coming. If she carries on being so nice, Marie is afraid she'll make a scene, collapse onto her chest, smear the silk with her sobbing.

'Sorry, my love. So sorry to startle you. I should have introduced myself. I am an old friend of your mother's. We worked together at the Alcazar. Beautiful voice your mother had, like a nightingale. Much better than mine. Shame she had to stop.' Go on, Marie tells herself. This is your chance. Gigi never talks about her time at the Alcazar, and even Papa became stony when it was mentioned. Ask her a question, ask her about Papa. She opens her mouth to speak, but it's too late, the lady is looking away now, out the window.

'Oh, look! There she is now! I'll be with you in a moment, Emma.' Madame Béranger shakes her head indulgently at the lady while other customers tut and moan. Then the lady goes to the door, rises onto her toes and hangs out of it, showing tiny silk flowers on her slippers. Everybody else in the shop scowls and stares at her but she doesn't seem to care, in fact she seems to enjoy it.

'Gigi! Gigi!'

Gigi turns away and pretends not to hear her. Why is she being so rude? But then the lady peels off a glove, puts her fingers in her mouth and whistles loudly, which makes the other people in the shop jump. Marie laughs at her daring. A man pushes past, huffing to himself, and several women in the queue start to mutter and cast disapproving glances. The lady ushers Gigi and Antoinette in and tells everyone they are old friends.

'Amélie,' Gigi says tightly. 'Amélie Reine.' She tilts up her chin and forces a smile. 'How – how are you?' They kiss each other awkwardly.

'I'm very well, Gigi. And all the better for seeing you.'

Gigi bristles at that. 'So, you aren't boycotting Emma for consorting with the enemy, like all the others.'

'No, Gigi, not at all. We all do what we can to survive.' Amélie's voice is soft now. Gigi sighs and gives her a lopsided smile.

Amélie. Marie turns her name over in her mind. Yes, of course, Amélie, the famous courtesan. Here she is, in person.

'You look as if life is treating you well,' says Gigi.

'Oh, you know. Can't complain,' says the lady, gesturing at her fine clothes as if she is embarrassed by them. 'And you?' Gigi shrugs and refuses to look at Amélie. Amélie has tears in her eyes as she smiles at Gigi. So they must have been very good friends, although Gigi never talks about her – well, only when she wants to stick the boot in. 'It's so good to see you, Gigi. So good. How could you disappear on me like that?'

Disappear, what does she mean disappear? Come on, Gigi, Marie thinks, please be polite at least, we have few enough friends left as it is. Marie likes this woman. Being with her is like somebody throwing the door open and letting bright sunshine into a long-forgotten room.

Gigi draws herself up, smooths her dress over her waist, tries to find something in herself, something to impress Amélie with.

'Well, I've been quite busy with my family,' Gigi says curtly.

No good looking to Antoinette for support. She is busy making eyes at Paul.

'Yes, of course. I just about recognise your two beautiful daughters. Haven't they grown up wonderfully? A couple of prize peaches! Oh, those long walks in the Tuileries gardens, Gigi, eh? Must be nearly ten years ago now, you and I swinging Marie between us? Remember that day when...'

Marie finds herself smiling like a lunatic while she tries to digest what Amélie has said.

'Do you have any children?' Gigi interrupts coldly. Everyone in the shop is silent, pretending not to watch but obviously straining to hear the gossip. Even Paul's stepfather has stopped with a tray half out of the oven. And Antoinette makes the most of it and blows a kiss at Paul.

'Lord, no. Not in my business. And it is a sadness to me. A great sadness.' Amélie sighs and strokes Antoinette's cheek. She speaks loudly, seems to be enjoying her audience. How wonderful to be so confident.

'What a lovely young woman you've turned out to be, my love. Such magnificent hair. And all real, if I'm not mistaken. Oh, she's just like you, Gigi!' Amélie reaches out and holds Gigi's hands, but Gigi pulls away and waves to Madame Béranger behind the counter as if asking for help. How can she be so rude? Marie wants to slap her.

Usually, Marie is able to place a Parisian as soon as she sees them and hears them speak. She can tell if they are from Montmartre or Belleville or Pigalle or one of the richer arrondissements in the south. The Montmartrois are used to dozy artists and a few drunken gentlemen on their way to or from whore houses cluttering up Rue Lepic, even a few foreigners and country people, but real Parisian ladies wouldn't be seen dead on the Butte. Amélie looks and smells rich, but she doesn't sound like a lady at all – rather than tripping lightly along like a well-sprung carriage her voice jumps up and down excitedly like a proper Montmartroise and is peppered with exclamations. And her emotions are not buttoned down, they are too much on display for her to be a true bourgeoise.

'What are you doing up here, Amélie? I thought you'd abandoned Montmartre long ago,' Gigi asks in an effort at politeness.

'Yes, that's right, Gigi, but sometimes I miss the Butte so much it hurts. Strange, really, but there we are. I still feel more at home here really, if I'm honest. But you don't find many counts or dukes offering you free accommodation around here. And I like to come and see Emma and the other women from the Vigilance Committee, make sure they're all still alive and well.'

'Amélie,' Madame Béranger calls over with a hard look which seems to tell Amélie to keep quiet, to stop mentioning the Vigilance Committee when her husband might hear.

'Oh yes, so sorry, my darling.' Amélie makes an apologetic grimace. 'Me and my big mouth!'

So, Amélie was on the Vigilance Committee too. Marie is surprised and delighted to find that out. People rarely even mention the Montmartre Vigilance Committee or anything to do with those three months of 1871.

'It was wonderful to see you, Emma, and I know I've said it before, but you make the best bread in Paris, and one day we'll find out your secret ingredient!'

Emma Béranger beams at that. 'Away with you, Amélie!'

Marie makes a point of saying very loudly how delighted she is to meet Amélie. Gigi scowls but Amélie exclaims that Marie is '*charmante*, just like your father'. It is a small victory, but it is something. Amélie kisses Antoinette and Marie on both cheeks and invites them to visit her any time they like. 'Boulevard Haussmann,' she whispers, 'halfway up, the flat with the parrots on the first-floor balcony.'

There is a very faint song in Marie's heart as they reach the bottom of the hill where the streets get wider, the houses straighter, the shops fancier. One day she will go and knock on Amélie's door. The thought is delicious, like a stolen bon-bon stowed in her cheek.

'Amélie says I look like my father,' Marie blurts out while they are waiting to cross Boulevard de Clichy. She knows it will annoy her mother, but she refuses to pretend nothing happened. Gigi stops short halfway across the boulevard.

'Well, Amélie Reine should mind her own fucking business.'

A smart carriage speeds past and the driver turns around and swears at them.

Marie hooks her arm through Antoinette's, and they start to skip and giggle at their own childishness while Gigi huffs behind them and tells them to slow down.

'Paul's so in love with you, it's so obvious,' she whispers.

Antoinette elbows her and tuts, but her eyes light up. 'I'm seeing him tonight – don't tell Maman.'

'I won't. Where are you going?'

'Martyrs Tavern. He says he's got something special for me!'

'Really?'

Antoinette nods. It's so good to see the light dancing in her eyes, to see her happy and excited.

'Do you think it could be…?'

'No, no. Nothing like that.' Antoinette shoves her away and calls to Gigi. But it's obvious to Marie that her sister is desperately trying not to hope yet hoping like mad all the same.

*

While she is putting on her ballet shoes in the dressing room at the opera house, Marie thinks about Antoinette and Paul, and what it would be like if they got married. The two of them silhouetted in the stained-glass window of St Pierre, Antoinette with her hair piled up, studded with diamonds, herself behind them as bridesmaid, dressed in white. She sighs and ties a tight bow behind her right calf. *Don't be an idiot!* she tells herself. Paul's stepfather would never allow it. He whacks Paul for talking to anyone who even looks like a Communard. He can't stand the sight of Antoinette – especially since she refused his advances – and has no idea she and Paul are courting. She must get those romantic ideas out of her head once and for all.

There's another blister coming up on her heel. It pains her that Antoinette could think of leaving her after all they've been through. Selfish. Typical. Both shoes on now, just the ribbon to tie around her waist. But what about Gigi? The ribbon is cool and silky in her hands, it sticks on the dry skin on her knuckles. How red they are. No, Antoinette wouldn't leave Gigi. Impossible. And anyway, if she and Paul did get married, they'd have to leave Montmartre, that's for sure. They might even leave Paris. Surely Antoinette wouldn't desert them. Surely she wouldn't leave Marie all alone with Gigi. *All alone.* Her stomach caves in at that, then guilt grabs her.

'Places, please,' the Crow shouts from the open doorway into the rehearsal room. Marie jumps to attention and notices that all the others have gone and are lining up at the barre.

Two weeks later, Marie is alone in the dressing room at the opera house. She passed the test for the seraglio scene and has been rehearsing hard every day. The ballet master has been even more agitated than usual, shaking his stick at the pianist, flapping his arms at the Crow, the wet patches under his arms growing with his temper. He made them repeat their steps again and again until somebody fainted.

So far, Marie has somehow managed not to faint, even though she is often dizzy with heat and hunger. There are girls even worse off than her, even skinnier and with hacking coughs that they try to cover up. The ballet master does not like girls who cough. He'll sack a girl on a whim if he's in a bad mood. Prettiness counts for a lot, of course. Much more important than ability. Also, if you are the favourite of one of the *abonnés*, the old men who talk through the performances and pay a subscription to ogle and smoke at the sides of the rehearsal room, you are untouchable. Antoinette has explained it all to her in great detail. Antoinette says that, while it's important to make a good showing at the Salle des Abonnés and in open rehearsals, the dressing room, closed rehearsals and backstage at the opera are a different matter. That's where you must be on your guard. She says she survives the manoeuvring of the little rats and their mothers by keeping quiet, not joining in with the gossip, keeping herself to herself. And it's true. Out on the street and in the bars, Antoinette is a big character, but here in the rehearsal room she is almost invisible. Antoinette once had an *abonné* who favoured her, but he moved away just before Easter and now she is in danger. She has also been late twice in the past few weeks, which doesn't help. No wonder Antoinette is hoping Paul will save her. If only she'd been chosen to be in the seraglio scene as well as Marie, then they could go home together, and she wouldn't be lumped with Blanche Balnar and her stuck-up friends and their sneering.

Marie's blisters are worse than usual, because of the heat. There is a particularly bad one blossoming on her heel. It is bearable with the shoe on, but when she takes it off she knows the skin will pull away and then she will have to hobble home. She pauses with her foot on the bench, hoping to find a moment of peace. No chance of that. When did she last feel peaceful? It is very quiet and pleasantly cool here at the back of the opera house, but she can't take in the silence, can't rest in it. There is a racket in her mind, a mass of shouted commands – five, six, seven, eight, pas-de-chats, pirouettes and enchaînements – and her stomach is growling at her, as usual. Her mind is as crowded as Pont Neuf on All Saints' Day, and she can't get away from it. And then there's that background rumbling, like the sound of clouds bashing into each other before a storm. The rumbling is always there, at her back. Best to ignore it.

'*Au futur, les filles, au futur!*' Papa used to command as he pointed forwards whenever she or Antoinette or Gigi talked about the past. Look to the future, girls, look to the future! He was entranced by modernity and often took her and Antoinette to visit the new railway station at St Lazare as part of what he saw as a necessary part of their education. He forced them to face the steam and screaming whistles when the new engines thundered in. 'This is the future,' he would say, 'and we must face it with courage. We must embrace it!' Poor Antoinette would always cry and complain and bury her face in Papa's chest, but not Marie, she held Papa's hand and forced herself to stand still. Oh, that taste of coal on her lips, the hot breath of the engines plastering her hair over her face, her heart racing in time with the trains. She always felt strangely peaceful then, in the midst of all that. She supposes it was because Papa was right there beside her and she knew nothing could go wrong. He never ran away from anyone or anything and she mustn't either. Papa promised to take them both for a ride on the engines to see the sea when the railway lines stretched that far.

But he never did, of course. So now she never would find out if seawater was really salty or not.

She sighs and drags off her slipper and winces at the flap of skin on her heel, the raw red patch underneath. *Never mind blisters*, one of the faceless people in her head says, *soon you'll be out on stage lit up by the gas lamps for everyone to laugh at!* The thought makes her dizzy. And if it doesn't go well both she and Antoinette will surely be for the chop. Concentrate, Marie. Concentrate on the steps. Double pirouette, wait two beats, lift the elbow and gaze left on the travelling steps. She must remember. She must. No, she can't. She can't! What if her mind goes blank on stage and she forgets everything? What if she faints, or falls into a gas lamp and burns to death? What if…?

'Here. For you. From Monsieur Degas.'

Marie is so surprised to see the Crow in the doorway that she yelps and drops the slippers on the floor, as if they are burning. She bends to pick them up and when she straightens up again the Crow is gone. Did she imagine her appearance? No. Because there on the bench beside her is a small white envelope with her name written on it in a strange squarish script. A letter! She holds it to her nose and inhales the smell of expensive paper. She hasn't held a piece of paper with words on it for years. Apart from *Fantine*, of course. And she hasn't even had the time or the appetite for that recently. Somehow just tracing a finger over her own name, there in the middle of the envelope, definite letters laid on thick cream paper, makes her feel more real, more hopeful.

CHAPTER FIVE

August 1878

Monsieur Degas' studio is at the bottom of the Butte de Montmartre, a stone's throw from Marie's house, although it may as well be the other side of the world; freshly swept squares with fountains, mellow-voiced ladies with parasols and pearls, smooth-faced houses with iron railings. She takes the letter out of her pocket and checks the address.

Best not to stop too long outside 3 Place Blanche in case she loses her nerve. '*Bonjour, Monsieur Degas.*' Or maybe just '*Bonjour, monsieur.*' Or nothing, just a nod, not to sound too familiar. She's not sure. She stashes the letter in her pocket and strides up the steps to the wide black front door, pulls hard on the bell rope and waits. '*Bonjour, monsieur*' is enough, she decides. It will be strange to see Monsieur Degas up close. Although she is sometimes quite near him when she is dancing, she can't afford to look at him. It is true she has felt him looking at her very intensely sometimes and has had to force herself to concentrate so she doesn't forget the steps, but always told herself she was just imagining it. Now he will be looking at her for hours. And she will be in her chemise or even naked. Courage, courage. Don't think about it. It's perfectly normal.

Artists draw naked women as part of their training. 'They see us like horses, not human beings,' Antoinette said. Marie is not sure if she is more worried about him seeing her naked or seeing her chemise. She has scrubbed the chemise and mended the holes under the arms, but it is still very tatty, and she can't get the salty sweat stains off under the arms.

A noise from inside makes her lean in. Two voices: Degas' low mocking tone and a lady's quick, light speech set against it. Footsteps on the stairs, the sound of a crinoline brushing against the wall in the hallway. A kissing sound as the big door opens.

'Aaah! Now, you must be Marie?'

Not Degas' big pale face, but a tall, very thin woman with cool hazel eyes. She's simply dressed in a black dress edged with velvet, her hair coiled into a bun in a black chenille net, jet buttons glittering at her cuffs. Marie finds her bare hand held in the lady's gloved ones. Something about her makes Marie's stomach clench. She reminds Marie of a spider.

'I am Mary Cassatt. *Enchantée.*'

Degas is hovering awkwardly behind the lady. He looks slightly annoyed, or amused, maybe. It's hard to tell. There are two shallow furrows between his eyebrows which may or may not be permanent and fine lines running from his nose to the edges of his wide mouth. But otherwise, his face is smooth, his eyes dark and unclouded. She had thought somehow that he must be older, but she can see now he is forty or forty-five, the age Papa would have been if he had lived.

'So this is your new model, Edgar? An interesting choice.'

The Spider looks into Marie as if she's searching for something. Her voice is as soft as her gloves, and she has a strange accent that is definitely not from Paris. Marie is not really taking in whatever it is that the Spider is saying, she just

63

wants to get in out of the sun and get the whole fucking thing over with.

Degas pushes back his floppy dark hair and raps impatiently on the wall behind the lady's head. His fingers are long and pale. One of his nails is broken and his hands look unusually rough for a gentleman. 'A shame you must be going, my dear Mary.'

Rich people's talk always sounds like they are competing for something, Marie thinks to herself. She smiles awkwardly and looks down to check her boots aren't too dirty. It would be embarrassing to leave mud on that freshly polished parquet floor in the hallway.

'Oh, don't be such a grump, Edgar,' coos the Spider. 'If you won't accompany me and Manet to Bougival and actually enjoy yourself for once, you could at least agree to come and sulk at Café Riche with my sister and me tonight.'

'All right. I agree.' Degas smiles. Well, not a smile exactly. Only one side of his full mouth twitches upwards for a moment before he pulls it back into shape. Is he enjoying this encounter or not? Hard to tell. 'Marie is waiting, Mary. And I have work to do, if you expect me to have anything at all to show at our next infernal exhibition. Now, go!'

Marie jumps aside as the lady stumbles down the steps, looks back at Monsieur Degas and hisses like a cat. She stifles a giggle. Papa always said that rich people never had to bother growing up and now she sees what he meant. The Spider snaps open her parasol and darts away into the crowds, leaving the gate wide open. Degas stares after her and Marie turns to watch her too, partly to put off the moment of facing Degas alone. When she turns back, Degas is frowning into the light and chewing his lip. He seems to have forgotten that she is there. She wonders if she

64

should shut the gate. No, of course not. It's not her job. Rich people probably don't worry about things like that.

'That woman is a nuisance. Come, Marie. Follow me.'

So he hasn't forgotten her and he even gives her a little knowing smile as if they are sharing a joke, which makes her feel slightly better.

At last Marie is over the threshold and following Degas through the deliciously cool hallway and up a long flight of stairs. Her boots creak loudly in the sudden quiet of the house. To stop herself thinking about standing naked in front of him, she takes note of his clothes: plum-coloured woollen trousers, a white shirt and a striped waistcoat in the most expensive brocade (she doubts he has ever had to stand naked in front of anyone, unless he wanted to, of course). Papa would have loved that waistcoat. Degas takes the stairs three at a time; she struggles to keep up with him, especially with the bloody blister on her heel which keeps getting rubbed before it can heal.

Degas opens a tall wooden door, and they are in a large room on the first floor. The light is almost blinding, and Marie stops just inside the doorway, while he goes to open one of the two sets of floor-to-ceiling windows. This must be his studio. At one end of the large room is a jumble of strange-looking things: rags balled up and bound with tape and string, canvases of all sizes propped up against the wall, interleaved with empty picture frames – some of them broken – alongside bits of wire affixed to planks of wood and teetering piles of books. Some kind of machine on a steel, three-legged stand and covered in a black cloth is placed in front of the pictures, presumably to stop them sliding onto the floor. In front of all this is an easel and a wooden table jam-packed with candle ends, chipped cups filled with brushes, saucers covered in paint and squished slug-like tubes everywhere. In the middle of the mess on the table, high on a pile of what looks like a balled-up bedsheet is a plate with a half-eaten sandwich on it, a knife precariously balanced on the plate. Marie has to stop herself going over and stuffing the bread in her mouth. God knows if he will feed her or even give her water. Surely he will. Even horses get fed, after all.

The walls of the studio are newly painted, no sign of damp, no cracks. A welcome breeze now from the open window. The walls are completely naked except for a few splatters of paint and one large, unframed portrait on the wall above his painting things. The gaunt-looking woman in the painting seems to be staring right at her from her ornate cast-iron bench in front of some sort of forest full of thickset fleshy-leaved trees. Marie drags her eyes away and steadies herself by inspecting the rest of the room. She is not about to let a lady in a painting unsettle her. At the opposite end to the portrait there is an old blue armchair with a pile of canvases on it and a red velvet chaise longue, with a Japanese screen next to it. Her heart lurches when she sees the screen and sure enough Degas makes a vague gesture towards it. 'Get undressed behind the screen please.' Luckily, he doesn't see her blush in response as he is already bounding over towards his easel. His heavy step unsettles a floorboard and the sandwich knife wobbles and spatters sunlight all over the room. It makes her dizzy. She wants to ask him if he would like her totally naked or in her chemise, but can't get the words out. Well, she can't put it off any longer. Hundreds, probably thousands of girls have done this before her, so she must stop making a fuss.

From behind the screen, there are noises of scraping furniture (is he moving his easel?) and a horse whinnying on the street. How long should she take? Is he waiting for her already?

She mustn't make him wait. Gentlemen hate to be kept waiting. She undoes her dress so fast that a button flies off and rolls under the screen. She hopes he won't notice, and she'll be able to retrieve the button when he is not looking. She can't afford to lose a button. There is no mirror behind the screen. *You look like a stray cat!* Antoinette's words come back to her. She smooths her hair with her hands, feels for the sweaty strands which always escape at the front and tucks them into her ponytail at the back. It is tied with one of Antoinette's ribbons. *Just this once you can borrow one*, Antoinette had warned her. *But if you get your greasy fingermarks on my precious ribbon, you're fucking dead.* Her bare legs are covered in bruises, no hiding that, and her feet are horribly ugly with lumps and blisters everywhere. Why would anybody want to paint her? Will he be disgusted by her? Will he send her away or laugh? Surely this is all a mistake. Oh no! Now he has gone silent. Does that mean he is ready? This must surely be worse than going out on stage (courage, Marie, courage). But of course, not as bad as walking into enemy fire. Don't be a baby, Marie! He coughs. Is it the dust, or is he politely telling her it's time? A rivulet of sweat is running down her back – what if it drips on the floor? No, no. Just think of the money: five sous an hour. Think of that. In three hours, that's fifteen. She will pop into the butcher's on the way home and buy treats for Gigi and Antoinette. *Now!* whispers the lady in the portrait and Marie raises her chin and steps out.

PART TWO

'An artist must not have a private life'

Edgar Degas

CHAPTER SIX

January 1879

'How was your trip to London?'

'I didn't go to London this time. Just a little coastal town. Horrible, vulgar place. I don't want to remember its name.'

'Brighton?'

'Yes, thank you, René. I thought you might know it. Your kind of place.'

'Yes. Forgive me if I enjoy pleasure and fresh air, joy and laughter.' René looks around at the rest of the group for affirmation, but they all look into their drinks. 'You should try it sometime, *mon frère*, instead of locking yourself in your cave.'

'You can't lock a cave, René.'

'Always the pedant. Did you sell anything?'

Degas shrugs into an awkward silence.

Marie is sitting in Le Rat Mort, a bar in Pigalle, with Degas and his friends. At least, she thinks they are his friends. They are an odd assortment of people, including Mary Cassatt, whom she is pretending to chaperone. How strange to be here for pleasure, she thinks to herself. Normally, she'd be here for business, eyeing up an easy target with her sister. It's hard to remember the last time she did anything for pleasure, apart from the occasional few minutes she spends in the company of Fantine and Cosette when Antoinette is not there, and she has enough light and energy to read before collapsing into sleep.

'I heard *In the Café* went down like a lead balloon,' says René.

Marie doesn't understand their humour, but she can tell Degas is getting agitated because he goes very still and there is a muscle twitching in his cheek. That's what happens when his sketching isn't going right. Sometimes, she thinks he must be ill. She waits and waits, holding her pose for what seems like an eternity, and then he suddenly breaks into action again.

'Durand-Ruel says I must rename the picture,' Degas says with a grimace. 'He wants the word "absinthe" in the title, thinks it will make it worth more.'

'Excellent idea. At least your dealer has some sense. Much more commercial. God forbid you should make some actual money out of this enterprise.' René lets out a dry chuckle, but the others don't seem amused. Mary Cassatt raises an eyebrow and a large man, the only one who greeted Marie and looked her in the eye, and who seems to be the ringleader, pats Degas gently on the back.

Monsieur Degas holds his glass up to the gaslight and tilts it right and left. No doubt studying the colours, lodging the image in his mind. Sometimes she thinks he sees the whole world as a painting. How strange that must be. Is she just an object to be studied and recreated by him too? Does he see her as a mass of lines and colours or as a real person?

As Marie watches Degas she reflects on the six months that have passed since she began modelling for him. She needn't have worried about posing for him in her chemise. He made no response when she appeared in front of him the first time. He didn't even look up when she stepped out from behind the screen shaking with nerves, he just kept banging a tube of paint on the table and told her to get into first, 'there where the light is'. She presumed that meant in the oblong of sunlight right in the middle of the room. Strange to remember how frightened she was of him then. Finally, he had turned to her and must have felt a little sorry or something because he apologised and softened his voice and told her to stay very still. He seemed to have given up on the paint and picked up a charcoal stick instead. Then he did look at her and she held her breath, waiting for – well, waiting for what? He didn't look her up and down, like the lascivious young men on the building sites. How did he look at her? Well, that first time, his attention was mainly on her left arm. He told her to hold the curve of it and not worry about anything else. It was strange the way he looked at her. It was if he was trying to work something out. For a very long time he scribbled on his pad, sometimes using light strokes as if smoothing the cheek of a loved one, sometimes jabbing at the paper as if he was angry, sometimes using his other hand to rub at his lines.

Since then, Marie has modelled for Degas once or twice a week. At first it was alarming when he got near to her and started prodding her calf or staring at her jaw, making her turn this way and that. But after a while she realised he didn't want anything from her. He was happy if she stayed silent and did what he said. It was the paper he was interested in. Not her. So gradually she found herself relaxing. She stopped thinking she ought to speak, stopped watching him so intently for signs of disapproval and just daydreamed or gazed around the room instead. Often, she stared at the picture of the lady, wondering what she was thinking and feeling, if she had been on that bench very long and why she was there.

In November, she was ill for a couple of weeks and almost fainted a few times. Once she was coughing so hard that Degas took pity on her and invited her to sit on the chaise longue. He sat with her and asked his maid to bring her hot lemon with honey and a ham sandwich. After that he let her take regular breaks. Sometimes he sat with her in silence, at other times he mixed paints or made objects out of wire and wood. The week before Christmas, he sat with her on the chaise longue, ordered the maid to bank up the fire and presented her with a huge slice of *bûche de Noël*. He laughed when she let out a childish squeal of delight and kissed her on the cheek, said he hoped she and her family would have a happy Christmas. Some chance, she had thought to herself – imagining her freezing cold house and warring mother and sister – and started counting the days until she would be back with him in his warm and peaceful studio.

'Do people really have to be led by the nose, like blinkered horses?'

Degas addresses the remark to Mary. She looks very elegant in a black damask gown with intricate lace edging. Valenciennes, by the looks of it. Mary is all angles, like a miniature version of Notre Dame, and the simple style suits her. Are they in love, she and Monsieur Degas? Mary doesn't flirt in the same way that Antoinette and Gigi do. But she flirts nonetheless. Marie wonders what she would look like in Mary's gown, what it would feel like.

The mood of the group changes. Mary makes horse ears with her hands which makes the ringleader splutter into his glass and declare that she is really too much. René looks offended by her behaviour. Marie can't help laughing along with the ringleader but stifles her uncouth noise when the others look at her. But then Mary and the other artists roar with laughter and Marie almost feels like she is one of them, which in turn makes her blush. How lovely it must be to sit in a bar and laugh with friends. And not be hungry or looking for business. René doesn't appreciate the joke at all. He just strums his stubby fingers on the table and tuts.

'It's the same with the critics,' Degas continues. 'I was skied at the Académie last year. The canvas was so high, you could hardly see it. Then I changed the background colour and put a dog in. *Et, voilà!* The picture is being taken seriously. The academicians are such low-minded sheep, *n'est-ce pas?*'

Marie's father took her to see the paintings at the Académie one year. They sneaked in and he pointed out the artists he liked. Did she see one by Degas? She was only four or five but remembers being bewildered by the huge rooms full of people staring at the walls and the thrill when they were thrown out and escorted to the door by a very tall man in a uniform of some sort.

Degas' friends nod and sigh together and look into their drinks as if they can see the future there.

'People must indeed be led by the nose, as you put it,' says René. 'You artists expect too much of people.' He says the word 'artists' as if it sours his mouth; his moustache tilts.

'And you expect too little, *mon frère.*'

This remark seems to make everybody sit up and be quiet and fiddle with their drinks.

Marie was surprised at the meeting place. She'd hoped for somewhere more glamorous, where she wouldn't know anybody. This is the first time she has been out of the studio in his company, and Marie can't help imagining herself as one of those artists' muses, or even a courtesan like Amélie Reine, feeding cake crumbs to her parrots. It wouldn't be so bad, would it? Some courtesans are said to influence politicians. She could snag a government minister and get a monument built for Papa and all the other Communards next to the damned new basilica, or instead of it. If she were one of those women, if she had money and a place in society, if she were visible, if she had a voice, she would raise it, to shout of the injustices heaped upon the poor, to force the bourgeoisie to listen, to make them understand, to make it impossible for them to ignore those less fortunate than themselves, or to see them as picturesque, or as deserving of their squalid fate. She grits her teeth and pulls herself back from such fanciful nonsense. Famous courtesans are to be seen on the arms of the most powerful men, or exhibited in open-topped carriages in the most extravagant clothes, but are most certainly *not* to be heard. Ever. The only woman she knows who is listened to by anyone outside her own home is Louise Michel. And she is hardly considered a woman at all. No! Marie pulls herself up tall. She is a Communard! Putting herself on the market, selling her own body in return for the right to swan about in silk and throw crumbs to parrots is out of the question.

Degas turns his broad back on his brother and huddles in with the other artists, leaving Marie on the edge with René.

'Forgive my brother's bad manners, my dear. He is obsessed with his art, if you can call it that. Now, may I buy you an ice cream? I bet you prefer vanilla.'

'Yes, yes, I do. Thank you.'

Degas had asked Marie to come to the circus in a way that was more instruction than invitation. Being in his company usually makes her feel solid and calm, but right now, she is feeling light-headed, a little giddy. She hopes somebody will offer her something to eat and drink before she faints. An ice cream is all very well, but she hasn't eaten anything all day and it would be lovely to tuck into a plate of veal and potatoes.

René goes off to the bar and Marie is all alone. It's very hot and the smell of sweat mingles with rosewater and a blast of horse manure every time the door opens. Degas and his friends are talking intensely; they don't even notice she is still there. Reality dawns. How idiotic she was to think all those hours in the studio with Degas meant anything to him. She is just an amusing sideshow, a doll, a horse, a bundle of flesh and sinews, a peasant, a nothing. Anger ripples through her. The same enlivening anger she used to feel in the atmosphere all around her at political meetings with Papa. Forget it, she tells herself. There's no point anymore. The battle has been lost. She looks over at Degas and his friends and feels even more lonely than before. She hasn't really got any friends, unless you count Paul and a couple of the other dancers who bother to say hello and goodbye. These days, there is no time or energy for anything but work and sleep and struggle.

She should really go home and check on Gigi. The thought makes her stomach stony. Gigi has been bad again the past few weeks. She says she's been looking for work but comes in late smelling of smoke and alcohol. Gigi's smile is hard to remember, and even Antoinette hasn't made her laugh for ages. Everybody knows work is thin on the ground and houses are being repossessed all around them, so it's no surprise there is no fun to be had anymore. Before, there would have been demonstrations; they would have gathered in basements and public squares and sung with their heads held high. But all resistance has been snuffed out since the Commune. Mostly, Gigi just sits in a tatty wicker chair Antoinette found on the street and stares into the fireplace. They rarely have enough wood for a fire and shiver with cold most of the time, wear all their clothes and keep their boots on at night. The three of them never sit down to a meal anymore. They stay away from their cold, dirty, joyless house, pick up what food they can and enough money to pay the rent most months. Antoinette is now secretly engaged to Paul and they are hoping to find a little place together. That will leave Marie alone with Gigi. Better not to think about it right now.

Soon, René will be back. He is so unlike his brother, short and wiry and light-eyed. She will have to make conversation, and she has no idea what you talk about with a gentleman.

'My brother has completely buried himself in his paintings since our mother died.' Luckily René starts talking as soon as he returns, stumbling as he places the ice cream in front of Marie. It has a long silver spoon. 'And he left the business in my hands alone, even though he is the one with a natural talent for it.'

Marie makes herself put down the spoon for a moment, in an effort at ladylike restraint, and looks over at Degas. He is sitting back in his chair with a serious look on his face, his long legs stretched out, his feet crossed, while the ringleader is drawing things in the air. What is Degas thinking? René is still speaking and looking at her intensely. She drags her gaze from Degas and makes herself focus on what René is saying. Something about a business. But surely Degas is an artist, isn't he? She scans around her mind for something to say and thinks of the lady in the picture in Degas' studio who seems to always be watching her. She is dressed in a very striking, short-sleeved dress covered in vines and huge yellow flowers and perched on an ornate bench surrounded by thick juicy leaves the like of which Marie has never seen. The branches seem to be coming out to get her. But she sits with her legs together, her slippers half-hidden under her skirts, unaware of it all. She holds a hairbrush in her lap. Strange for a lady to hold her own hairbrush. Surely her maid would have taken care of her hair. The lady looks straight at Marie from under a wide-brimmed bonnet covered in yellow feathers to match her dress. Her face is unusually brown for a lady and the softness of the feathers is in stark contrast to her eyes, which are dark and hard as coal. So dark that they keep drawing you back to them. She is not smiling, not frowning either. There is no invitation to sit down next to her. Quite the opposite. And there is some kind of animal at the edge of the picture. Marie can't decide what. She went close up to the painting once when Degas went out to get paint. The eyes were just splodges of purple and blue against white and yellow. But when she stepped back again, they came alive. It was startling. And whenever she moves, to go behind the screen and get dressed or go nearer the window when the light fails, the eyes seem to follow her. It is the only picture in the studio.

'Do you know who that lady is in the portrait in your brother's studio?'

The question seems to jar René.

'Oh, that. That's our dear mother.'

Of course. How could she not have known? They have the same colouring. The same sense of stillness about them. Like cats waiting to pounce.

'What was she like? Your mother, I mean.'

'She died a long time ago, so it's hard to remember. I'm afraid she had nervous problems and I was a small child, so – well, it's hard to ascertain her character. She had her good days.' René looks uncomfortable now and starts strumming his fingers on the table.

Marie says nothing and then René shifts in his chair, licks his lips, seems to be deciding something.

'Some say Edgar has her disposition.' René looks over at his brother and his nostrils flare, then swivels back and slaps on a toothy smile. 'She was a famous beauty in her time. You have a look of her, my dear, similar complexion. He puts out a hand as if he is going to touch her face then snatches it back. 'Not the same character, I am sure. Anyway, her family are much grander than my father's, so she was quite a catch. Edgar did that portrait when he was twelve, the year before she died. It's good, isn't it? He should have stuck with the society beauties, instead of painting miserable old tramps in dirty cafés.'

René puts a warm, damp hand on her thigh. Marie wants to move away but stops herself. She needs to keep him talking, find out more.

'No offence, my dear,' René continues. 'I didn't mean you. I am sure his portrait of you will be absolutely charming. How could it not be?' René leans in and twists a smile at her. She forces a smile in return and fiddles with the ribbon around her neck. Gigi would be proud! But she cannot stop the blush rising up her neck. How on earth do girls do this stuff without feeling like performing bears? Perhaps they like being performing bears. She hopes it is too dark for him to notice. She hears Gigi urging her on; go on, show your neck, brush a lock of hair off it. She resists.

'Are you well, mademoiselle?'

'Yes. Just a little, er, hot.'

A loud peal of laughter breaks out from the artists and René snorts in annoyance.

'Children!'

His hand moves from her thigh and picks up a clump of her hair. He eyes it like a length of cotton at the market. For a moment Marie considers reaching into his pocket and seeing what she can steal but then fears she can see Degas looking over at her from the corner of her eye. She smiles but he doesn't notice. What is he thinking? He is so hard to read. Even though she has the chance to watch him for hours at a time at the studio, and thinks about him for hours after she has left. She must drum up the courage to speak before René changes the subject. She wants to know about Degas' mother.

'She looks terribly sad. Your mother, I mean.'

René drops her hair and sits back, looking slightly annoyed that she has brought up the subject again. He wets his lips and takes a long swig from his glass. He crashes the glass down so hard that the table wobbles. He is obviously drunk.

'Our mother? Yes, I suppose so. Poor Papa was very patient with her. Too patient. He adored her. But she only had eyes for her beloved Edgar. He was her pet. The thing was, she was too clever for her own good. Women should not be over-educated; they are best left as natural beings. Like you, my pretty one.'

René leans into her and runs his finger along her jawbone. He smells of cigar smoke and alcohol. She dares herself not to draw back.

'Did she read a lot?'

He draws on his cigar, coughs out smoke and bats it away from Marie's face.

'What a strange question! I suppose so, mainly because she didn't like parties, preferred to stay at home with Edgar and her books. That was part of the problem. She couldn't stand reality. Every appearance in public was a chore. Our father brought the best doctors in from Paris and Amsterdam. The last one was a specialist in female maladies from Turin. He made her get rid of all her books, confined her to her bedroom and gave her some very strong medication. After that she got worse, if anything, hardly spoke and just stared out of the window all day.'

René draws on his cigar again and lets the smoke out in one long whistling sound, like a train coming into Gare St Lazare. How awful for Degas' mother. How awful for René and Edgar too. She knows exactly what it's like to have to take care of your mother when you are still a child yourself.

'She was always calling for Edgar to sit with her. He became an awful mummy's boy, I'm afraid.' René stubs out the cigar and pulls at his moustache. 'He stopped playing with me and I was left entirely alone with our savage of a nanny for much of the time.'

It makes Marie's temples tight to hear about the lady in the painting being kept like a caged animal. There's no earthly reason why she should care about Degas' deceased mother, but somehow, she does. Maybe ladies don't have it as easy as it seems, after all. At least Gigi is free to come and go as she pleases, even if she only comes and goes to the Martyrs Tavern. It makes Marie furious to hear René drawling on so heartlessly. She almost feels she is there in that strange garden. She can feel the heat. Her mind starts to swirl. Quick, name things. Bring yourself back. Glass. Spoon. Table. Marie sucks the spoon and lays the cool metal of it on her forehead to stop herself fainting. René is staring at her. She must ask a question. Keep him talking.

'What do you mean, about your brother having her disposition?'

'Well, I shouldn't tell you this. But he shouldn't have been allowed to spend so much time with her as a child. She was a bad influence on him. A dark influence. He hides from the world like her. All that morbid poetry and sitting in silence. But he was the only thing she could stand towards the end, just Edgar. He brushed her hair, attended her in the bath.'

René looks over at Edgar with something like hate. He twiddles the ends of his moustache. 'Strange for a twelve-year-old boy, don't you think?'

Marie has no idea what to say to that. She looks at the two brothers. They are so different. It reminds her of herself and Antoinette. René looks like a sulky twelve-year-old boy himself. She steals a glance at Degas, and she is sure she catches his eye, but he doesn't show any sign of recognition, just looks down and starts scribbling something on his notepad. She tries to imagine him as a young child, taking care of his difficult mother.

'Thank you for—' Marie says but is interrupted by a waitress with a bowl of nuts and dried fruit. She throws restraint to the wind and dives on them.

René doesn't seem to have heard her or notice her wolfing down the nuts. He stares into his greasy glass, makes lines in the condensation, and carries on as if talking to himself. Marie considers slipping the spoon into her pocket but decides it's too long.

'He was like her, never liked the outdoors. She said she liked it when he sketched her. It soothed her. She was always quiet and docile with Edgar. And my father would have given anything for that – we both would.'

René draws himself up as if from a dream and clinks the glass with a huge emerald on his index finger. That would be worth stealing, but it looks very tight on his finger; even Antoinette would have trouble getting that off him.

'I'm sorry,' she says gently, for want of anything better to say.

83

René coughs violently, steadies himself on the table, fiddles with his ring.

Marie can't work out whether she likes him or not. Then she looks beyond him and sees Degas staring straight at her. A crease between his brows, his dark eyes tunnelling into her. For a moment she feels glad, but then realises how angry he looks. How dare he look at them like that, as though they have done something wrong. At least René talks to her like a human being. Perhaps they are right about Degas after all. His terrible temper, his haughtiness. People tell stories about how he threw one girl's clothes out the window onto the street and left her to go out after them completely naked. She is too soft on Degas. What would Papa have said if he'd seen her letting herself be seduced by the soft manners and false attentiveness of the bourgeoisie?

She turns to René and smiles, hoping that Degas will see.

'Thank you for telling me all that, about your mother.'

'Oh, it's my pleasure. I wouldn't usually be so free, but I'm enjoying your company. You are rather charming, little Marie.'

He tucks a sweaty lock of hair behind her ear and squeezes her thigh. His tenderness touches her and repulses her at the same time.

'René!' Degas is there beside them. His voice is so angry and loud that people all around them stare. 'Stop rattling on to poor Marie.' He puts a hand on his brother's shoulder and René pushes it off.

'He wasn't rattling on. We…' Her mouth is dry, and she stops mid-sentence. Degas turns his face from his brother to her and he is so close that her throat constricts. He seems very angry, and she is scared.

'Come with me, Marie.' She is on her feet and being dragged by her arm out of the bar. When they are outside, Degas stops, rakes his hand through his hair. His nostrils are flaring. She is almost scared he will hit her. Then something changes in him.

'I am sorry, Marie. Please forgive me.' His voice is so soft and serious now. His words hang in the fleshy dark. 'I was watching you with René and I thought he had said something to upset you.' There are ragged pools of light under the gas lamps.

'There is nothing to forgive, monsieur.' He looks so upset, the furrow between his brows coming and going. She was angry with him a moment ago for being so rude, but that has gone completely. His feelings seem to drag him about like a drunken friend. She has to stop herself reaching up to touch his cheek.

'No. No. There is something. There is.'

His mouth twitches as if he is embarrassed, as if he is reining himself in. The rest of the group tumble out of the bar behind them. One of the artists does a somersault and the others applaud. The moment is broken.

'We must go, *mon brave*, the show is about to start. Goodness me. Are you quite well? Here, take my arm.' Mary Cassatt whisks Degas away from her before she can ask him what he means. She stands still, unable to move, watching him go. Degas stops short under a gas lamp and looks back at her with the strangest expression on his face. A memory – a pale face turned towards her in a dark street – darts through Marie's mind, but she can't grab hold of it. Degas raises his big pale hand to her, and the rest of the world disappears.

Somehow, Marie finds herself at the circus. Mademoiselle La La is suspended above Marie's head. The famous acrobat's stockinged legs dangle out of daringly short orange pantaloons, and she hangs onto a rope with her teeth. It feels like a dream. People all around her are gasping at the sight above their heads.

The women are fanning themselves furiously. She steals a glance at Degas. He is sketching away in his book, oblivious to everything but lines and colours. She stares at his hand on the pad to make sure. And she knows at that moment that she is right. He is the ghost. It was his gesture when he turned to her tonight in the dark and raised his hand. Just as he did that night. He is the ghost. The tall pale man who stood next to Monsieur Béranger in her house the night Papa died. He followed Papa's body out into the street and turned to wave to her and Gigi. That was why she recognised him when he first arrived in the rehearsal room.

How could she not have known it before? He must know how Papa died. He must know where he is buried. But why didn't Gigi say anything? She knows Marie has been modelling for Degas. Yes, she is sure she said his name. Or did she? And what about Antoinette? Surely she must have known Degas if he was a Communard and friends with Papa?

The moment of recognition is like the bell the hypnotists on Pont Neuf use to bring people back from their reverie. Marie feels awake and full of energy now. She cannot bear sitting in this stuffy theatre any longer. She must find out. She must make Gigi and Antoinette tell her the truth. She will force them if she has to. As soon as the lights go up for the interval, she pushes past the tutting crowds and runs outside.

'You have to tell me. If you don't, I'll tell Gigi about your stealing.'

Antoinette has moved on to bigger things since the watch. Blanche Balnar said she'd heard a rumour that Antoinette broke into a shop and stole from the till. Marie defended Antoinette vehemently, but she knew it was true. One day, Antoinette will get caught. The police love catching the families of ex-

Communards. And recently the police have been given new powers to stop anybody who looks suspicious and interrogate them. One of the girls at the opera was pulled away from rehearsal last week to be questioned. She came back shaking and was promptly sacked. It was horrible. She was crying so hard, crouched on the floor, begging to stay, while the pianist tried to carry on and they danced around her. And she, Marie, did nothing, just watched and let it happen. She wanted to run to the girl, pick her up. One glance from Antoinette made her think again. She could have stood up for her, spoken for her, for her rights. That's what Louise Michel would have done. In the days of the Commune, people used to stand up for themselves and each other. The Red She-Wolf inspired everybody around her to be more fierce, more wolfish. She left Paris and took all the courage with her. Since her transportation and imprisonment in New Caledonia, it seems like they have all become sheep again.

'Hush, Marie. *Calme-toi!*'

Marie and Antoinette are lying side by side in bed, hissing at each other, so as not to wake Gigi up.

'If you really want to know, he was a friend. Well, not a friend really. More of a hanger-on. Not an actual Communard. He didn't fight, he just tagged along with his sketchbook. I never understood why they all put up with him. Maybe he donated money to the cause or had friends high up in the Garde Nationale. I don't know. I didn't have much to do with him, but Papa wouldn't hear a word against him. He came to the house once. Maman was furious because Papa hadn't let her know and she was all tired and sweaty from the laundry. Degas insisted she carried on working while he sat on the floor and sketched her. You were tiny then. You kept grabbing his charcoal and getting it all over you. We all laughed a lot, even Maman.'

A big sigh comes from Antoinette. 'Anyway, that's all behind us now.'

Degas on the floor, laughing. It's hard to imagine. That world in his studio and this one, all mixed up. Since Papa died everything feels shattered into bits, and it is Marie's job to try and gather the pieces together, make something whole and real. It is still raining and the drip from the roof is getting worse. Antoinette gets up to move the pisspot under it.

'He came here, to this house?' The thought is unsettling and thrilling. 'And he was there. He was actually there, when Papa died. Answer me, Antoinette.'

'Yes, he was there, Marie.'

No argument at all. Just a statement of fact.

'Why didn't you tell me?'

'It's not important.'

'Not important! How can you say that?' Her voice is getting too loud now. If she keeps it up, Gigi might wake up and Antoinette will just clam up, refuse to say anything; that's what she always does. Better to stay calm, ask gently.

'Will you tell me the story? Please?' Her throat is tight, and her heart is beating so fast, she is surprised Antoinette can't hear it. She has to force the words out, make herself carry on.

'He was my father too, you know. I – I want to know. You must remember.'

'No, no, Marie. I don't remember.'

'Where were you? You know, when it happened?'

'Shut up, Marie. Shut up! I don't want to fucking remember. And you can't make me, Marie. Nobody can.' Antoinette's voice comes out like gunfire, like an accusation, as if it is all Marie's fault.

'How did he die, Antoinette? Just tell me! How did he die?'

'No! Shut up, Marie – you never know when to fucking shut up, do you?'

Antoinette turns over her pillow, beats it with a fist and flings herself down on it.

'I should never have told you anything. Just shut up and go to sleep. I'm exhausted, Marie. Aren't you?'

'But—'

'Leave it alone. *Nom de fucking dieu*, Marie, leave it alone. Please leave it alone…' Antoinette's voice peters out like a pigeon coming to rest on a chimney. The rain has stopped and there is silence except for the sick baby crying next door.

'*Bonne nuit*, Marie. Sweet dreams.'

How dead Antoinette's voice sounds. Words drained of meaning.

Questions press at Marie's throat, but she shuts up as Antoinette has demanded. She knows she won't get any more tonight. Next time she sees Degas, she will ask him. She will drum up courage and ask him straight out. She will.

The rain has stopped, and a smudged moon appears in the skylight. She imagines her aching body is sinking into it and dreams that she is covered in charcoal and being pushed down a well by a man in a dark coat.

CHAPTER SEVEN

September 1879

It is the afternoon before the opening performance of *Yedda* and Marie has a few hours off before she is due back at the theatre for costumes and make-up. Her neck is aching so much – from trying to stop the ornate headdress she has to wear as a Japanese courtier falling off while executing perfect pirouettes at yesterday's dress rehearsal – that she can hardly turn her head. What's more, since Blanche Balnar was chosen to come forward to proffer a flower to the Mikado at the end of Act I, she's been even sharper with her elbows in the dressing room.

Marie is sheltering from a sudden rain shower in the Passage des Panoramas, a covered arcade off Boulevard Haussmann. She can't afford to get her hair wet – especially as it might drip onto her face and wash off the heavy face paint she must wear – and anyway it's a good excuse to gaze at the shop windows and inhale the smell of expensive chocolate and perfume. Through a chocolatier's window, she notices a haughty shop girl disappearing out the back, leaving the shop unattended. She could just run in while the girl is gone and pop a few chocolate-covered almonds in her mouth. No, it's not worth it, too risky without Antoinette as a diversion. This area is rife with plainclothes policemen on the lookout for prostitutes and petty thieves.

Marie leans up against the window of a reading room and peers in at the newspapers laid out under green lights. But the windows are steamy and it's impossible to make out the headlines. She hasn't read a newspaper or leaflet for years now, just managed to gobble down a few pages of *Fantine* when she can stay awake to focus on it, and even then, she feels guilty about burning a candle for something as frivolous as reading. A sigh gutters through her. A vague memory of feeling like things had meaning, those words marching and dancing on pamphlets and in books, crowds of bright-eyed people gathering in squares, daring to hope that things could change. All gone now. The only thing she looks forward to is being with Degas and he has been away all summer. Degas' studio is not far. She could go and ring on the door again. But only yesterday the house was completely closed up, with the blinds closed and no sign of life at all. After he'd been away a month, Marie asked the Crow if she knew where he was, and the Crow told her that he would probably be back some time in the autumn. Marie felt sick when she heard that. Not only does it mean that money is even tighter than before (especially with the rent rise that the goat-faced landlord announced when he came threatening eviction at the weekend) but now she has lost her chance of confronting him about the night Papa died. She had been meaning to ask him since the night of the circus but somehow it didn't happen.

For the first few weeks after the outing to the circus she'd told herself it wasn't a good time to tackle the subject of Papa because Mary Cassatt kept arriving unannounced and haranguing him about some exhibition they were preparing for and Degas was very irritable, seemed to have forgotten about giving Marie any breaks at all. And then, one day just before Easter when she was gathering courage to ask him outright, however awkward it felt, Degas started working on his contraption and nothing was the same after that.

Marie had arrived one freezing-cold day to find that Degas didn't even come down to greet her as he usually did but got his maid to let her in and called to her excitedly to say he had something to show her. When she arrived in the studio, she found it was strewn with bits of wire and tubing and paintbrushes with their bristles cut off in a precarious pile on Degas' painting table. 'Look! Look, Marie!' he shouted, wild-eyed, as if he'd seen a vision of the fucking Virgin Mary herself. In the middle of the studio were two bits of metal in the shape of a cross, attached to another bit of metal in the shape of an upside-down U which in turn was planted on a wooden base. The whole thing came up to Marie's shoulder. It looked to her like some kind of drying rack. While Degas talked – he didn't even look at her, didn't notice she was shivering with cold – he went to the old armchair, which now had a big hole in it, as if mice had got into it, and started digging out wadding and putting it in a pile next to the chair. He told her he was going to create a figurine of her from everyday materials, the like of which nobody would have seen ever before. Over the next few months, he'd worked like a man possessed, only stopping to poke her and prod her, to look at proportions. She was rehearsing for the new ballet, felt comfortable in Degas' company – despite his moods – and time seemed to fly by.

The drying rack started looking more like a little person about two thirds the size of Marie as Degas wrapped rope loosely around the top of the upside-down U-shaped section (which turned out to be legs) and filled the spaces with the wadding from the chair. The whole thing became an organised mess of wire, rope, wood, metal and wadding. At one point Degas told her to hold still and disappeared upstairs, came back with one of his shirts, balled it up and stuffed it in behind some coiled rope. 'Haha, Marie! This will do for the stomach – see how it adds weight but not too much.' Marie had stroked her own slightly rounded stomach and couldn't help laughing.

Degas had been so distracted that she hadn't dared ask him anything at all, let alone tackle the subject of her father. She reasoned with herself that if she came out with a sudden question, it might sound like an accusation. It might not even be true; Antoinette might be mistaken. In his volatile state she'd told herself it was too risky to challenge him – he might throw her out for good and then where would she be? She couldn't afford to anger him. Those are the excuses she has made, but really, she realises now as she thinks back on it, she'd been too comfortable, too distracted by rehearsing for the new ballet – she'd shied away from doing what needed to be done, backed away from her promise to Papa. She hates herself for it now.

Marie massages her right hip. The pain is terrible from the hours spent perfecting arabesques with her right leg in attitude for *Yedda*.

Degas disappeared without warning at the end of June. At first, she thought he must be on a short trip to the coast or to the countryside, as that's what rich people seem to do in the summer. He was so absorbed with the sculpture that he surely wouldn't be away long – at least that's what Marie told herself. But weeks turned into months, the first autumn leaves appeared and still there was no sign of him. Recently Marie has started to wonder if he will ever come back, if he's moved away like Antoinette's sponsor at the opera. The thought of never seeing him again is unbearable. She still waits every day in the dressing room after rehearsals hoping for a note from him, gets in early – her heart thumping like horses' hooves on sand – but it is as if he has disappeared into thin air. His wicker chair by the piano lies empty and abandoned, except for Zou-Zou, the ballet master's dog, who takes a nap on it every now and then. Once she was sure she heard, above the din of the rehearsal room, the tip-tap of one of Monsieur Degas' collection of canes on the great marble stairs which run up to the *abonnés* entrance (and which the little rats are banned from using). But the noise turned out to be the metronome on the piano. She was so disappointed that she forgot the last pirouette and ended up with high-pitched threats from the ballet master and a hard thwack on the calf from the Crow. To be fair, the Crow has been quite restrained, strangely restrained. After the thwack, she even gave Marie a sympathetic wink. A knowing wink, she would call it, although she has no idea why that would be. It seems everybody has secrets. She has noticed that recently.

It's hard for Marie to imagine herself asking Degas about her father now, even if he does eventually return. It would be easier just to forget Papa ever existed, like everybody else has. Keeping his memory alive is such a lonely task, kindling that tiny flame of truth, cupping her hands around it. And for what? Nobody but her seems to care about truth anymore. Another luxury, she supposes, to even think about abstract things like that. She could just let his memory gutter and die, but even the thought of that makes her recoil. She has made a pact with Papa, in her mind, and she can't break it. He is the one who matters, not Monsieur Degas, she must remember that. The fact is that she doesn't want to spoil things between her and Degas. Their time together is so precious to her now, she looks forward to it so much, that she is terrified of shattering it, of her life going back to what it was before. She crosses herself and makes a silent pact with God that if He brings Degas back to her, she will find out the truth no matter what.

Marie leans her forehead against the cool, damp window of the reading room and allows herself to think over her time with Degas, to try and work out why he left while she waits for the rain to stop. In May, he'd become very restless and irritable. He kept tutting and raking his hand through his hair and getting her to change position every few minutes. When she gathered the courage to ask if she was doing something wrong, he very gently asked her to forgive his childish tantrum and carried on. This went on for weeks. She didn't really mind, as it was always more comfortable to change position and he was quite magnificent to watch, with paint in his hair and his beautifully pressed shirt coming untucked. Finally, he sat back in his chair, declared that he was an imbecile to even think of trying to make this infernal sculpture, that Mary Cassatt was right, that none of the poses worked and that he would have nothing at all ready for the next exhibition, nothing at all, that he would be a laughing stock, like his lumbering failure of a brother.

When his rant was finished, he looked up at her from his daze and said she could have five minutes' break while he 'composed himself'. Then he got up, turned to his mother's portrait and seemed to be muttering something to her, a prayer by the sounds of it. She feared he had lost his mind. Artists were known for their wild tempers and Marie could take it, could understand wild emotions better than most, but this was extreme, even by his standards. She stayed quiet and took the opportunity to stretch out her shoulders and upper back by lacing her hands behind her. It felt delicious, the flesh of her back folding in like dough, her ribcage pushed forward like a robin about to sing, knots unravelling along the sides of her neck, life rushing back into to her tired, parched body. She was heaving a great sigh when—

'STOP!'

His voice made her jump. He was back in his chair in an instant. 'That's it. May God be praised. That's it! My prayer has been answered. Yes, hold it there, Marie, exactly like that.' He sounded like a man who had won a fortune at the races. But why? She was in a loose fourth position, her feet a metre apart, turned out. But it wasn't a proper posture, the alignment not precise. She pulled up her front knee to make it more correct, less knobbly, hoping he wouldn't notice.

'No! No! I don't want that. Stop fiddling! What is that position called, Marie?'

'Er, it doesn't really have a name, monsieur. It's just something we all do when our backs are aching. Or when our shoulders hurt from holding our arms above our heads for too long.' It felt very intimate to be telling him that and she cleared her throat to free her breath.

'What does it feel like? Why do you do it?' He was staring right into her.

'Well, to stretch my bones, I suppose. They get squashed up.' It felt a silly thing to say but it was all she could come up with.

He nodded slowly and smiled softly at her. 'I see. Yes, I see.'

He started running his gaze over her as if he was measuring her and she was embarrassed. Surely he was mistaken, and wanted a pretty fourth position with arms held high above the head in an oval? 'Maybe if I bring my arms up…?'

'No!' he stamped his foot and raked his hair. Her heart lurched. How was she supposed to please him when he was like this?'

'It's the arms I've been struggling with. There was no balance. No – no beauty. Just go back to what you were doing before.' He must have seen she was about to cry then because he softened his voice.

'Pardon, Marie. Yes, like that. You see, I want to see you as you really are. You know, when you are backstage or in the dressing room. No, relax your knee. Stop trying to impress me. Yes, as if you are in the wings right now. That's it. I am not here. Just you. Yes, yes. That's perfect, my little Marie. Perfect. You are a treasure, really you are.' They both let out a huge sigh at the same time, once she blanked out his presence and settled back into the position, warmed by his praise. She couldn't help watching him as the line disappeared from between his eyes and his movements became graceful, as if the cage door had been flung open, the lion breathing in the wide horizon. All his tension gone, just like that. He seemed to drop away from her, like he always did when he was concentrating, as if he was entirely alone and all that existed was the lines he made on the paper, the wire and wood in his hands. As if the lines on the paper, the wire and the wood were part of him. It took her back to when she used to sit with Papa while he was stitching.

Degas seemed much happier after they'd settled on a position for the sculpture and they relaxed into a comfortable routine again. He told her he planned to cover the armature with clay. She'd felt a little disappointed as she'd been picturing a bronze statue like the one of Napoleon that the Communards had pulled down.

The Passage des Panoramas is thundering now as hailstones land on the glass roof. Two gentlemen rush in, pour water off the brims of their hats and laugh uproariously. Marie steps into the doorway of a pipe shop and stares blankly at the packets of

Chinese tobacco laid out in the window. She and Antoinette made off with two handfuls of these a few days ago and sold them for the price of a cheap supper. She'd better move on before she's recognised. She strolls further into the passageway and stops outside a jewellery shop, wonders how much she'd get for Papa's rings. So far, she's managed to hold onto them and her copy of *Fantine*, persuaded Gigi not to sell them. The thought of losing the rings makes her sick but imagining the three of them out on the streets is worse. Marie's not even sure if she can trust Gigi not to break her word and sell them without asking her anymore. A lady passes by, shakes out her umbrella and sprays her skirts with water.

'Fuck you, *salope*!' she shouts after the lady. Marie realises with a jolt that she's starting to sound more and more like her mother and sister. Luckily the hammering rain muffles her voice, but the tight-lipped lady is exactly the type who might call the police on her. Marie rushes on just in case, stops again outside a café, bends down and pretends to lace up her boot. She must be careful, or she'll end up like Fantine.

Stirring up her memories of being in the studio combined with her hunger and the clammy atmosphere in the Passage des Panoramas has made Marie dizzy. She straightens up and clings onto a wrought iron railing.

Five o'clock sounds at Notre Dame and brings her back to reality. Only two hours to go and she will be on stage. Where in God's name will she find something to eat? She could go home, but it is not likely there will be anything there. The thought of home makes her utterly exhausted. The landlord has been in yet again, threatening to evict them, and Gigi is chasing another man. Rain will be pouring into her bedroom again. Best not to think about it, easier to stay on the streets. People are bracing themselves and gingerly stepping out onto the boulevard now, chins high, like dancers back on stage after a welcome break in the wings.

As the storm peters out and sunlight pours into the Passage des Panoramas, a desire rises up in Marie, a desire to do something wild and foolish. She pauses at the ornate entrance onto the boulevard. An exotic thought wings its way into her mind. Or rather, not a thought, a name – Amélie Reine – on Boulevard Haussmann, the flat with the parrots on the first-floor balcony. It is only when a gentleman shoves her in the rear and looks back, making a winding motion at his forehead to suggest she is mad, that she realises she has spoken out loud. Oh well, it is not illegal to talk to yourself, not yet anyway.

Boulevard Haussmann is very long and lined with stucco villas. The roar of water rushing into brand-new drains is deafening. The whole of Paris used to be united by mud before the great boulevards were built. Papa used to delight in the rainstorms which would bring butchers' scraps and drowned rats into the smart parts of Paris. Now the drains are like great barricades keeping any reminder of the unpaved poorer parts of the city far away from the rarified atmosphere of the boulevards. Marie peers up at the balconies on the first floor. Most are empty, a few are filled with ornate topiary. Nothing like the washing-strewn, crumbling, child-filled monstrosities of Montmartre. Ah, there! A cage and what looks like a giant bird flapping in it. But, as she gets nearer, she realises that the bird is a person. A woman with long grey-blonde hair in a white silk kimono, throwing seeds into the cage. She looks like she's in costume for tonight's performance of *Yedda*. Well, now or never. The worst that can happen is that Amélie turns her away. Marie dodges the flow of carriages, crosses the boulevard and rings hard on the bell pull.

A torrent of footsteps and the door kisses open. It is Amélie, but she looks quite different. Her face is naked apart from a wash of white powder, which makes beads on her pale lashes and clings to her lips. Amélie's blonde hair is streaked with grey and falls to her shoulders in frizzy waves and she clasps the edges of her kimono together over her chest. Marie is so shocked she can't speak. But Amélie's eyes, though a lot smaller without the kohl and shadow, still light up and crinkle when she smiles. 'I thought it was the Count!' Amélie hisses with a wink, drawing Marie inside. 'It is Marie, isn't it?' Amélie takes Marie's hand and carries on chatting while she leads her through a courtyard and up several flights of wide, shallow stairs. 'Yes, well, come up. I'm afraid you have caught me in the middle of my toilette. I start work at five p.m. usually, but there's some meeting at the Palais de Justice today so the Count won't be here for another hour, so we can have a nice little chat, *ma petite.*'

They are in front of a huge double doorway now. Marie looks behind her and sees her muddy footprints on the white marble staircase, hopes that Amélie won't notice. Marie curses herself for having such a stupid idea. Amélie seems half-crazed, and she is sure she can smell alcohol on her breath. She is on the point of making an excuse when Amélie kicks the door open with a bare foot. Marie can't help staring at the foot. It is so smooth; no cuts, no blisters, no dry skin. Nails clean and perfect like little soldiers.

'Welcome to my humble abode!'

Marie gulps. The room is huge and sparkling white. Maman was right about that. The ceiling with its ornate crenellations, the walls, the window frames, the long silk curtains, the marble floor – everything is white. A tiger skin is spread out in front of a gigantic roaring fire. There are two armchairs in the middle of the room, one upholstered in black velvet, the other in white satin with bows. There is also a grand piano laden with perfume bottles, pins and boxes overflowing with ribbons; opposite it stands an imposing rosewood double wardrobe with two full-length mirrors. Gigi would kill for that wardrobe.

'Excuse me, angel, but I must get on. You sit there. No, not on the white one, it shows the dirt. Yes, that's it.'

The black velvet is deliciously soft. Marie has never sat in a soft chair before, only seen them in the window of furniture shops. She lets herself lean back and pushes the fine nap of the velvet on the arm of the chair back and forth with her fingers, watches how it changes colour. Then she kicks off her damp old boots and wiggles her muddy toes, finds herself relaxing, despite herself. Amélie comes over and kisses her on both cheeks, says she is delighted to see her, and Marie thinks she means it, but cannot be sure. Then Amélie stands by the piano and turns to face the mirrors on the wardrobe. She unties her kimono and lets it drop so that she is completely naked, her eyes narrowing, fixing on her reflection.

'Not too bad for a woman of my age. What do you think – will I do?'

Marie nods even though the question is not really directed at her. She has seen other women naked of course, at the bathhouse, and Gigi and Antoinette undressing at home. But not like this. The women she knows push themselves in and out of their clothes, huffing and puffing. Amélie turns and admires the profile of her full breasts in the mirror. The women she knows are more likely to curse their bodies for being too weak or too thin or too old. Amélie smiles at Marie and then turns her head and kisses herself softly on each shoulder, as if she is kissing a beloved child good night. The gesture is so tender that it makes Marie's stomach lurch. She grabs onto the velvet armrests so she doesn't burst into tears and presses a hot blister onto the cool marble floor.

'Well, if we can't love ourselves, they will never love us, will they?' Amélie coos to herself. 'Where we lead, the cosseted rich arseholes follow, eh, Marie? There, I have given away one of the secrets of every successful courtesan!' She breaks into a cackle and slaps her thigh.

Marie can't help laughing along with her. It is such a relief to be with somebody who isn't irritable as a wounded cat all the time, to be able to sit back and not mind every word that comes out of her mouth. She sighs, lets her body settle and soften into the chair.

Even though Amélie is Gigi's age she looks at least ten years younger. Her flesh is still firm and creamy; her skin has no blemishes or bruises from manual work or rashes from sweaty clothes. It makes Marie sad for Gigi, thinking that this could have been her, if things had turned out differently. Amélie seems to notice her spirits drop. She comes over and squats down next to her, looks into her eyes.

'Are you hungry?'

Marie makes herself nod, as her voice does not seem to be working.

'Of course you are. That was a stupid question. I can hardly remember it now, Marie. Being hungry all the time. But I was hungry for so many years, I didn't know what it felt like to be full.' She strokes Marie's cheek. 'You have a lovely face, my child. An unusual face. But your cheeks are a little sunken. I'll send the *portresse*'s daughter out for some food, and a jolt of the Green Fairy for me. She's always happy to earn a sou or two.'

Amélie strides over to the window, ample buttocks wobbling like blancmange, wraps herself in a curtain to protect her modesty and leans out over the balcony. A strange voice says, '*Bonjour, madame*,' and Marie realises it must be one of the parrots and finds herself bursting into giggles. How long is it since she has giggled? Amélie tells the parrot to shush, then puts her fingers to her mouth and whistles like a carriage hand. A door grinds open below. Amélie gives the order and then disappears into a side room and appears with a lace-edged chemise half over her head. She pulls it down and goes over to the piano, picks up a stick of rouge and starts applying it by the mirror.

'Anyway,' she continues, 'as I was saying, yes, being hungry. Horrific. And I swore that one day I wouldn't have to worry about where the next meal would come from, or the one after that, for the rest of my fucking life.'

Amélie explains how she started in the business. Men used to hug her when she was with her father at one of the big dirty bars in the outer suburbs. Her father was always drunk and whenever Amélie slipped away from him to beg food or kindness from strangers, he would chase her and beat her. Some of the customers would hug her and hide her from her father, but they weren't much better, hands in all the wrong places. 'I got used to the feel of them behind me,' she says, her mouth full of hairpins. 'If you get used to something when you are young, good or bad, you seek it out later.'

Marie stuffs a cake into her mouth, pours a bit of absinthe into Amélie's mouth ('I don't want the smell on my hands'), wipes her hands on one of Amélie's beautiful lace handkerchiefs and helps Amélie lace up her red velvet corset. Amélie explains that she got a leg up from an old courtesan who wanted to pass on one of her customers and trained her up in the art while she was still very young. When Amélie's hair is up and oiled and a yellow silk dress smoothed over her shaped figure, she applies kohl to her eyes, asking Marie to check if it is straight 'because my eyes are going'.

The transformation is fascinating. Before, Amélie was a slightly shabby pigeon and now she is a tropical bird. Marie wonders if she could do that.

No sooner has Marie closed the door to Amélie's world – with her sing-song voice, the feel of the velvet chair, the possibility of becoming beautiful still dancing through her mind – than she bumps right into Paul Béranger. His face is very red, even allowing for the heat.

'What are you doing here?' he asks. Now her face is going as red as Paul's, as if she has been found doing something she shouldn't.

'Is something wrong?' she asks to distract him.

Paul attempts to blow a lock of light brown hair off his eyes. For no particular reason, they both break into giggles, like children. Paul is such a sweetheart, always has been. She has always had an affection for him. No, not just affection; admiration, to be more precise. He is one of those people who manages to keep an even temper and a sense of humour whatever happens.

'I'm just running an errand for my lecherous fucking bully of a stepfather, Marie. When I get back he'll start whacking me around with a palette knife because the trays haven't been cleaned. Then I'll be up 'til midnight, preparing things for tomorrow while he sits on his arse and counts the takings.' Paul wipes his hands on his apron and lets out a long sigh. 'Sorry, I don't mean to dump my worries on you, you've got enough of your own…' His voice trails off and Marie knows he is thinking about Antoinette. He seems awkward and uncomfortable. He takes her arm and draws her down to sit beside him on the step, looks around as if to check that nobody is watching them. His arm brushes against hers.

'Anyway, listen, I'm glad I met you, Marie, because there's something wrong. Don't panic, it's not serious. Well, not yet. But, well, the police are sniffing around.'

'What? The police? What police? What do you mean?' The rush of people and carriages on the street is making her dizzy. She needs to get to the theatre. Paul is sweet but she can't work out what he is saying. Antoinette often says how easily scared he is, how he tries to stop her 'having fun'.

She gets up. 'I have to go. The show starts in an hour. I'll be in trouble.'

Paul grabs her arm so hard that she yelps. He apologises, but draws her down again. 'Listen. I heard your *maman* talking to mine. The police have been to your house, investigating a series of thefts in the quartier. They want to speak to you and Antoinette. They say it's urgent.'

Marie's stomach drops. She doesn't know whether to be angry or scared or both.

'Look, I know Antoinette got in with some low types a while ago.' Paul swallows hard. She can tell he is worried. 'She told me about that, that little slip-up. But she's over all that, isn't she? She hasn't been stealing recently, has she?'

'No. No, of course not,' Marie manages to mumble. She hates lying to Paul, to cover up for her sister. Paul thinks Antoinette is a reformed character, is out modelling for an unknown artist in Pigalle every night. He has no idea about her

105

stealing, none at all, and Marie is sworn to secrecy. Well, maybe she should tell Paul the truth about his fiancée. She knew the thieving would do them no good, that Antoinette would get caught in the end. She warned her. Only the other day she'd come back drunk and boasted about how stupid rich people were, how she'd soon have enough for a decent wedding dress and the whole neighbourhood would look up to her. Marie had tried to make her see that it was best to tell Paul the truth, that one day he'd find out. That Paul loved her enough to understand, that he'd forgive her if she told him now. Why did she waste her breath? Antoinette just scoffed and told Marie, in her usual superior way, that she knew nothing of the world.

'Anyway,' Paul continues, 'your mother has gone to Madame Robert's boarding house, she'll come home as soon as she can. And you mustn't go home tonight either. They might come back. The police, I mean. They've obviously got it wrong and I'm sure it'll blow over but best to be sure. And if anybody finds out the police even suspect you, you'll lose your jobs. They're always looking to frame people like us. Marie. Marie. Are you listening?'

She makes herself nod.

'Come to the back of the boulangerie after the show. I'll wait for you. Knock on the door. Two double knocks.'

'The rhythm of "*La Marseillaise*",' she finishes his sentence for him. Her voice is flat, all life drained out of her. The coded knock they used during the Commune. *Here we go again.* The hiding and running, the secret signals. The fear. How could Antoinette put them all in danger again? She must have been careless, talked about it to someone when she was drunk. How could she?

'But, what about your stepfather, Paul?'

'He won't know, don't worry about that. He sleeps at the top with Maman. Six cannons outside the door wouldn't wake up that old bastard! You can bunk down with Antoinette in my room in the basement.' Paul obviously sees the fear in her eyes because he puts a floury hand on her thigh and draws her head onto his shoulder, like he used to do when they were little and she was crying about something stupid. 'Don't worry, *petite soeur*, I've got it all worked out. It won't be for long. They'll soon lose interest, move on to some other poor beggar.' He squeezes her tighter. 'And anyway, a few croissants are always spoilt and need eating up every morning.' It is typical of him to be so brave and kind and offer to help them when it puts him at risk. He is really much too good for Antoinette.

'Thank you, Paul. See you later then.'

There is nothing else to say. She gets up and walks away before he sees the tears in her eyes. Marie doesn't know how she will have the energy to even reach the theatre, or how she will remember the dance steps when her heart is galloping like this. A few minutes ago, the world looked brighter than it had done in years and now it all looks lifeless and unreal again. What's the point in hoping? What's the point in living? Everything always turns out wrong. Everything.

By the time she gets to the theatre she has managed to calm herself down enough to get into her costume and find her way to the wings. *March on for him. March on for him.* But Louise Michel's words sound empty, the drumbeat distant.

Marie worries whether Paul will be able to get her things from the house. The thought of losing her copy of *Fantine* forever makes her feel sick. The rent hasn't been paid for four months. Antoinette gave the landlord a watch in lieu of some of the arrears but it's not nearly enough. Soon enough his patience is sure to run out. And with rent prices soaring as people flood in from the provinces, they'll never find somewhere they can afford. They will be out on the streets, like so many others. And she doesn't even want to think of Gigi being at Madame Robert's, a place that is well known for offering much more than lodging. Oh well. She is past caring and is watching herself from outside again, just as she did the night Papa died.

The other girls are stretching and whispering. The Crow is fussing about, adjusting headdresses. Marie feels like she isn't really here. The whalebone on her bodice is cutting into her ribs, she will probably have a bruise tomorrow. She could ask the Crow to mend it. But why bother? Tomorrow there'll be another bruise, another blister, another reason to be scared. She leans against one of the flats and waits.

Down below in the simmering dark of the orchestra pit, where the musicians are coughing and tuning up, she can see a few accents of brilliant white: the conductor's sheet music, the diagonal line of his sharply parted hair, handkerchiefs in freshly pressed jacket pockets. She finds she can't even be bothered to worry about the dance steps now. She will get them right or she won't. She might collapse on stage and die, and it doesn't really matter. Nobody will care. Nothing really matters.

She is starting to feel dizzy again so she makes herself watch the scene she can see between the wings: the theatre is filling up, top hats bobbing along the aisles, fans fluttering, the gaslight nestling on strings of pearls and shooting off the metal tips of gentlemen's walking sticks. How ridiculous all these rich people are, preening and chatting about nothing. Most of them couldn't give a fucking sou about the ballet itself, they are here for the return of the great Rita Sangalli, to show off and gossip; they probably wouldn't notice if the girls all danced naked. Well, the gentlemen might, she supposes. The world is completely absurd, no meaning in it at all. How could she ever have thought things mattered, that she mattered?

She looks at her hand to see if it is still there and finds she has been picking at the cuticle on her thumbnail and it is bleeding. She sucks it so she doesn't get blood on her silk skirt. Right opposite her, in the audience, a pale-faced lady catches Marie's attention and she finds she can't take her eyes off her. The lady is gesticulating all around her as she puffs up her black crêpe de Chine dress and settles into her seat in one of the boxes at the front of the auditorium. She takes off her gloves very slowly, folds them, admires her pale fingers. Could it be? Yes, it is her. Mary Cassatt, the lady-artist, the friend of Degas. She is leaning out over the edge of the box now to show off the lace edging on her deep décolleté, the light glinting off her auburn hair. A quick glance behind, to see if her companions have arrived. Mary drapes an arm over the green velvet of the box edge to show off a collection of flashing rings. Now she tires of that and snatches up her opera glasses, looks for people she knows. A door opens behind Mary. A gentleman enters behind her. His top hat is tipped down low over his face.

Is it him? Could it be? No, of course not. Don't bother getting excited, she tells herself. But her deadened heart starts to flicker anyway.

The gentleman is turning around now, carefully closing the door of the box. Just a tall figure in a top hat. Could be anybody. The musicians have stopped tuning up, the conductor raises his baton, the audience mutter and shush each other.

'Places please. Places please.'

The call has come, and she must line up with the others. In

a minute. In a minute. No! Don't snuff out the lamps. Not yet, not yet.

The lady in the box beckons the gentleman with a sharp circling gesture.

Yes, hurry up, hurry up!

The gentleman is turning towards Mary, taking off his hat. Now he is pushing his hair away from his eyes. With his left hand. Always the left hand! Yes, leaving his right one free to grab something to draw with. His coal-black hair has grown even longer. Well, that must be very uncomfortable for him in this autumn heatwave. Yes. Yes. It is him. His long horsey nose and purple-black eyes. The angle of his long back when he sits, the slight frown when he concentrates, which she can't see but can imagine. He has come back to her. Degas is back. Edgar is back.

It feels daring to call him by his Christian name, even in her head. She says the name out loud to herself, over and over again. The sound is a flourish, a perfect pirouette. It is a magic spell bringing life back to her, bringing her back to herself. She finds herself smiling and stepping forward as if he will just walk out of that box and come and embrace her.

A sceneshifter rushes by, carrying a papier-mâché fountain, trips over her extended leg, swears, and hisses at her to get back out of the light. Well, he will have to wait.

Degas flips out his coat-tails and sits down next to Mary with a slight dip of the head by way of greeting. He doesn't seem at all interested in the other people or even Mary. He just looks straight at the stage. Surely he is looking straight at her? He is very still, like a cat about to pounce. Just like he is sometimes before he picks up his charcoal or his paintbrush. That strange hush where nothing is happening, but everything is happening. She feels elated, like a woman saved from the guillotine at the last minute.

'Places. Marie! Attention, Marie! Places!' The Crow's stick comes down hard on her calf, but she doesn't even feel it.

The houselights are all down. The bright green light, like a monster's eye, is lit at the front of the stage and Edgar and the whole auditorium dissolve in the glare. The only thing that is real is that Edgar is here. He is back.

She will dance for him. For him alone. Nothing else matters after that. Nothing.

CHAPTER EIGHT

October 1879

Another session. As soon as possible!

Marie is standing on Degas' doorstep, reading his note for the hundredth time, just to prove to herself that she hasn't imagined it. When the Crow handed Marie the envelope at the end of rehearsals yesterday it was so hard to just smile and take the note in front of the other little rats, to stop her hands shaking, to hide the blush rushing up from the pit of her stomach.

One long week after Marie saw Degas at the opera, he appeared in his chair in the rehearsal room and then two weeks after that she received the note. All that kept her going in that first week when she was hiding at the bakery – terrified that the police would find her or that old Fumble Fingers, Paul's stepfather, would storm in and throw her out on the street – was the hope that Degas would appear. Every day after that glorious day arrived she stayed behind after rehearsals praying that the Crow would bring her an invitation to come to Degas' studio. She's been back at Rue Lepic for three days now, ever since Paul brought word that the police had given up on nailing down anybody in the impenetrable community of lowlifes in Montmartre and were now obsessed with tracking down a murderer in Bellevue. So at least she's been able to change her chemise and wash her hair. She also managed to stop herself tearing the envelope open while she walked home so she could steam it open over a pan of water and keep the whole missive from Degas pristine forever, stashed safely inside *Fantine*.

Marie wonders now, as she fingers Degas' elegant scrawl, why he is so short with her. Why no 'Dear Marie', no 'please', or 'thank you'? Is his familiarity a good sign as it shows he is talking to her like he might talk to Mary Cassatt – or is it language he reserves for servants?

Tant pis! Marie mutters to herself as she stashes the envelope in the pocket of her old coat along with her doubts and tugs at her sleeves, tries to hide her pale bony wrists. Her arms and legs have grown like weeds recently, but she hasn't eaten enough to flesh them out. She can't remember the last time she ate meat. Some slight shift of the light makes her look up at the house. The shutters are all up and the doorstep has been washed, so he must be back for a while. The low autumn sun is dazzling on the washed windows; it makes her quite dizzy.

Marie is aware that she can't stand here dithering on a gentleman's doorstep for much longer. People will think she's a thief. Or a beggar. Or worse.

She slows her breathing, raises her chin, and smooths her long thick plait down her back. Let them think what they want. The main thing is that he is back. The thought makes her heart bloom. So what if she is hungry and exhausted? So is half of Paris.

Her palms are sweaty on the bell pull and she loses her grip and sets off two embarrassingly jangly rings, pictures him tutting and huffing at such a clumsy interruption.

And then he is there, right in front of her.

'Bonjour, Marie. You look wonderful!' A bead of hair wax clings to a clump of hair on his forehead.

'Bonjour, monsieur. I... I hope you have had—'

She is stopped short because Monsieur Degas steps forward and kisses her very gently on each cheek. He is slightly prickly, as if he hasn't shaved for a day or so. Then he is holding her shoulders and looking at her. Not at her. Into her. Her face is level with the elaborate knot of his yellow silk cravat. His chest is rising and falling; he must be puffing a bit, probably from running downstairs from his rooms on the second floor – he rushed to see her.

She makes herself look up at him again. His right eye, the one that seems to bother him when he is painting, is slightly bloodshot. She is unaccustomed to looking at his face close up. There is a dab of blue paint on his right cheekbone and a small cut on his wide forehead. She can't help reaching out to touch the scab.

'Did you hurt yourself?'

'What was that, Marie?'

Her voice seems to bring him out of a trance, to annoy him slightly. He frowns and blinks as if he's just woken up from a dream and then moves her hand away, clasps it in his own. His hand is soft and warm. Can he feel the chapped skin on her knuckles, does it disgust him?

They stand in the dark hallway next to the collection of walking sticks he keeps stored in an elephant's foot. Degas squeezes her hand and squints into the sun, his bad eye twitching a little. It is as if their positions are reversed; it is as if he is on stage, and she is in the dark of the auditorium. He looks nervous, almost as though he is scared of her.

'Listen, my sweet Marie. There is something I must tell you.'

His voice is so soft that she can hardly hear what he is saying against the whinnying of some frightened horses outside. He has never spoken to her like this before. With such tenderness. The creases have appeared between his eyebrows again, there are beads of sweat on his forehead.

Then something changes. He drops her hand as if it were a lump of hot coal and clears his throat. And now he is looking past her out into the street and drawing himself up, pressing his cravat into his yellow and blue striped waistcoat with a sharp sigh.

Somebody is coming up the path towards them. Marie turns to where Degas is looking, a sudden tight smile pinned to his face, all softness gone. She sees Mary Cassatt – damn her – waving her black fringed parasol before her, her carriage shining behind, the four liveried horses stamping in the street. So, it was her horses making that noise.

'Ah, I see you have a visitor, Edgar.'

'No, no. Come in, Mary. Come in.'

Mary steps in before Degas has finished speaking, squeezes Marie's chin and kisses her on the forehead as if she were a child. Marie has no choice but to step back against the wall and let Mary swish past her.

Mary kisses Degas briefly on both cheeks, steals a look at herself in the hall mirror, lays a gloved hand on his cheek and whispers something Marie cannot catch. Marie watches Mary's hand there on Degas' cheek, as if he belongs to her, and feels somehow bereft, shut out of an intimacy she cannot understand. She hopes for a look from Degas. Just a look to let her know that he knows she is there, that he will tell her what he wanted to say later, when they are alone again. But he gives her nothing. He is too busy leaning in and listening to Mademoiselle Cassatt telling him how hot it is for October, how he must be in need of an outing, maybe to Bougival with her. Now she has made him laugh. Leaning over him like that, pretending to flick a bit of fluff off his shoulder. Surely he'll send her away, tell her he has work to do.

'Marie, go upstairs and get ready. I'll be there in a moment.'

She stomps upstairs as loudly as she can. Not that they'll notice. She jumps when she sees the Creature. It's now a lumpy, terracotta-coloured thing, with a roughly shaped head. She goes to touch it and recoils, realises that it's clay and is still slightly wet. The arms that Degas constructed with broken toothbrushes and wire are joined onto the body, a few bits of wood still sticking out where the elbows should be. She steps loudly towards the screen where she should be changing and creeps back on tiptoe to lean over the banister so she can hear what Degas and Mary are saying. As soon as Degas comes upstairs, she'll dart back behind the screen.

'I don't want to come to Bougival, Mary. I am perfectly happy here.'

The banister presses painfully into a bruise on Marie's hipbone but, leaning out, she can see the top of Mary's tiny off-centre hat now, black of course and studded with jet.

'But you don't look well, my dear Edgar. And we've hardly spoken since you returned – I could be forgiven for thinking you are avoiding me on purpose! Did something happen in New Orleans? Come now, a bit of fresh air would do you the world of good, wouldn't it? Might get you working again,' coos Mary in that strange foreign accent of hers. The pointed tip of her silk slipper appears from under her petticoats and hits the elephant foot as she steps towards Degas.

'Why don't you come and join us for a little painting *en*

116

plein air, rather than stewing in your studio every day? Come on, Edgar. Enjoy yourself for once, *mon brave*!

'I should love to visit Bougival sometime. But I hate the idea of working outside, as you know. I have everything I need in my studio.' Degas digs in his pocket and dabs his brow with a bright white handkerchief. The sight of it gives Marie a jolt. The handkerchief over Papa's face so bright and clean in the shuttered gloom. Obscenely clean. The scene is inside her all the time, knitted into her bones. Papa lying out on the stretcher, his feet bare. The image lives in her. Just when she thinks she can step forward into the future, the past grabs her like a thief. She grips the banister and pushes the panic away, concentrates on the scene below.

'Now, I really must get on.' Degas grabs the handkerchief and stuffs it in his pocket, turns away from Mary.

Good. He is getting rid of her. But Mary Cassatt won't let him go so easily. She clasps his shoulder and deepens her voice.

'What on earth were you doing in New Orleans anyway? I had no idea you would be gone so long.'

Degas shrugs off her hand. 'I had family matters to attend to, Mary. And I just needed to get away from Paris, from everything. Please stop asking me questions.'

'René again?'

'No, not René. Well, not directly. I just wanted to visit my uncle. And to get back to Louisiana for a while to restore my spirits.'

'Do you need more money, Edgar?'

'You Americans are so brutishly direct! No, no, I do not need any more of your money, Mary. Now please just go and let me get on.'

'Did you enjoy being in your beloved Louisiana with your country people?'

'Not as much as I'd hoped. It's full of awful Americans like you. Hardly any Creoles left.'

Marie can't help noticing that Degas seems to be enjoying Mary's little show.

Mary chuckles lightly, then clears her throat and draws herself taller.

'I'll let you go in a moment, I promise. But first I need to ask you about *Le Jour et La Nuit*. Have you thought about it at all, Edgar? I really think it could be the making of us – there's no other magazine devoted to printing and I have some new ideas for it, which I think you'll like. Perhaps you could come over later and discuss it. Mother would be delighted to see you. We have some decisions to make *now* if we are to launch it at the spring exhibition as agreed. Well – Edgar? Look at me, Edgar. You seem terribly distracted.'

'I'm sorry, Mary. I haven't thought about it; I'm very busy with other projects.'

'Oh, Edgar!' Mary stamps her foot and hisses at him. 'You promised me, Edgar. You are utterly impossible sometimes. I spend weeks getting our little magazine together – the magazine *you* were so enthusiastic about – while you swan off to New Orleans to – to mope, and to quench your insatiable thirst for the exotic, no doubt. Why can you never finish anything? Anything at all?'

'I'll get back to it soon, Mary, I promise. But I'm busy at the moment. With – with…'

'Your little monkey girl! That's it, isn't it? Come on, admit it! Why in God's name are you so obsessed with that creature? It seems somewhat perverse to me.'

Marie watches Mary's slippered foot tapping lightly on the floor now, making the elephant's foot wobble slightly. 'Do you really think that strange little doll is going to push our project forward? Are you unhinged?'

'My little dancer is coming along very well, I think. And she's not a doll, Mary, stop calling her that. In any case, the armature is almost finished. I've nearly completed the clay layer.'

Mary's tapping foot quiets itself. And she seems to quieten with it.

'I'm sorry, Edgar. Standing in your hallway haranguing you when you're so busy! Very selfish of me. The truth is I'm a little overwrought. My sister is unwell again. Mother has hardly left the house for two weeks. And I've missed you.'

'I'm sorry to hear that, about your sister.'

Mary claps her hands together lightly and holds her fingers on her chin as if she's praying. 'Anyway, let's start again. How are you, my dear Edgar? Is your eye hurting again?'

'Yes, it is a bit sore.'

Their two heads move together, and Marie is afraid they are kissing, but it seems that Mary is just inspecting his eye.

'Same old injury?' she asks softly.

'Yes.'

'Well, if you will go out to join a mad band of Communards and start shooting muskets and God knows what else, you only have yourself to blame!'

How easily she teases him, twists him around her little finger. So Antoinette was not lying. Degas must have been in the Garde Nationale. Now Degas is finally back, she must steel herself and ask him about Papa as soon as she can. Perhaps if she does, she will finally be able to walk away from that scene and be free. As soon as Mary has gone, she will be brave. She will ask him flat out. Maybe it was Papa that he wanted to tell her about.

'The folly of youth, Mary. The folly of youth,' Degas says with a snort.

'Your eye does look terribly bloodshot. I'll arrange for my doctor to see you again. You can't possibly work with that, or it will get worse and then you won't be able to work at all and you will be responsible for the failure of our great exhibition. I know you don't want that!'

No answer from Degas, just a long and exasperated sigh. 'You are impossible sometimes, Mary!'

'I know! I've got it!' Mary's voice is louder now. She slowly draws her parasol out from the elephant's foot, as if she is drawing a sword from a sheath, and pokes it into Degas' polished shoe. 'I need a new hat. And you know how you adore Madame Pavlovski's.'

'I'm not in the mood, Mary. I…'

'Come along now, my dear. Just wash that paint off your face and come with me now, Edgar. I insist. Come and help me choose a hat. Your little monkey girl can come with us as my chaperone. Oh, please, Edgar. Please!'

Degas lifts Mary's parasol off his shoe.

'Oh, very well, Mary. You win again. I'll be back in a minute.'

Damn, thinks Marie. Now she won't get Degas alone and will have to listen to Mary's simpering instead. But at least she'll get to see inside a real milliner's shop. Antoinette will be very jealous. Better get back behind the screen before he comes upstairs. There's a half-eaten sandwich on his painting table. She grabs it and darts behind the screen to devour it. Monkey girl! The words are a kick in the stomach for Marie. She mutters the words to herself as she pulls on her clothes. How dare she? How dare that rich bitch call her a monkey? Her own burst of anger nearly trips her over. Degas bounds up the stairs straight past the studio and calls to her to get dressed and come downstairs.

'We are going on a little outing, my dear Marie.'

Well, at least he didn't call her 'monkey girl'.

Mary takes Marie's arm in the hallway while Degas selects a walking stick. Marie finds it hard not to flinch from Mary's touch. She licks her lips to check there are no tell-tale crumbs and peers up at Mary. She is only a little taller than Marie. Her neat, pale face is dusted with freckles, her nose small and uptilted. Her silk slipper is tapping under her skirts with impatience, making a little black rose-bud dance. She smells of lemons and freshly pressed linen.

Mary snaps open her black fringed parasol and makes a string of jet jump on her narrow throat.

'The sun is still terribly bright, isn't it, Marie?' she mutters, wrinkling her little nose at the impudent sun.

'*Oui, mademoiselle*,' says Marie, thinking that it is no brighter than usual.

Degas walks a little ahead of Marie and Mary. He is very different out here on the wide new pavements, his unruly hair covered by a top hat, stick tapping like a metronome. Even the way he walks is different; his back is straighter and his footsteps heavier and more definite. She doesn't like this version of him. It is as if he is on stage, in costume, in character. Far away from her. She prefers the backstage version of him, with his uncertain gestures, the paint in his hair and his shirt untucked.

They pass Rue des Poissoniers, where Mary gasps and holds her nose at the whiff that comes from wash-down at the slaughterhouses.

'Talking of printing, Edgar—'

'Were we?'

'Yes. *Woman with a Fan* is nearly finished, you'll be glad to hear. The distemper was difficult to work with, but well worth it, you were right. It really does have the look and feel of a traditional Japanese woodcut, Edgar, but with a sense of modernity as well. I struggled with the line of the woman's back for weeks and deliberated for much too long over the colour tones, but I think you'll have to admit that it works pretty well.'

'I'll come over later to take a look. I just hope it isn't too light.'

Mary stops short and raises her voice. 'Light! Light? Is that all you have to say, Edgar? Edgar! Come back here and explain yourself.'

Two gentlemen in top hats push past Marie and Mary. They frown at her shrill tone.

Degas turns reluctantly on his heels and comes back to face Mary and Marie. He takes off his top hat, smooths back his sweaty hair and replaces it.

'What now?'

Marie turns her head away in embarrassment. She fingers the pockmarks of bullets on the wall next to her. Bullets that had already been through a body. A line of ragged soldiers, begging for their lives. Then screaming, silence falling like a guillotine, a wall turned red.

'Do you really have to make a scene, Mary?' Degas asks softly. 'Must I always be praising you and encouraging you as if you are a child? You know I admire your work, don't you? I wouldn't have let you into the group if I hadn't thought you were an exceptional artist. No woman has the right to draw as well as you, Mary, it's quite extraordinary.'

Mary seems to soften for a moment and then decides against it, pushes her chin up, lets out a sharp sigh. 'I know you mean that as a compliment, Edgar. But can't you see how insulting it is? Presuming *you* have the right to tell me what my rights are, in your usual high-handed way. I may be a woman, Edgar, but I am not your wife. You think you can proclaim on what I've created, tell me what I should do next, dictate which colour tones I use. And – even though I'm funding the damned exhibition – I do what you suggest. I've had enough of it, Edgar. I am an artist in my own right, whether you think I have the *right* to that or not.'

Degas jabs at a crack in the pavement with the tip of his stick. Marie can't tell if he's angry or sad.

'But I wasn't saying...' Degas reaches out his hand to her. Mary bats it away.

'No, don't stop me. Don't you dare silence me! Don't worry, I'm not going to cry, Edgar. You've taught me such a lot; I'm not disputing that. I'm very grateful for it. The thing is, I *like* my pictures of children and mothers, Edgar. You may think women are *fleurs du mal* – born of pain, only beautiful in their noble and quiet suffering. But I disagree. I *like* depicting female elegance and charm and confidence. And ease. I think it's beautiful and I think it has value. And dignity. And, may God forgive me, I *like* lots of light!' She lets go of Marie's arm now, squares up to Degas and balls her hand into a fist as if she's going to punch him.

'If my surfeit of femininity disgusts you, then so be it!'

Mary's voice breaks and she steps past Degas, pops open her parasol and strides away from them with her head held high.

'Will you go after her, Marie? She gets terribly overheated sometimes and I can't help her.'

The look on Degas' face is desolate. She remembers the lonely figure of his mother on the wall in the studio, all alone on that bench. Degas as a little boy, desperately trying to make her happy and protect her.

Marie rushes to catch up with Mary; she links her arm in Mary's to show her that she understands how she feels, steers her around the careering cart of a delivery boy. How strange to understand how a lady feels, for Marie's heart to go out to her.

'Oh, Marie,' Mary throws her a sad smile. 'Sometimes I fear our voices will never be taken seriously. However hard we scream, however sweetly we sing.'

Mary is right, Marie thinks to herself. What a beautiful way to put it. Louise Michel and the women of the Union des Femmes used to say something very similar. She wonders if any woman can have a life independent of a man, even a rich woman like Mary. She has always thought all the rich women she saw gliding past in their shining carriages or striding about laughing in their sumptuous clothes must be very happy, but it seems she was wrong. She looks up at Mary. Mary is biting her lip and her tightly corseted chest is heaving with the effort to regain her composure after the argument with Degas. Being a woman and wanting to be free is exhausting, thinks Marie. Mary seems to read her thoughts, because she strokes her cheek and nods slowly. 'You're very sweet, little Marie.' They both have tears in their eyes. But now Degas is striding towards them and the moment has gone. Mary has already pasted on a bright smile, and they all face forward and set off again as if nothing has happened.

The three of them walk in silence through the freshly swept new streets, which are filling quickly with ladies and gentlemen out for their evening stroll, the ladies fanning themselves and exclaiming at the heat. In between them boys rush past with carts and seamstresses dart by with huge baskets of clothes.

They stop for a moment at a crossroads.

'Have you seen my designs for the posters, Edgar? Do you approve?'

'You seem very fond of green and red at the moment, Mary.'

'Are you referring to my frames at our last exhibition, Edgar, the frames around *all* those paintings I sold?' Mary raises a finely arched eyebrow at Degas, flashes him a tight smile. Degas snorts.

'I suppose your design will make our little poster stand out from the crowd. So I suppose I do approve, yes.'

'Good – oh, and neither Berthe nor I want our names included on the poster. It doesn't seem right to advertise ourselves when we paid for most of it.' Mary starts humming a tune now. She obviously feels she's won a small victory.

Marie is uncertain whether she will get paid for this outing. If not, she and Antoinette will have to go hungry again tonight. She looks at her reflection in the sparklingly clean shop windows. The wide, flat Belgian cheekbones, the thick black fringe that Antoinette cut for her recently and that only makes her face look broader. She hardly ever bothers to look in the mirror, she leaves that to Gigi and Antoinette. How does she look in Degas' eyes? And why on earth has he chosen her as his model?

The narrow green milliner's shopfront proclaims the proprietress's name in curly gold letters. Marie pushes aside a heavy sadness that has lodged inside her and presses her face up to the window while Degas and Mary fiddle with hats and gloves. Bonnets float, ribbons trail. A huge yellow hat, its brim laden with apples and pears, is balanced on a faceless wooden head in the window display.

Degas opens the door, tips his hat and clicks his heels (why must he put on such a show?). Mary chuckles, puts her hand on Degas' shoulders and whispers, 'If you must know, Edgar, I left a dark section in the upper corner of *Woman with a Fan*, just to please you. And it does improve the piece, loath as I am to admit it.'

Mary and Degas exchange meaningful looks. They seem to have made up after their argument. Artists are extremely fucking childish sometimes, thinks Marie to herself, as she watches them. Mary snaps her parasol shut sharply, steps into the shop and starts inspecting the displays with her back to them. She sticks her hip out and leans on her parasol to display her figure, no doubt. Marie wipes her old boots on the doormat while Degas holds the door for her. It makes her nervous to have a gentleman hold a door for her. She trips on the shiny brass footplate and Degas catches her arm.

'Thank you, Marie,' he whispers into her ear.

He is so close she feels the warmth of his breath. And the tenderness in his voice. Marie. Her name sounds so beautiful when he says it like that. His words dissolve the icy sadness in her chest, like spring rain on snow.

It is quiet and cool in the shop after the hot hum of the street. Red velvet banquettes are arranged at angles around the small room and among them wooden poles at different heights topped with hats and a full-length mirror, tilted and smeared. Mary tries on a huge-brimmed straw hat loaded with fruit and makes a face. Marie can't help laughing along with them both.

'Shh! Here she comes,' Degas says, and they all wait in a line.

A rustling from the back of the shop, a peek of lurid purple crinoline between the heads. A gasp and a cluck and the rustling grows frenetic as Madame Pavlovski sails towards them.

'Ahh, Monsieur Degas,' she drawls.

Her eyes are tiny new coins in a huge head with a little red taffeta hat perched at a precarious angle, covered in jet and lace, and secured around her thick neck with a wide-ribboned bow even bigger than her entire face. Her body is a shiny barrel of purple silk and her feet look bigger than Degas' in bulging silk slippers. Marie has to stifle her giggles, and a sideways look tells her that Mary is suppressing her laughter too. It is so wonderful to feel laughter bubbling up inside her so naturally.

'And Mademoiselle Cassatt,' Madame Pavlovski practically drools as she intones their names, her head on one side, counterbalancing the hat. Then she turns to Marie and frowns, scans her body as if it is a cheap bonnet, wrinkles her fleshy nose in disgust at the knot in Marie's broken bootlace.

'And – and this is…?'

'Mademoiselle. Van. Goethem,' Degas barks in her face. Madame Pavlovski is the same height as Degas and much wider.

Marie has to stop herself throwing her arms around Degas and thanking him for standing up for her. Madame Pavlovski is wonderfully flustered now, her face bright red. She repeats Marie's name, says she is very welcome and apologises twice. Madame Pavlovski reminds Marie of Madame Thénardier. The thought makes her grit her teeth to stop herself bursting out laughing. Degas hands Madame Pavlovski his hat and Mary's gloves. Now he is reaching out for Marie's coat. They will all see the ripped lining, the sweat stains under the arms, yet she has no choice but to give it to him. Degas doesn't seem to notice; he folds the coat up carefully, as if it were as beautiful as Mary's satin jacket, and hands it to Madame Pavlovski with his own.

Marie sits on the velvet banquette while Degas and Mary wander around looking at the hats. Everything around her has a glow. She and Antoinette used to press their noses against the windows of places like this and pretend they were fine ladies choosing a new outfit until they were chased away. And now, here she is with the snooty shop-owner being forced to bow and scrape in front her. Who cares if Degas saw the tatty lining on her coat. He doesn't seem to care about these things. *Un vrai gentilhomme.* That is what Papa would have called him. And Degas and Papa fought together in the siege of Paris, shoulder to shoulder. Papa trusted him so why shouldn't she? The temptation of giving in to the situation, of letting go of her constant vigilance, just enjoying herself, is enormous.

'What do you think, Marie?'

Mary is standing in front of her in a wide-brimmed hat, turning her head to the side. It's obvious she is really posing for Monsieur Degas who is standing behind her pretending to study the ribbons on a green felt bonnet.

'*Vous êtes belle, mademoiselle.*' It is true. Mary looks beautiful. The curve of the brim sets off the graceful line of her jaw and the mounds of purple berries bring out the colour in her dark eyes. She is sure Degas sees it too.

'And what is the expert's opinion?' Mademoiselle Cassatt swings around and Degas comes towards her, squinting a little.

'Turn the other way. Hmm.'

'Well?' She dips her chin, looks up from underneath the rim, eyes glittering.

'It is certainly quite striking, my dear.'

Degas smiles at Marie and seems to wink, although it could just be that his bad eye is bothering him. Mary smiles tightly at them and her voice is a little too bright when she turns to Marie.

'Here, Marie. Why don't you try it? I am sure Edgar would enjoy that.'

Marie swallows and gets up. She is half excited, half terrified at being so exposed in front of Degas. Mademoiselle Cassatt unties the fine purple ribbon from beneath her little pointed chin and places the hat on Marie's head, steers her towards the mirror and holds her there by her shoulders. Degas follows and stands behind them.

Marie gasps when she looks in the mirror. She almost looks like a real lady. Her monkey face looks almost pretty, framed in this sumptuous hat. Degas is watching her in the mirror with a strange expression on his face. Maybe he will see her differently now she is dressed like a lady, like one of his own kind.

In the mirror Marie sees Mademoiselle Cassatt studying her.

'She has an interesting face, Edgar, a little like yours in a strange way. That would explain your extreme attachment to her.'

Edgar looks angry now. Why can't the bourgeois just say what they mean like normal people, rather than dressing up everything they say in wry smiles and riddles? Marie wonders. The hat is tight on her head, but the hatband is made of the softest velvet. Mademoiselle Cassatt ties a bow under her chin a little to the side, steps back and gives her a wink.

'*Charmante. Très charmante.*' She looks at Degas when she speaks, and her smile contains a question. But Degas' expression is fixed on Marie. Emotions she can't read flicker over his face like cloud shapes over the Seine. The pulse next to his ear starts, the one he gets when he is frustrated or angry. But why? Why is he angry? Is he angry with her? She must do something to make him happy again.

Madame Pavlovski rustles over and adjusts one of the brown silk leaves on the brim. Marie is starting to feel a bit sick. It feels like Mary is playing a game she doesn't understand.

'The berries are made from the finest glass from Nîmes. Each one modelled by hand.'

'Yes, yes,' Degas tuts and shoos Madame Pavlovski away.

This is her chance, she must show Degas that she is a woman, a lady, not just another little rat to be used and thrown away. She thinks of Amélie, how she poses in the mirror, and tries to copy her, dips her chin with a small smile and puts her hands on her hips. Now the thing where you turn this way and that to show your figure. It's like remembering steps at the opera: glissade, pas de bourrée, enchaînement.

'Mademoiselle is very elegant,' exclaims Madame Pavlovski, clasping her huge fat hands in joy at the prospect of a sale. Marie knows her game but can't help enjoying her praise anyway. She ambles across the shop and behind the hats on their sticks, turns around and around. Another customer stops to watch. She can feel Degas' eyes on her and it feels wonderful. Maybe she can play the coquette after all.

Mary claps and cheers her on, tugging at Degas' sleeve, telling him not to be such a sourpuss. Degas shrugs her off.

'Oh, you are too adorable, Marie. Isn't she adorable, Edgar? Let's buy it for her. Edgar... Edgar.'

'Take it off.' His voice is a gunshot. Marie stops short. He looks furious. 'Take it off now, Marie!'

The way he says her name now is not affectionate at all. He is full of disdain. It feels so bitter in her chest that she can't breathe and starts to cough. How foolish she was, dancing around the shop like that, thinking he was enjoying it too.

A customer on the other side of the shop looks around at

the commotion. Marie's stomach sinks. Why is he so angry? She looks to Mary and sees that she is shocked too. The light in Mary's eyes retreats and gathers further back.

'Calm yourself, Edgar,' she hisses. 'Come here, Marie. I'll help you take off that hat.'

'She looks ridiculous, Mary. Ridiculous! Take it off now, Marie! I should never have let you lure me here.'

Marie tears at the bow under her chin, fingers shaking, while Mary tries to help her and Degas just stands there, stiff as one of the hat stands. She wants to cry. Her fingers won't work properly; she is just tightening the knot and making it worse. She can't look at Degas. She has made such a fool of herself, thinking she could be a lady, daring to believe he might care about her. The Red She-Wolf was right when she said working people were like carthorses for the bourgeoisie. Marie was only four or five when she heard those words – Louise Michel standing on an apple crate in Place du Marché, she on her father's shoulders imagining the feel of metal in her mouth, her head drawn back, the tightness in her jaw. That is exactly how she is. A carthorse. How could she imagine otherwise? She would live her whole life 'in harness'. Mary is freer than she can ever dream of being. She's a lady. She can afford to tease and be rude and upset Degas without losing him.

'Well, I think she looked charming, Edgar. I thought you loved to see women in hats and ribbons, looking pretty for men. Just your sort of thing,' snaps Mary.

'Not her. Not Marie,' says Degas.

'Why not? Why not Marie?' Mary's accent sounds much stronger now, her voice higher. 'I've never seen you so protective, Edgar. What in God's name is so special about your…' She catches Marie's eye. She was going to say 'monkey girl' but stopped herself, that much is obvious.

131

So that's what Mary was up to. She didn't really think Marie looked good in the hat; she was just using her to tease Degas. She feels so stupid, so stupid for responding like this to anyone who shows her a bit of kindness, even if it's false.

Mary smooths her skirts and tries to compose herself. 'About Marie?'

'Some creatures need no adornment. They have natural elegance and beauty, unsullied by artificiality.'

Now his voice is soft again and he gives Marie a soft smile that seems to say he is sorry for hurting her. Is 'creature' supposed to be a compliment? She will not forgive him that easily. She holds his gaze but refuses to smile.

Mary fiddles with her jet necklace. Her mouth twitches. A vein at her temple starts to pulse. She shouts out to Madame Pavlovski to get their coats, that she will not be purchasing anything today, but will be back when she is 'in better company'.

There is a silence stretched between all three of them. Marie daren't break it, even though she needs to know if she is allowed to leave and if she will get paid for this jaunt. Mary taps her slipper impatiently.

'How is your picture of that cabaret singer with the huge scarlet mouth and vulgar gestures going?' She turns to Degas and resumes her conversational mode as if stepping into a well-known dance.

'*La Grande Nathalie*?'

'Yes. One could hardly imagine a more artificial creature.'

'She at least is honest in her artificiality, whereas most of your sex are merely artificial in their honesty.'

As he speaks, he strokes the grainy forehead of one of the heads by the door, traces the chin and pinches the nose. '*La Grande Nathalie* is a *fleur du mal*, a fascinating blend of the delicate and the gross. I search for *l'honnête femme* and find that she is as rare as an academician with taste.'

'Do you find it in yourself?' asks Mary.

'Good taste?'

'That I take for granted. No, I meant honesty.'

'Honesty is only useful in a woman. For a man it is superfluous, a distraction. The painting must be true, but the character of the man who paints it is irrelevant.'

Marie is only half-listening. She is still wrestling with the monstrous hat. She frees herself just in time for Madame Pavlovski, who is trotting towards them laden with coats.

Degas and Mary continue their argument about painting outside the shop as if Marie is not there. She could slip away but she's not going to make it that easy for Mary. Better to wait until Degas remembers she's there and gives her some money.

The sun has dipped behind the building, and an autumnal chill has descended. The street is unusually crowded for this time of day. What are all these people in working clothes doing here with their muddy boots and exhausted faces? They are far from the workshops and factories, only shops and smart houses here. A woman arm in chubby arm with two other red-faced women pushes her in the back, tells her to get out the way, laughs loudly. They are obviously drunk. It must be a festival or feast day because the mood is excitable, eyes are bright and flashing, footsteps quick and light.

The ladies and gentlemen start to look a bit concerned at the invasion. A lady waves her parasol at a girl who comes much too close and snatches up her hatbox, fearing the girl might swipe it. Madame Pavlovski's face appears in the window, straining to see what is going on, and she slams down the shutters. Marie flattens herself against a wall as the crowd thickens and starts to stream past. Degas and Mary are still talking but she can't make out what they are saying above the hum of the crowd. Men in overalls, women wrapped in scarves, some singing, some shouting. A woman thrusts a leaflet into her hand, another knocks it onto the ground. Where is Degas? He and Mary are being dragged away by the crowd now. Just the top of his hat bobbing in a sea of people, Mary's pale face looking startled. She tries to move towards them, but the current of people is taking her away. 'Monsieur Degas! Monsieur Degas!' It's no good, the crowd is too thick, and she is scared. People are starting to run.

'Police. The police are coming!'

Now she is running too. She feels a hand on her shoulder and panics. The sound of hundreds of footsteps pounding up the Butte that night. That metallic smell of sweat and fear.

'Marie! Marie. It's me, Paul.'

What a relief it is to see dear Paul's face. He takes her arm. In his pocket she sees a stack of rolled-up pamphlets.

'What's happening?' she shouts above the din of police whistles.

'Didn't you see her, Marie?' Paul's eyes are shining as if he is drunk but she can't smell drink on him.

'Who? Antoinette?' Please God she isn't in trouble.

'No. Not Antoinette. Louise Michel! She's back! She was speaking in Place Goncourt just now. I thought you must have been there too. Oh, Marie. It was wonderful.' Paul pauses to embrace an old man with a long white beard. 'Hurry, monsieur. You don't want to get arrested now!' The man replies that the police wouldn't dare arrest him and spits into the gutter.

'She's going to fight for us again, Marie,' Paul continues. 'I thought it was all over, but it isn't. The Red She-Wolf is back! And she is howling as loud as ever. Aren't you happy? Marie, you must be happy! You should have seen her. She looks just the same, even after her years in New Caledonia. Remember when she played the organ while they fired cannons at St Pierre? Remember the soup kitchens? Remember queuing up in the snow that awful winter, you and I? But there was always enough for us all. Because she made sure of it. We stuck together, we looked after each other. Not like now. Everybody out for themselves, the government setting us against each other, like dogs fighting over crumbs.'

Paul talks on as they cut down a side alley and make their way towards Montmartre. Marie can't really concentrate. Degas was washed away from her by the crowd, and she doesn't even know when he wants her to come back to the studio. Oh, she should have spoken up and interrupted his stupid argument with Mary Cassatt. Why is she such a coward, such a good monkey girl? She didn't even get paid. Maybe Paul can get her some bread, but it's so shameful to have to keep asking.

'We are setting up soup kitchens again, Marie. Will you help? Marie! You're not listening. What's wrong with you?'

'Oh, sorry, Paul. I was thinking about other things.' They have stopped to catch their breath before climbing up the Butte. 'Yes, yes. Of course I'll help.'

Paul stands opposite her, holds her shoulders in his big warm hands, narrows his eyes and smiles, just like he used to do when she agreed to some mischief when they were little children. The truth is she could happily never see a bowl of soup again. Oh, for a plate of thick meat stew! But she must do something. At least it will distract her from thinking about Degas. Half the people in Montmartre are starving. And the other half are either prostitutes or thieves. Papa would not have

135

stood by and let it happen. At least she can make him proud by doing something for her fellow citizens.

'Do you ever think of your father, Paul?' she whispers.

Paul's arms drop to his sides and his smile sinks. He looks like a lost child. The light goes out of his eyes. They are back there. She knows it. Both of them. They are staring into each other's eyes, looking for a way out, knowing it doesn't exist. Monsieur Béranger, Paul's father, the panic in his eyes when he begged Louise Michel to let him leave and go to his family. But he didn't escape in the end. He was rounded up with the others and executed the day after Papa. She can see that panic in Paul now. They are both stuck with that aching loss that nobody talks about.

It is too painful to keep him there, to keep them both there. She must look away and break the silence.

'I'm sorry, Paul. Forgive me for asking. I am cold. And hungry. It's wonderful that Louise Michel is back. Miraculous!'

She tries to take his arm so they can break this awful spell and continue. But Paul won't let her. He shoves her away, grips her shoulders again, fixes her in his gaze.

'Yes. I do think of my father, Marie. I can't help but think about him. I think of him every day. But thinking, going over and over it, does no good.' He shakes her shoulders, and his voice is so loud now that passers-by are tutting at them. 'That's why I'm carrying on the fight,' Paul continues, 'for him. You should do the same, Marie. Otherwise, what did they die for? What did they fucking die for?' Paul shakes his head; his eyes are wild. 'For nothing, that's what. For fucking nothing!'

He grabs Marie's arm sharply and starts to drag her up the Butte. All she can hear is her heart beating in her ears like the drums the soldiers played on the way to the mass burials. Sometimes the past and the present seem so close together they get mixed up in her mind. She wants to apologise to Paul again but hasn't got the energy to speak. He is right. It is up to them, the children of the fallen, to keep their memory alive, to march on for them. *You must march on for your father, Marie. March for him!* That's what Louise Michel said that night.

'I will help in the soup kitchens, Paul. I'll do whatever it takes.'

Paul squeezes her arm. 'Good. We're having a meeting at St Pierre tomorrow night. Six p.m. sharp. Come in the back door and don't breathe a word to my mother. Or Antoinette.'

Somehow, Marie feels taller now she has promised to help Louise Michel. The night is clear, cut with a thumbnail moon. She lays her head on Paul's shoulder and yawns, lets him march her up the Butte. If Degas is not at rehearsals tomorrow, she'll just go to his studio anyway. What is there to lose?

As they round the corner into Rue Lepic, Paul pulls her sharply away into a side street. She takes her head off his shoulder. 'Where are we going?'

'I'm taking you to the Veau à Deux Têtes for a plate of chops,' Paul says. His voice is soft and kind again, eyes sparkling.

The Veau à Deux Têtes. She hasn't been there for years. The cheapest and best chops in town, smothered in thick gravy and served with fried potatoes. A thrill of pure happiness snakes up inside her. Then she thinks of Antoinette and happiness rapidly turns into guilt. Antoinette and Paul are putting every penny aside to leave the bakery and Paul's monster of a stepfather and find the first month's rent for a room of their own.

'But you can't – I mean, you have to save for a room for you and Antoinette.'

'I got a nice tip from your friend Amélie Reine today. So, it's on her. Antoinette doesn't have to know a thing about it.'

137

CHAPTER NINE

December 1879

The table in Degas' studio is covered with beeswax candles. Some tall and thin, some short and squat. The flames are doing a mad dance in a draught from the open door and the sweet smell of beeswax makes Marie think she is in church. As if she should make the sign of the cross to Degas' mother, there in the picture on the wall behind the table. Madame Degas seems to come alive in the flickering light. Her clasped hands loosen slightly, her dark eyes glow as if she wants to get up from her wrought iron bench at the edge of the tropical wood, step out of her frame and say something. Is she smiling? Marie finds herself smiling back.

She's been waiting here for five minutes at least, and her hands are still numb. It was the housekeeper, Sabine, who opened the door to her and sent her up.

'Monsieur Degas is expecting you, mademoiselle.' Sabine put a strange squeeze on the 'mademoiselle' and gave her a knowing smile, as if she was hiding some secret knowledge in the deep crinkles of her kind old eyes.

The butter-coloured wax is oozing onto assorted saucers and plates. Some are almost overflowing. What on earth is Degas up to? Is it some kind of bizarre artist's ritual? Nothing would surprise her anymore. But what a waste! All these candles burning at once when it's not even dark yet, when at home they all have to share one measly stump, cradling it from room to room.

She sits down on the chaise longue by the fire to warm her hands and hopes Degas won't make her pose nude. Paris has been under snow for two weeks and at night she shivers so much she hardly sleeps. She scrunches her toes in her wet boots. The chair is not quite as soft as Amélie's chair, but if she leant back, she would probably doze off straight away.

The Creature at the other end of the room keeps grabbing her attention, even though she doesn't want to look at it head on. It is unnerving, seeing a miniature version of herself in clay. The whole armature is covered now. Nobody but Marie and Degas will ever know what lies beneath the surface; it will be their secret. Forever. The thought warms her a little. She's been coming to Degas' studio for almost a year and a half now, though it feels like a lifetime and a single day all at the same time. She's seen the Creature grow from a few rough sketches into a strange metallic monster, she's watched Degas meticulously flesh out this skeleton and affix the arms so that they extend backwards at the correct angle – she had to hold her arms still for what felt like hours at a time while he fiddled with various sorts of wadding, including part of a mattress he'd found on the street somewhere to create the right impression of musculature at the shoulder. And now the Creature is fully coated in clay, whole and complete, and she *still* hasn't asked Degas about her father. The silence and sense of deep concentration on their shared task in the studio feels impenetrable.

Maybe she could just close her eyes for a couple of minutes. Feel the warmth of the fire seep through her boots onto her aching feet, watch the shadows making ragged shapes on her closed eyelids.

She's in no rush to go home. Last night was so awful. Another row. Gigi and Antoinette at each other's throats over money, Gigi's humiliation at having to beg for work, her hands shaking as she dropped the candle, the sob in her voice as she shouted at Antoinette for 'bringing nothing but trouble'. Worst of all was Antoinette's cold fury.

It's too painful to think about it now. She used to try being peacemaker, but she's given up. When she went to Gigi's room last night to offer comfort, she found her splayed out on her bed, fully clothed and snoring with a repossession notice in her hand. It is not the first. So far, they have managed to talk the landlord, who is an old friend of Papa's, into letting them stay, but it can only be a matter of time. Rents are soaring, the streets of Montmartre are full of homeless people sheltering under shop awnings and begging for food. She and Paul had talked about how Louise Michel will lead the fight for rent control, for workers to be treated with dignity once again. Their conversation had fired her up, sitting there in the fug of the Veau à deux Têtes, filling her belly with meat and the most delicious gravy she has ever tasted.

Since that night she has attended several public meetings with Paul and even started going to the weekly meetings at the Martyrs Tavern with Louise Michel and her inner circle. Gradually she has started to feel at home with the raggle-taggle bunch of comrades, and their impassioned discussions about justice and fraternity never fail to stir her blood, to make her feel more alive, if only for a few hours.

Oh, it is so boring being gloomy and hungry all the time. Better to be marching on, to be fighting for the rights of her neighbours and friends, to help Gigi keep her dignity and Antoinette out of prison. But now, sitting on this chaise longue with the churchy smell of beeswax and the crackling of a full fire, it all feels too difficult and the idea of staying here, warm by the fire forever, feels too tempting.

'Marie!'

Degas bursts in. Shirt untucked, eyes wild. Marie leaps up, ready to greet him.

'*Bonjour, Marie.*'

She could swear Degas addressed himself to the Creature before he turned his gaze on her. He is busy fiddling with the overflowing candles now. He pours the molten wax into what looks like a large Flemish pisspot (white porcelain with blue figures) and starts mixing it with some sort of oil.

She sits down again, feeling stupid and deflated.

'Shall I get undressed?'

'I am sorry, Marie. For – for this!' He gestures at himself and then at the candles. 'Thank you for coming. I must catch this wax, you see, while it is the right consistency. No, no. Don't bother getting undressed. Not today. Just sit there for a moment and take your boots off. I'm going to start with your feet.'

Marie supposes that Degas must be planning to cover the clay figure with a layer of wax for some reason. She smiles. Degas makes her feel safe somehow, even when he is raving like the mad one-legged organ-grinder on Pont Neuf.

He doesn't look at her while he speaks. He is bent over the table now, trying to pour the wax into the chamber pot while keeping the candles lit and not setting fire to himself. His white shirt sticks out under a yellow silk waistcoat, the same colour as the beeswax, and he keeps pushing back his hair, depositing more and more wax in it.

'Have you seen Louise Michel again, Marie, since that day we got separated by the crowd? I used to be involved with her before the Commune and still have great admiration for her. Is she well?'

Degas speaks while hopping around the far side of the table to catch the wax from an overflowing plate with a gold rim.

Marie is not sure how much to tell Degas, if he can be fully trusted.

'Well... I have seen her a few times, yes.'

Degas is looking at her with so much interest now that she finds herself opening up despite herself.

'I – I do what I can to help. We have plans to help homeless people find shelter for Christmas – and I'm helping set up soup kitchens. And – and I'm in the new Montmartre Vigilance Committee. Although nobody is supposed to know about that so...'

'That's good, Marie. Very good.'

But he doesn't seem to be listening anymore, he's dipping his finger in a pot of molten wax. He has an amazing ability to slip out of conversation like a thief in the night.

Degas starts to mix the brew with a palette knife. It reminds her of Amélie, doing her make-up for the Count. The look of concentration and excitement on her face, the strange liquids and pastes being mixed up to create an illusion for the audience to come.

'I apologise, Marie. I will be with you in a moment. I must hurry, you see. Otherwise, the mixture will set before I can apply it.'

'What is it for, monsieur?'

'It is flesh, Marie!'

'Will I – will she be naked?'

Marie is struck with the horrific thought that she – or rather the Creature – might be put naked in a shop window for everyone to laugh at.

'No, there will be a bodice and ballet skirt. Mary has already found a wig-maker and I wanted to ask if you might have a spare ribbon for the hair, Marie? I'd like it to be one of yours.

'*Oui, monsieur*,' she mumbles, thinking how well that will go down with Antoinette when she sees one of her precious hair ribbons stuck on a statue in a backstreet gallery somewhere, but also pleased that he's asked her.

Degas looks up at her, palette knife in mid-air, and smiles. He looks like an alley cat with his hair all standing up and matted with wax. She basks in that smile. Not the one that is manufactured for Mary Cassatt, but this one, where his usual composure cracks open and his delight breaks through. Even though he is over forty, he looks like a boy. Did his mother see him like that, did he light up like this with her?

Marie pictures the young Edgar sitting alone on that bench at the edge of the tropical forest with his mother. She wonders if he knows where his mother's grave is, if he visits it sometimes. How lonely he must have been. That pain of being suddenly left alone with nobody who understands or appreciates you is all too familiar to her.

Some of the smaller candles have spluttered and died before Degas finishes putting the wax on just one of the feet. Not that he would notice. He is entirely in his own world. It seems to Marie that she could be watching him through a window and would have to knock to tell him she is there. Of course, in reality, he must know she is there as he keeps looking at her foot and then rushing back to the armature, prodding it with his fingers to form a toe, digging it out with his palette knife to make little caves at the heel (she's certainly never noticed how complicated her foot was before, how full of ridges and curves). But her foot, her whole body, is now just something there for Degas to meditate upon. She is there to give life to the Creature. Is that all she is to him? What if he is taking the life from her with his palette knife and wax and somehow transferring it to the Creature? After all, the Creature will be alive long after Marie is grown up, maybe even after she is dead. The thought gives her a chill. She holds a hand out towards the fire to warm herself. To check that she is real, that she can still feel.

'Are you cold, Marie?'

Marie is grateful for his question for though she loves to be with him, her feet are now growing numb and she's sick with hunger.

'I am a little cold, monsieur. And – and a little hungry.'

There, she's said it. It shames her to mention it, but she feels it doesn't quite count as begging.

Degas wipes his hand on a cloth and tucks his shirt-tails back into his trousers. He walks over and sits down beside her on the chaise longue. She can feel his warmth, smell the sweat on him from all that lying on the floor and jumping up again, mixed with that lemony smell that must be some gentleman's *eau de cologne*. It is quite dark in the studio now. She dares herself to look up at him. His eyes look sore.

'I am sorry, Marie. I should have thought. I was carried away. But it is working. The mixture is just right.'

They sit in silence for a minute, both staring into the fire. What is Edgar thinking? He's obviously agitated; he strums his long strong fingers on his thighs, sighs and huffs like a horse who has just won a race. Why is he still sitting here with her? What is he waiting for?

144

Well, she can't wait for him any longer. Now is the moment, if ever there was one. She can't call herself a revolutionary, she can't claim to care a sou for solidarity if she doesn't even have the courage to find out what happened to her papa. Especially now she knows for sure that Degas is an ally.

'Monsieur Degas!' Her voice must be loud because he is startled out of his reverie and looks at her as if he sees her for the first time. 'You – I hope you don't mind me asking, but you – you said you had something to tell me. It was a long time ago, you probably don't remember, but you did say it, you said you had something to tell me, but you didn't say what – and – and I'd really like to know what it was.'

He blinks and rubs his bad eye, shifts on the chaise longue. 'Did I? Oh, it was nothing, Marie. Nothing important.'

Marie swallows hard, thinks of her papa, forces herself to march on.

'Was it about my father?' She speaks to the fire, knowing that if she looks at Edgar, she won't be able to speak. 'About the night he... he died.'

Silence. She feels him breathe in and out. Then the whinny of a whipped horse out on the street, carriage wheels speeding past, the sound deepened and dulled by the snow.

He reaches out and holds one of her hands in his. She pushes him away. She must shut him out or she will just dissolve into tears. She draws herself up straighter. *Courage, Marie. Courage.*

'I know you were there, monsieur. That night. And when you held up your hand to me the night of the circus, I remembered. You went out the door and looked back. And raised your hand. And I'll never forget it. Will you tell me what happened that night?'

She turns to face him. It is so dark now that it is hard to see his expression. He is very still, silhouetted in the dying light at the window. A log shifts and collapses in the grate. Something seems to shift and settle in Degas too. He holds her hand in his again and this time she lets him. His hands are warm and rough. Just like Papa's.

'I – I need to know what happened to my father.'

It feels as if she has been writing that sentence in her mind forever. Or rather that it has been trying to come to the surface of her mind, to be born. Her plea hangs in the crackling air between them. If he refuses, if he pushes her away, how will she bear it? He is looking right into her now; she can feel his gaze in the pit of her stomach. The corner of his mouth twitches slightly. He seems to be weighing something up in his mind. Half of her hopes he will agree, the other half hopes he will refuse so her heart can stop thumping and she can pretend nothing happened and come back up to the surface.

'You are braver than I am, Marie. I was just sitting here trying to drum up the courage to talk to you. But I am such a coward, I couldn't.'

His voice is soft. He rubs his bad eye again with the back of his hand and lets out a sharp snort. As if he is angry with himself.

'Really, monsieur?'

He picks at a lump of wax on his forearm. Marie pictures him as a little boy, caught out by his father for daydreaming.

'Yes. Don't look so surprised, my sweet Marie. Why do you think I spend all my days hiding from the world in my studio?'

If I had a roaring fire and a housekeeper and plenty to eat, I might never move from this chaise longue, Marie thinks to herself.

'The world is too much for me, Marie. It must sound utterly ridiculous to you, I know. But the thought of being out in the cut and thrust of the world, as you are every day, fills me with absolute horror,' he lets out a dry chuckle, 'and fear.'

He strums his index finger on his thigh and frowns. 'It's hard to explain. What I mean is that I can't face the full glare of the world, I must look at the world as if through a keyhole and paint what I see. But you…!'

He holds her face in his hands and kisses her forehead. She is sure there are tears in his eyes but cannot for the life of her understand why.

'This may sound ridiculous to you, but in my eyes you are heroic. Just like your father.'

She feels his warm lips on her right cheek. 'I am proud of you.' Then on her left cheek. 'You give me hope!'

Marie can't help thinking that there is nothing heroic about dancing for drunken men while imagining the taste of bacon and longing for sleep.

He is still holding her face in his hands and staring at her. The tension between them is too much. It must be broken. She closes her eyes, both longing for and dreading what might come next.

'And that is why I am making this little statue of you, Marie.'

Of course. The statue. He loves the statue. Not her.

'I – I don't understand.'

Degas takes his hands from her face and spreads them on his thighs, stares into the fire.

'Of course you don't, Marie. How could you? Why on earth should you?'

They both look into the fire, as if for an answer.

The reflection of Madame Degas' portrait floats in the mirror above the fire. An angular figure in a dark forest. She seems to be watching them both, expecting something. Then Degas looks up and their eyes meet in the mirror. He shifts a little, looks like he is about to get back into his shell and dismiss her.

No! She will not let him escape. She puts her hand on his shoulder to stop him getting up and he looks down at it. In surprise or disgust, she cannot tell.

'So, will you tell me, monsieur? I need to know.'

Hail hits the window with a sound like distant gunfire; they both jump and crack into a smile at the same time.

'Yes. Yes. I surrender, Madame Commissaire!'

He traces the line of her jaw very lightly with his fingertips. His eyelashes are long and dark; they make shadows on his cheeks in the firelight.

Is he admiring her or thinking of the Creature? Perhaps he doesn't even know himself.

'I will tell you, Marie. My brave girl, I promise I will. You deserve to know the whole story of that night.' Degas sits back now and slaps his hands on his thighs. 'But first of all, we must get you something to eat. I shall call Sabine and she will prepare something. And we shall throw more logs on the fire and have a picnic right here. And I will tell you everything.'

Within minutes Sabine has banked up the fire – oh, the glorious heat of a proper fire – and laid a plate of cakes on a table in front of them. Degas sits up straighter and looks at Marie. A muscle is pulsing at his temple.

'I'll tell you what happened, but you must stop me if it gets too much. Ready?'

Marie nods and swallows hard. 'Yes, I'm ready.'

'We were hiding behind a wall next to Pont Neuf. Six or seven of us, including your father.'

Degas stops for a moment and glances at Marie then looks back at the fire.

'The battles had become concentrated in a few places by then – by the third day, I mean. Deathly quiet in most of the city. Just occasional bursts of distant gunfire, all the houses and restaurants shuttered up. Everybody in Paris was holding their breath, waiting to see if the Commune would hold.'

Marie remembers hiding with Gigi, peeking through the gaps in the wooden boards nailed over the window, willing Papa and Antoinette to come trudging up the hill.

'Rain had just started to fall, as I remember. The rest of us were exhausted after three nights with hardly any sleep. Morale was low. But Serge, your father, didn't seem to mind at all. He never seemed tired, always had absolute faith – it was quite amazing. Absolute faith that we would triumph. His faith kept us all going, Marie.'

A sigh shudders through Degas. He holds Marie's hand, asks if he should go on. She nods again but she can't look at him, makes herself stare at the fire instead. If she looks at him, she might lose her nerve. She might soften and crumble like one of those dry logs in the heat of his gaze.

'I had my sketchbook out as usual; I was drawing one of the men curled up on the ground. I can't remember what everyone else was doing exactly. Checking their guns probably – and trying to get some sleep. We knew we had to go up and defend Montmartre with our comrades in the morning. Your father volunteered to be lookout, I do remember that, because it wasn't actually his turn and one of the men – who was in a very bad way with an injured leg – argued with Serge about it, but eventually gave in. If only Serge hadn't volunteered maybe—'

Degas breaks off suddenly and sits forward, elbows on his thighs, and rolls up his shirtsleeves. He keeps tensing his long fingers, making the ridges of muscle on his long forearms twitch. Blobs of dried paint and wax are caught in the fine dark hairs of his right forearm. A deep silence settles on them. Just the hissing of the fire, the scrape of a chair downstairs. Couldn't they just stay like this forever? Did she really want to hear what he was going to say? Why make Papa's death real when Gigi and Antoinette were so determined to erase it from memory, like a blood stain on a white cotton bedsheet? She could just scoff down the cakes and talk about something else. He's allowing her to choose that. Perhaps he's willing her to ask him to stop. But she doesn't. She can't. It's as if she is pinned to the chaise longue like one of those butterflies on the green felt at the Museum of Curiosities. And only the truth Degas is about to tell her will bring her back to life, let her escape.

Degas grabs the poker and strikes sparks off a log. Only a gentleman would waste wood like that, Marie thinks to herself. The two creases between his eyebrows deepen for a moment and he seems to forget she is there. He seems to be deciding on something. Then, the shift as he seems to come back to her. He nods at the poker and puts it back in the stand very slowly, sits back on the chaise longue and gives her a little smile. The real one. She smiles back and half-nods, to tell him she's fine, to urge him on.

'Serge's cry was so loud it made the rest of us jump and grab our guns. "Antoinette! Antoinette!"' One of the men tried to drag him down below the wall, told him to stop shouting. I stood up and I saw her, Antoinette, running towards us. Her red hair flaming out behind her on the deserted grey street. She was only a little thing, Marie. None of us knew what to do. We all froze. A few of the men cursed her; I beckoned furiously at her to come to us. But she didn't see us. Serge didn't hesitate. He dropped his rifle, jumped over the wall and ran to her. He made himself a sitting target, Marie. It was hopeless. They embraced and Antoinette was sobbing. He picked her up and started to carry her towards the wall. It was only seven or eight steps away and then...'

Marie's breath keeps stopping and starting, her mind scrabbling around trying to make sense of what Degas is telling her. But – but she always thought Antoinette was at the Bérangers' that night, that's what Maman said. She remembers how Antoinette always said she wanted to fight alongside Papa, how she cried and cursed and banged her fists on Maman's chest when Papa left to fight. She must have run away from the bakery without anyone even noticing. She used to spend half her time at the bakery in those days.

'What happened then? You must tell me, please... please tell me.'

Degas stares into the fire.

'It was deathly quiet as they edged towards us. We were all holding our breath, hoping against hope that the snipers were distracted or that they wouldn't shoot a man carrying a child. They were nearly there, nearly safe, Marie – only a step or two from the wall. I reached over to take Antoinette. And then...'

Degas breaks off and breathes out hard, seems to compose himself.

'And then I saw the glint of metal from a window, and... and heard two shots. They fell instantly, Marie. Serge on top of Antoinette. He was already unconscious, probably dead – I don't know – when we got to him. I don't think he felt any pain.'

'Antoinette?' Marie's voice breaks as she says her sister's name, imagines her there. 'What happened to Antoinette?'

Degas strokes Marie's hand. His fingers are rough, like Papa's.

'Antoinette crawled out from underneath his body. She was unhurt. Serge's body shielded her. We tried to save him – your father, I mean. We did everything we could. A few of us carried him to the ambulance station halfway up to St Pierre. But he was dead before we got there. That's when we brought him to your house and then on to the mass graves at St Pierre.'

'What happened to Antoinette – why didn't she come with you?'

'She ran off. By the time we noticed she'd gone it was too late. We had no choice, Marie, we couldn't go after her. Do you understand? We had to carry... we had to carry on towards Montmartre.'

Marie's heart is beating so loudly she thinks Degas must be able to hear it. Antoinette didn't come home for days after Papa died. She must have been too upset, too ashamed. She thinks of Papa lying on the street, all the life gone out of him. Even thinking it over now makes her feel faint. She tries to imagine the scene, to put herself in Papa's body, to feel the shots. The handkerchief over Papa's face on the stretcher – it belonged to Degas. Yes, that lace around the edge, the monogrammed initials.

She grabs onto Degas' arm then to stop herself fainting or floating off. He doesn't push her off. She makes herself breathe deeply and take a bite out of a cake; it tastes like sawdust.

'Marie. You are pale...'

His kindness, the tenderness in his voice, is tipping her over the edge. The storm that has been building in her since she was five years old is about to break, she can't hold it back anymore. She turns to Degas, expecting him to be in his own world again. But he is looking right at her, his purple-black eyes catching blue, red and orange reflections from the fire. He reaches

out his arms to her and she collapses onto his chest and cries
uncontrollably for what feels like days.

CHAPTER TEN

January 1880

'We must remember. Do you remember the restaurants on Boulevard Haussmann, comrades? They served up the contents of the zoo, while we sautéed the remaining rats!'

Louise Michel is standing in the pulpit at the old church of St Pierre. A tall, solemn, bony-faced figure with arms held aloft, a red scarf wrapped around her head and neck. She looks just like the pockmarked statues of the saints who stand in alcoves around the walls of the church.

A few people mumble and shuffle. A man shouts out that the revolution is over. Louise ignores him.

'Do not act like sheep, that is what they want. Speak up!'

Louise was always famous for her loud voice and the years in New Caledonia haven't taken away any of her power.

It's absolutely freezing in the church of St Pierre. Marie clenches and unclenches her toes to stop them going numb. Nobody comes here anymore. Not since they started ploughing money into the white monstrosity of the Sacré-Coeur around the corner. Gusts of hail-spattered wind from the large hole above the altar batter the crowd of fifty or sixty people. Everybody is wrapped in scarves, so it's hard to see if there's anyone she recognises, apart from

Paul. Marie has been looking for a chance to talk to Antoinette since Degas told her the truth about what happened to Papa three weeks ago, to tell her she knew the truth, that she forgave her, that she was not to blame. But Marie and Antoinette haven't talked properly for ages. Antoinette comes home very late at night if she comes home at all. Marie sees her in passing at the opera, but talking is strictly forbidden in the rehearsal room and whenever Marie goes up to her in the dressing room, Antoinette averts her gaze and pretends to retie her shoe ribbons or starts talking to one of the other girls. It's as if Antoinette started running away the night Papa died and has never really stopped, Marie thinks to herself now as she wraps Gigi's old scarf more tightly around her shoulders. She went to the bakery for the tenth time to see if Antoinette would talk to her but found Paul instead. He told her he's hardly seen Antoinette in the past few weeks either, says she's busy working – little does he know. 'You are coming with me to a meeting,' he said before she could object, linking his arm in hers. 'No, don't bother telling me you won't – you're coming, like it or not. And afterwards, we'll go to the Veau à Deux Têtes again, see if you can eat a little slower this time!'

She was too tired to resist. And wasn't it a sign? Because the meeting was here at St Pierre, where Degas had told her Papa was buried. So, she let Paul drag her to the meeting. But her head is full and noisy, and this isn't the place to find peace.

Louise Michel bangs a bony fist on the lectern, making it wobble precariously, and raises her voice above the pounding of rain. Everybody flinches at the wind whipping through the hole in the roof. Everyone except Louise Michel.

'We shall tell the truth about our twenty thousand comrades who died for us. We shall not forget them. Their fight is our fight. What greater memorial to our loved ones can there be?'

Paul winks at Marie and she manages a smile.

What Degas told her about how her father died still hasn't fully sunk in yet. It was like a force of nature in her. This desire for the truth. Like this blasted wind. She couldn't help being moved by the tide of it, even if it brought nothing but trouble. Her heart stammers at the thought that she might now have opened up something that cannot be closed again, something that will cause hurt and suffering to Antoinette and Gigi. Yet to have left it closed would surely have been a betrayal of Papa.

Louise Michel is painting a picture in words of a future utopia now.

'We will control the means of production. Just imagine it, comrades! Food will be delivered to us through pipes under the ground. Women will be freed from domestic enslavement.'

'*Vive la Commune!*' shouts an old veteran with one leg. He blows kisses at Louise. She blows one back to a cheer from the crowd. An old woman next to Paul calls out, '*Vive la Louve Rouge!*' and soon others join in until their din drowns out the sound of the storm.

Louise Michel has them all in the palm of her hand now. The chant becomes so loud that even Marie is caught up in it and forgets her worries for a moment. After a while, Louise signals to the crowd to quieten down, lowers her voice and starts describing a world where everyone has a home and enough to eat, where doctors provide medicines for free and the price of bread is permanently fixed.

On her way into the church just now Marie had glanced at the long raised mound of earth behind the iron railings just outside St Pierre, where Degas said Papa and others were buried in mass graves – 'All the bodies were put into makeshift coffins made of planks of wood nailed together; there were no markers because the authorities didn't want any sign of the Commune to remain.' She'd grabbed onto Paul to stop herself fainting.

I love you, Papa. I will march on for you. I will continue the fight.

She'd said the words out loud without realising it. It felt strange telling Papa she loved him like that, after all this time. Even though she felt dizzy at the thought of his body there in the earth, it also made her feel more solid. Her heart flared in her chest. A big smile appeared on her face, so bright that Paul asked her what was wrong with her, 'grinning like an idiot and muttering to yourself, Marie. Are you drunk?'

It was true. She'd felt light-headed, exhilarated almost, that she'd found him. That there was a physical place she could visit. Not just the shifting, flickering land of her memories where she seemed to lose her footing.

Marie blinks her eyes, makes herself focus on Louise Michel and what she is saying. Paul elbows Marie every time he thinks Louise has made a good point and occasionally winks at her or rubs her arm to try and keep the chill off. She cannot help but feel warmed by him. He's like a big brother. Yes, that's what it is. And if Antoinette comes in later from wherever she's been, smelling of drink and humming a dance tune, when she takes whatever it is that she's stolen out of her deep pocket created especially for that purpose, and stashes it in her lockable box and jumps into bed, putting the key under her pillow, Marie won't pretend to be asleep. She won't pretend she doesn't notice what Antoinette is up to. She will tell her that she knows, that her pain is no longer a secret.

She moves closer to Paul and links her arm in his. They are comrades now. The pull of the past is strong, but the present isn't so bad anymore. She's part of something good, something meaningful.

'We must not forget, citizens. We must not forget! To remember is to honour the dead!'

Louise's words warm her heart. She will remember Papa. She will piece all the bits of his story together and make something whole. She looks around at all these good people gathered in the tomb-like cold of St Pierre and feels that she belongs, that she is doing something good with her life.

Louise leaves a pause, pushes back a greying chunk of hair, looks around at the people in the crowd, waves to a few people she knows. What a heroic woman she is. Standing proud, like the carved figurehead on the bow of a great ship. People stand stock still, faces raised as if they are receiving holy communion. Louise must be nearly fifty by now, but her face is the same, just very brown with a few wrinkles around her eyes. Everyone knows what happened to Louise. After the fall of Montmartre, she turned herself in when they threatened to shoot her mother. She asked the guards to shoot her, but they refused. They knew she would become a martyr, so they sent her off to the colony in New Caledonia instead. Nobody thought she would ever return.

'The stockpiling profiteers stole the bread from the rest of us. They had plenty for all, but they kept it all for themselves. The government refused to ration flour. They preferred to let us starve. They still refuse. But one day, change will come. Change WILL come.'

A huge cheer ripples through the crowd. Marie cheers too. It is almost as if Papa will appear beside Louise in a moment. Then they will all go to someone's house and drink wine and laugh and plan the revolution.

That winter of the siege of Paris was awful. Marie can't remember much about it, except that one day just before Christmas, her tutor at the free school here in the back room of

St Pierre told them all to take their desks home and burn them to keep warm. There was no wood left in Montmartre. After that they had to sit on the floor.

'I remember.' A woman's voice breaks the silence and the crowd turns towards her. 'I remember the queues that winter. Children freezing in the snow. I watched them starve. I can see their faces now. And we didn't have enough bread. I couldn't feed them all.' Her voice starts to crack.

'*Oui, madame!* Yes, citizen!' Louise peers into the crowd, fixes on the woman. 'You were one of the brave ones. You shared your bread; you did not seek to make a profit on the back of misery.'

Louise is wearing the same uniform she has always worn: a man's black greatcoat with tarnished brass buttons and a red scarf knotted around her neck. Hair scraped back, long face grim and fiery. Her fist lands on the wooden edge of the pulpit and the whole thing wobbles again. It is full of woodworm; please God it doesn't collapse.

'Isn't Louise magnificent, Marie?' Paul's eyes are twinkling now.

She nods and squeezes his arm. Louise is indeed magnificent. It is impossible to resist her.

Louise casts a bony hand over the heads of the crowd as if she is calming stormy waters. Everyone is silent now; she makes them wait.

'Comrades, it is time for action. We have heard stories of the past, we have imagined a better future. But now is the time for action. Now! Who is with me?'

Fifty hands are raised, and others cheer half-heartedly, realising that the meeting is almost finished, and start to make their way towards the door.

'If the government will not give us bread, will not listen to our pleas, we will take the bread for ourselves. That is our right, that is our duty.' More cheers ring out from the usual people. 'We have decided that it is time to liberate the bread that is being hoarded by greedy bourgeois bakers all over our city and give it to unemployed workers. There will be a series of demonstrations outside bakeries in the more affluent arrondissements in the next few months. If you are unemployed or if you want to be involved in this noble campaign, please speak to one of our officers at the back of the church.'

After the meeting, Marie joins Paul and a few others at the Martyrs Tavern to discuss the new campaign. They all huddle around a table in the back corner and whisper in case there are any government spies around. Marie is happy to be squeezed in next to Marceau's comforting bulk, even if he does smell slightly of the slaughterhouses where he works. On her other side is a small lady wearing a red turban whom Marie hasn't seen before. Louise Michel introduces her as 'a friend and comrade from New Caledonia' and the lady embraces Marie so hard and with such warmth that Marie has to stop herself bursting into tears. Louise talks through the timings for the looting of the first bakery and Marceau, Marie and Paul are tasked with organising and leading the demonstration outside. It's the first time that Louise has called on Marie by name, given her a leading role.

On the way out, Louise grabs Marie by the shoulders. 'You have grown up beautifully, *ma petite*! I see the fire in your eyes is still burning. Your papa would be proud of you. Very proud.'

Marie nods uncertainly and starts to turn away but Louise pulls her back.

'I'm going on a speaking tour of England soon and I wanted to invite you to join me. We have funding to sponsor young comrades so it wouldn't cost you anything. We leave on the first of April. No need to decide now, but I hope you will join us.'

Paul is obviously impressed that the great 'Red She-Wolf of Montmartre' has singled Marie out for praise. He claps her on the back and makes her cough. They both laugh and her heart swells in her chest; she hardly feels the rain lashing down as she and Paul make their way to the Veau à Deux Têtes.

When Marie gets home, she's surprised to find Antoinette already curled up in bed. She creeps in beside her, wipes her mouth with the back of her hand to make sure Antoinette won't smell the gravy. Now Antoinette is finally here, she must not falter. She must not slip into the old fog of forgetting. She calls up Louise Michel's face, tries to steal some of her fearlessness.

'Hello, stranger!'

No answer. The bundle next to her shifts a little.

'It's freezing in here, Antoinette, give me some blanket.'

Antoinette doesn't move. Marie pokes her arm. 'I know you're awake.'

'Did you go?' Antoinette's voice is sharp and accusing. She's obviously been awake the whole time.

'Where?'

'You know where, *Marie*,' she hisses.

Marie tugs at the blanket but Antoinette ignores her. 'Why don't you turn around, Antoinette? I can't talk to you with your back to me.'

Antoinette mutters that she doesn't want to turn around.

'Yes. I did go. If you must know. How did you know about it?'

Marie hopes Antoinette doesn't know about the dinner afterwards as well. She shouldn't have gone. It was a mistake. Next time she will say no.

'Everybody fucking knows about it, *Marie*.'

If only Antoinette wouldn't keep saying her name like that. As if she's the stupidest person in Paris.

'You should have come. It would make a change from thieving.'

As soon as she says it, she regrets it. But it's too late. She can feel Antoinette stiffen, as if she's holding her breath.

'Louise is setting up a soup kitchen. Antoinette. Antoinette?'

She prods Antoinette in the back. No answer. Marie props herself up on her elbow and gently touches Antoinette's arm. Antoinette doesn't speak but she doesn't shrug her off either.

Now! She must speak now, then everything will be different. But somehow the words don't come out. It's as if they are frozen in her mouth, as if Antoinette has put a spell on her, as if she has the power to silence Marie by just being there.

Then Antoinette shrugs off Marie's hand, huffs and puffs and punches the lumpy old pillow to show she doesn't care, that what Marie thinks is of little interest.

'Goodnight, Marie.'

'Things will get better, Antoinette. They will. Do you remember that freezing winter?'

She can't bear it that she has lost this chance. That Antoinette is slipping away from her again.

No answer. Marie shakes her sister.

'I know you do. We helped each other and we all survived, and we were strong. And happy— ow!'

Antoinette is pinching her arm so hard it makes her wince.

'Shut up, Marie. Shut up.'

Now Antoinette's face is right up against hers. She has a bruise on one cheek and her eyes are wild.

'I don't care about that troublemaker, Louise Michel. The Commune was a huge stupid mistake. Everybody knows it.

And you've put us both in danger, Marie. You should never have gone to that fucking meeting. And I know Paul was there too. So don't try and hide that from me. What if old Fumble Fingers finds out?'

Marie feels herself blushing and her shame sharpens her tongue.

'Is that all you care about? Keeping that fucking bastard sweet and saving up for your fancy wedding dress and leaving us all homeless?'

Antoinette pinches her again and turns her back.

The moment has passed. It's too late now, she's spoilt it by getting into a row. Better just go to sleep and try again tomorrow. She turns her back on Antoinette and tugs at the thin blanket.

'There is no wedding dress.' Antoinette's voice is soft and flat. She sounds like a little girl.

'What? What do you mean?'

'I had to give the money to Madame Robert. For Gigi. That's how it works – you pay upfront for your place and earn the money back from customers.'

The thought of Gigi earning money like that is horrific. Marie hasn't really let herself think about it before. Too caught up with Monsieur Degas and the opera. How selfish she's been!

Antoinette's red hair is spread out on the pillow, like a scream. Her profile looks terribly pale and thin. And now, poor Antoinette doesn't even have her dream of a great wedding at St Pierre to keep her going. Marie buries her face in her sister's hair. It smells of lavender and woodsmoke. She wraps her arms very slowly around Antoinette's tiny waist. Please don't push me away, she prays. Antoinette freezes for a moment. Then she grabs Marie's hands in her own and bursts into tears.

CHAPTER ELEVEN

February 1880

'Well, he did call me heroic.'

'Heroic!'

Amélie laughs and stamps her slippered foot. The two parrots in the cage next to her jump and squawk in fright. A few passers-by far down below, on Boulevard Haussmann, look up at the racket, but Amélie doesn't care. She tosses a few crumbs into the cage.

'That's hardly a compliment, *ma biche*,' she says. 'Oh, Marie. *Ma chérie*. You are too sensitive. Don't look so sad!'

Marie doesn't know what to say. Her stomach sinks. She has confided in Amélie because she has nobody to talk to. It's been two months since Degas told her about what happened to her father and she hasn't been able to confide in anybody. There's nobody she can trust. Antoinette is too distracted and Maman is gone. Friendship is a luxury she cannot afford anymore. There was a time when she used to have friends. She, Antoinette, Paul and a gaggle of other children used to stroll along the river in those hours before dinner, when everything was calm at home, when she knew a bowl of something hot would be put in front of her, when she didn't have to watch out for the bailiffs, when her mind wasn't busy with working out where the next meal would come from. Now Antoinette is too caught up in her own troubles to care about Marie's, to be a sister to her. And Paul is more of a comrade than a friend now. Maybe there's no difference, maybe comrades are the only friends worth having. Maybe friendship is a bourgeois luxury only the rich can afford. The only peaceful time she has in the company of another person is with Edgar in his clean, warm studio. His breathing is often the only sound she hears apart from the occasional carriage passing by. Long deep sighs when he is struggling with something in his head, that faraway look in his eyes. Then impatient snorts when he's lying on the floor, smearing wax onto a knee, chipping it off, smearing it on again, cursing under his breath. She couldn't stop herself smiling at his antics earlier this week. 'What is it?' he asked, looking up at her, blinking. And then, when he caught her eye, he broke into a wide smile and rubbed his eye with the back of his hand. 'You must think I am completely mad, Marie.' Then he cleared his throat, lowered his head and disappeared back into his chiselling and scraping.

Amélie is looking right at her now. Marie can feel it, even though she is pretending to look down at the street.

'Are you in love with him?'

The question stops Marie's breath. Her heart is racing, and she can feel herself reddening as she tries to word her denial, but it won't come.

'The artist, I mean. Isn't he a bit old? Well, the older ones are kinder. And less demanding. Look at me, Marie! You are! You are in love with your artist! Come on, admit it, my little *chouchou*.'

'I... I...'

Marie can't look at Amélie. She can't order her thoughts at all. The world down below on the street looks unreal; she grips the railing hard to calm herself, to stop everything spinning out of control.

'Marie?' Amélie puts a hand on her shoulder and Marie turns towards her. 'Oh, Marie!' Marie grits her teeth to stop herself blushing. She meets Amélie's gaze and finds she can't stop herself smiling. Amélie smiles back and embraces her.

'He kissed me,' she whispers into Amélie's neck.

Amélie holds Marie away from her like Gigi used to do when she had something important to ask her.

'On the mouth?'

'No, on the cheek. Oh, and the forehead.'

'Hmm… the forehead. I see.'

'Is that bad?'

'Not bad, no. It could be good, I suppose… Hang on a minute, Marie.'

Amélie is distracted now. She taps her long manicured nails on the railing of the balcony, adjusts her gaping dressing gown and leans out. 'Look!'

Marie leans out with her. She's never been so high up; it makes her feel a bit sick. Amélie points down to the entrance of the arcade opposite. 'That's my friend, Caroline.

'Oi, Caroline!' Amélie puts two fingers in her mouth and whistles so loudly that the parrots jump and mutter. A woman below them with very long dark hair looks up, drops her skirts and waves up at them.

'She's an old friend, one of the tarts who works the patch outside Café Balthazar. Thank the good Lord I'm out of all that. Terrible business for the past month or so, apparently. Police everywhere. And that'll be you, Marie, if you don't net that artist.'

'I'll never…'

'That's what they all say. They all say they'll never sell their bodies. Until they do. No woman can earn a crust from honest work anymore. Everybody knows that.'

Amélie has a point. Marie thinks of Gigi. And Antoinette. In fact, she doesn't know anybody without a man in the family who manages to survive for long without 'supplementary earnings'.

Marie is starting to regret having confided in Amélie. She doesn't understand; she sees love as something to be traded, her body and soul a piece of jewellery to be pawned. No! Marie's whole self rears up at the thought. It's degrading, it runs counter to everything she believes in. Everything the Commune stood for. Edgar is fine and noble, nothing like the jeering gentlemen on the street below. He does not see her like that, like some piece of meat. She is sure of it. The smiles they exchange, the time they share in the studio, is real and good and she mustn't doubt that.

Caroline and the other tarts with their whitened faces are parading outside Café Balthazar now. From her vantage point high on Amélie's balcony Marie observes how they completely change as they round the corner into the boulevard, as if stepping on stage.

'The show begins.' Amélie sounds sad. She looks so young squatting on the ground with her chin resting on the railing and no make-up on. But the lines on her neck show her true age. Marie squats down with her. Oh, it feels so good to stretch her back like that after hours and hours practising the same damned glissade across the rehearsal room. 'You are supposed to be birds of paradise, not scabby pigeons!' shouted the ballet master. 'Bend! Bend more!'

Marie takes a deep breath in and reties the laces on her boots. Some hope of being a bird of paradise. She'll always be a scabby pigeon. Even her laces are tatty and threadbare. She sighs deeply, inhales an acrid smell from the parrot cage mixed with the stomach-tickling whiff of sautéed onions being prepared in the cafés below. Her mouth waters despite herself. How degrading it is to be hungry; it drowns out thought and finer feelings. She lives on food given to her by other people these days. Degrading or not, she must survive.

Amélie elbows her hard and wakes her from her daydream. 'Watch and learn, Marie. See how they sway their hips. And then you must laugh, look like you are having a ball, even though you are probably feeling sick and need to scratch between your legs.'

A drunken gentleman drops his hat on the street below and stumbles to fetch it. One of the tarts, a skinny, sick-looking one, runs to fetch it for him, holds it out with one hand and raises her skirts with the other. He tries to pull the hat out of her hand, but she resists and pulls her skirts higher until he shoves her away so hard that she falls over, starts clutching her knee and wailing. Marie turns away; it's too awful to witness her desperation. It must be horrible to have to beg for attention like that, she thinks. At least when you steal, you don't have to humiliate yourself like that. But then again, it's much riskier. There aren't any police sniffing about on the Butte at the moment, but they could come back at any time. Rumour has it that another purge of prostitutes and beggars is overdue.

'*Salaud!*' spits Amélie, raising her fist at the gentleman.

Marie wonders if all Louise Michel's protestations about women's rights are in vain. Be it at the opera or in the street or in the bedroom, that does seem to be the way of the world. Marie's stomach sinks at the thought. All her grand thoughts about love are deluded. She is no different to the skinny tart with the sore knee. She, Marie, contorts her body to Edgar's orders just as the tarts contort themselves for their customers. She's closer by far to those tarts on the street than she will ever be to Edgar and Mary Cassatt. She's not Jean Valjean fighting for justice and liberty. She's not Cosette, destined to be saved by the love of a rich man. She's Fantine. Of course she is.

Now Caroline is chatting to a waiter outside Café Balthazar. She plonks herself down at a small table occupied by a mother and child.

'Let's hope somebody buys her a drink to numb her for the night shift.'

Amélie yawns and pulls herself up to standing. She turns away from the scene on the street below with a sigh, peers into the parrots' cage.

'We are safe here, my beauties. We are safe. Nobody can hurt us.'

Oh, to be safe! To come home and know there won't be a notice on the door, that you can sleep in peace without being half ready to pack your things and run. It would be worth doing almost anything to feel safe again.

Amélie takes Marie's arm, steers her back into the apartment.

'Now, where were we? Oh yes. *L'amour.*'

Marie asks herself which she would choose between safety and love and has no answer. Then she realises that both are out of her grasp. The only choice she has is between thieving, selling her body or starving. As the thought sinks in, something in her riles up against it. No! Her father fought and died so that there was hope, so that working people could have the chance of happiness and friendship and dignity. She must not betray him, betray the struggle with her cowardly thoughts. The Communards threw safety aside, raised the red flag high and walked into battle in the hope of a better life for her, for Amélie, for all women, for everyone. They marched for love of humanity. The only love that truly matters, that can be trusted. She must not drop the flag and run away in exchange for comfort, for safety, for some paltry semblance of love. She is no deserter.

Marie helps Amélie get ready while Amélie insists on giving her 'a lesson in coquetry'. It's pretty much like the advice Gigi gave her that night at the Moulin. All about prancing like a pony, teasing and laughing prettily. When Marie says that 'the artist' (as they both call him) won't like that, Amélie huffs and insists that all men like their women vivacious and light. Marie thinks about that. How Mary Cassatt was when they went to the milliner's, how Edgar seemed entranced by her silliness – and admits that, sadly, Amélie might be right. Then Amélie offers Marie a cake and persuades her to take a swig of absinthe to wash it down. It tastes disgusting but makes her feel pleasantly fuzzy. No wonder Gigi loves the Green Fairy.

Amélie shows Marie how to sway her hips like Caroline and her colleagues. But Marie can't get the hang of it. She's just not built for it. Amélie says she looks like a duck and they both double up laughing again until Amélie realises the time, says her Count will be there any minute and shoos Marie out, pulling her back to reassure her that plenty of gentlemen take a fancy to a pretty piece on the street. Especially the artists. It makes them feel they are doing something noble. Takes away from the guilt of paying for love and doing the dirty on their wives, apparently.

*

Out on the boulevard a slight drizzle has started.

'Watch out, *petite saloppe*!' shouts a cab driver. They drive so fast on the wide boulevards, she didn't even see him when she stepped off the high kerb.

Marie catches a glimpse of herself in a café window, smooths back a couple of strands of hair that have escaped from her plait, tilts her head and thrusts out her chest as Amélie demonstrated. Would Edgar take care of her if she let him make love to her? It might not be too bad, if he was her first. And he has plenty of room in that house. She wouldn't be any trouble. He would hardly notice she was there. She could fetch paint and brushes for him, polish his shoes. Then he could sculpt her whenever he liked for nothing. The comforting images flood Marie's mind and she is disgusted by them. The absinthe seems to have weakened her ability to keep these treacherous thoughts at bay.

'A kiss on the lips!' Amélie's shout from the balcony jolts Marie out of her reverie.

She refuses to look up, concentrates on her feet instead, tries to steady herself.

'Promise me, Marie. Don't you dare come back here until you've done it!'

The people on the terrace at Café Balthazar look up and tut while Marie scuttles past as fast and as gracefully as she can.

CHAPTER TWELVE

Marie stumbles home up the Butte, her mind fogging and her mood sinking into the mud with every step. She calls out for Gigi when she goes in, hoping against hope that she'll be there for once. Just calling for her out loud hollows Marie out. It must be a month since she's seen her mother, several months since they shared a smile or an embrace. It's so lonely here without her or Antoinette. Not a home at all. Spending time with Amélie has made her realise how much she misses them. First Papa, then Gigi, now Antoinette. All of them have abandoned her. All of them.

She goes into Gigi's empty, stale-smelling room, collapses face first on the bed and lets herself cry until she thinks her heart will break with her longing for human affection. Touch. She's starved of it. She's even jealous of the fucking Creature, how Edgar strokes it, the attention he gives it. Sometimes she imagines it's her. Her whole body shivers when Edgar touches her briefly to adjust a strap or a finger, or even when Paul links her arm on the way to a meeting. She's like a stray cat sidling up to any passerby and getting kicked aside.

She turns over and reaches under the bed for Gigi's cotton-reel box, finds a bottle instead. It's still half full of red wine. She sniffs it, decides it might assuage an incipient headache from the absinthe she'd drunk with Amélie, and glugs down the lot. Then she reaches under the bed again. *Bon dieu!* The box is still here. And there are Papa's rings. If only he was here. It's hard to even picture his face clearly anymore. Marie pushes strands of tear-soaked hair off her face, slides the silver one onto her middle finger. It's very cold.

'One for the Commune,' she speaks into the gathering dark. The ring is loose, and she moves it onto her thumb where it fits snugly. She's sure Papa would be proud of her, going to meetings, carrying on the struggle. Even if Antoinette disagrees.

It's so quiet in the house. Not the studious, comfortable quiet of Edgar's studio, but a neglected, deadened type of quiet.

Gigi must be at Madame Robert's and Antoinette – well, Antoinette could be anywhere. Best not think about either of them. She sniffs the bed. It hasn't been slept in for a week at least; the whole room is strangely, eerily tidy. Gigi has moved nearly all her remaining things out, obviously preparing for the worst.

Marie lies on her back on the bed, stares up at the stained ceiling. She holds her hand out into a slice of late sunlight from the skylight to get a better look at the ring. It looks brand new. Marie moves her finger so that the ring spatters sunlight on the walls and onto a tatty wicker-bottomed chair that Gigi must have picked up on the street somewhere. And underneath that she sees the blue and white porcelain chamber pot. The pot is the one pretty thing Gigi has managed to keep hold of. The pots at Madame Robert's must be the cheap, breakable ones. That's why she's left the pretty pot here. Imagine how much use Madame Robert's pots must get. All that vinegar they use afterwards, to stop getting pregnant or diseased, or both.

Amélie told her about that. It must be what makes them want to scratch between their legs.

Gigi's old chemise is draped over the wicker chair, waiting to be mended. It's been there for months. Apparently, Madame Robert provides all the 'girls' with new chemises, edged with expensive-looking lace. It's a perk of the job. She hopes it gives Gigi some pleasure; she used to be so proud of all her things: the china dogs, the little fringed lamps, that onyx box she kept by her bed. All sold long ago. She wishes she could go over to Madame Robert's right now and drag Gigi back home. If only she had the energy. Or the courage. If she became Edgar's companion, perhaps she could provide for Gigi and give Antoinette enough money to marry Paul and set up house and stop thieving. She slides the silver ring off her finger and puts it back in the box. No. Papa would despise such a life of voluntary servility, of dependence on a rich man with no certainty that his whim would keep her safe.

The gold ring is there too in the box. *One for the family.* The ring feels heavy, substantial, as if it could never be broken. But her family itself is shattered. And as for her home...

Home. She says it out loud. The word falls flat in the neglected room. This house hasn't felt like home for a long time. And if the landlord sends in the bailiffs, as he has kept threatening that he will, her only home will soon be the streets. Or Madame Robert's if she's not too young. Or too ugly. She grabs Gigi's chemise from the chair, curls up on the bed and buries her face in it. She doesn't even manage to take her boots off before sleep takes her down.

The rush of noise at sunset jolts her awake. The last carts rumbling down from the building site at the Sacré-Coeur, brakes squeaking on the steep cobbled street, the shouts and coughs of workmen released from a hard day's graft. For a moment she thinks Edgar is next to her and lets out a gasp, confused and blushing at her own dreams. She must've fallen asleep and now she's already late for the meeting. Paul will be there right now, watching the door, waiting for her to arrive. The thought brings her to attention despite herself, like a soldier rising to the sound of the bugle. She slips Papa's rings into her pocket for luck and forces herself up, wipes her chin with the back of her hand in case it's still got dribbles of red wine on it.

The crowd at the church of St Pierre grows at every meeting. People are squeezed up against the walls, a few children sit on the floor at the bottom of the pulpit. She manages to find her way to Paul. He squeezes her hand and whispers that a sympathetic printer has been found to make flyers, the soup kitchen will be up and running in the next week or so and various committees are being formed. His eyes are shining. He seems bigger, he has pride in himself. It's good to see him like that, after looking like a beaten dog in the boulangerie, cowering at Fumble Fingers' every command.

'How did the meeting about the special mission go?' Marie whispers.

'I'll tell you later.' Paul cups a hand around his mouth. 'Don't mention it to anybody else. It doesn't exist.'

Marie nods as if she understands, but she doesn't, not really. Then she remembers Papa and his secrecy. How Gigi used to push him to tell her where he was going. One evening he came home all dirty, his best work trousers ripped around the knees. Gigi flew to him and started sniffing him all over. Marie had laughed out loud, thinking it was a joke. Gigi shouted at her to shut up. It's all coming back to her now: the feeling in her stomach as if somebody had kicked her, the relief when her father told her mother to leave Marie out of it. The fear swirling again when Gigi started to cry, 'I can smell it. The gunpowder. I knew it. I just knew it. How could you, Serge? How could you put your whole family in danger?' Papa just held Gigi's hands until she broke away and went upstairs. It was later that night that she sat on Papa's knee and he told her about his two rings and let her try them on.

Louise Michel is in full flow up in the pulpit. She's talking about her trip to England. A grand lady with excellent ideas about female suffrage has invited her. Louise says a republic must not have borders; the republic she seeks is international, for the benefit of workers all over the world.

'Our sisters over the water lack *l'esprit de la révolution*. We must give them a kick up their British arses.'

A young woman stands up and starts talking about petitions. A few people mumble in support and others shake their heads and roll their eyes. Louise holds up her hand and insists that everyone must be heard. She warns them about a new police effort to track down and arrest insurrectionists. They must all stay alert. A nod to the door-watcher whose job it is to watch out for police. So far, it's all gone smoothly.

A man raises his hand from the thick crowd.

'We've had enough of petitions. People are starving on the streets. We must take arms, kill the thieving bastards who killed our brothers. They're still lying outside this church in unmarked graves, and you talk about petitions, about women being allowed to vote!'

Marie is half-listening, dreaming about the chop and gravy she might get later, going over her conversation with Amélie. Papa is out there in the ground somewhere, she says to herself.

Wake up, Marie. Pay attention to what is being said, in his honour.

Louise Michel holds up one of her huge white hands to hush the shouting man. 'Patience, comrade. Patience. The time will come. We shall in time have a grand memorial to all our fallen.'

'On top of the damned Sacré-Coeur!' Paul chips in and several people cheer.

'We shall not forget!' Marie finds herself shouting out. Several people repeat what she says. Paul squeezes her arm and winks at her. At least somebody is proud of her.

'Yes, indeed, citizens,' says Louise. 'The marble monstrosity will forever be a monument to the massacre of our comrades. We shall never forget.'

A round of applause, which sets Marie's head thumping. Paul rubs her arm, asks her if she's well. She manages a nod, can't help feeling touched by his concern. Does Antoinette know he's here? Probably not.

The meeting ends with Louise Michel reciting one of her poems and rapturous applause.

'Shall we go to the Veau à Deux Têtes?' Paul asks as people file out. 'Louise asked me to write a flyer for the demonstration for the unemployed outside the bakery on Rue des Cannettes. She said I should get you to help because you are your father's daughter and she trusts you to come up with the right words. And I'm too stupid.'

'That's not true, Paul!'

But she knows it is. The thought of being asked to help makes her want to jump for joy. Paul was never interested in learning. While she pored over books and learnt lists of new words for fun, Paul and Antoinette and most of the other children tapped their feet and looked out the window.

Marie kisses Paul on his cheek. It's much bristlier than Edgar's and smells of baking instead of paint.

On the way out of the meeting, Marie touches her heart and bows to the figure of Jesus on the wall (who himself looks like he could do with a good meal). Not only chops and gravy but a chance to write. Louise Michel trusts her to find the words to inspire people. Marie's exhausted heart swells with pride. How good it is to feel proud. Antoinette doesn't understand how it gives life true meaning to do something, anything, to change the world – to make things better, or at least try to. It makes you forget your hunger. And your loneliness. If only for a moment.

CHAPTER THIRTEEN

At the Veau à Deux Têtes, Marie is tucking into a Toulouse sausage, piling soft, oniony potatoes into her mouth while Paul laughs at her and begs her to pay attention to the task in hand. The windows of the café are steaming up as workers crowd in, stamping muddy boots and cursing the rain.

'I was so proud of you when you spoke up today, Marie. Your father would be proud too.'

Marie raises her breastbone, allows herself to breathe in Paul's compliment and let it warm her heart a little. Of all the feelings raining inside her, the anger and fear, the desperate hunger and longing for love, pride is like an anchor, something strong and solid at her centre. Like her spine. Like Papa.

'Are you ready to step up, Marie? Are you brave enough?'

'Yes. Yes, I think so. What is it?'

Paul looks around and leans in towards her. His breath is warm on Marie's cheek.

'Remember when our fathers used to disappear off some evenings?'

Marie thinks back. Papa was always disappearing off, going for 'walks' to St Lazare, and Maman hated it.

'Is it true that they were testing out bombs? Maman used to say she could smell gunpowder, but Papa always denied it.'

'Yes. They were testing out bombs, Marie. Over at the building works at St Lazare, in the days when there was all that open ground. It was such dangerous work. My father told me they could never get it quite right. If they had, we might never have been defeated. But now it's easier, the triggering mechanism is much better.' Paul leans in and cups his hand around his mouth. 'I'm going to suggest to Louise that we bomb the Palais de Justice.'

Marie finds herself choking on a potato, having to spit it out.

'What? What are you talking about, Paul? The Palais de Justice. Really?'

Marie notices that her voice has gone loud, her arm is gesticulating wildly, and a blob of gravy drops off the hunk of bread in her hand and lands on the floor.

Paul puts his finger to his lips and scowls at her and Marie realises she's speaking much too loudly.

She stares into Paul's eyes to see if he was joking and realises he wasn't. He's deadly serious. A scene appears in her mind. The day when the women and children of Montmartre helped defeat the army. She sat on top of a cannon, Papa's arm around her waist, while they all chanted '*Vive la Republique*' louder and louder. Everybody thought they were fools, that the army could not be stopped, that they would all be arrested. But they were wrong. After a while, the soldiers dropped their rifles and slunk away, and it opened the way for the Commune. Why not bomb the Palais de Justice? Why not? She wishes she'd suggested it herself.

A waiter rushes over with a cloth and curses Marie. She shrugs her shoulders, almost falls off her stool, and rights herself, laughing.

'Hush, Marie!' Paul hisses. 'Are you drunk?'

She shrugs her shoulders again. 'Maybe, a little.'

'Look at me, Marie.' Paul's strong fingers are under her chin now. She looks into his eyes. She's never noticed how blue they are before. Paul seems to soften, a jolt in her stomach. 'We have to do this. For our fathers. We must finish the work they started. But you must calm down and keep quiet.'

Now he's just being bossy again and the way he's tipping her chin is making her head hurt even more.

'Yes, yes. I know. I understand,' she says, shrugging him off. How dare he tell her to calm down and treat her like a child? It strikes her that men are often like that, all soft and tender one moment, trying to crush your spirit the next. As if you are a horse that needs taming and blinkering. Only a few women, like Louise Michel, manage to escape and stay wild. Even Amélie changes and becomes all tame when her Count is about to arrive.

'I shall do whatever is necessary.' Marie puts down her knife and fork, draws herself up and holds the edge of the table to keep herself steady. She is almost as tall as Paul now.

Paul gets the waiter to clear away their plates and wipe the table. The waiter huffs and puffs, obviously hoping they will leave soon as the café is starting to empty out and they are waiting to close. Marie smooths the paper out on the table in silence and decides to forgive Paul. He is tired and probably scared and God only knows what life is like with his stepfather. At least she doesn't have to live in fear of a beating.

The rain has started in earnest now; the waiter puts a big pan on the floor beside them in anticipation of a leak from the stained ceiling. The newspaper stuffed into the holes in Marie's boot will do no good against this. Her feet will be soaking by the time she reaches home. And there's no way they'll dry out before morning.

'"Bread is a human right." Is that good?' asks Paul.

'No. No,' says Marie. 'Hold on. Yes! No! I've got it: "We all have a right to our daily bread"?'

A miserable-looking man in a greasy cap looks up from his table and curses them. Paul reaches over with a napkin and pats at the gravy oozing out of Marie's mouth. 'Ignore that rubbish about the Palais de Justice, I was getting carried away.' Marie shrugs. They are friends again.

'What was it Louise said at the end of her speech, when she was talking about enshrining the right to be properly fed and housed?' asks Marie.

'I can't remember.'

Marie is sketching out a few phrases and ideas. She writes with a pencil she managed to steal from Edgar's studio. At first, she goes very slowly, moving her fingers around the pencil, struggling to find the right position. It must be seven years since she has held a pencil or a pen. But it all comes back to her quickly, as if she's carrying on where she left off at the free school in St Pierre. Those hours spent creating letters in squares, then sentences and finally whole paragraphs. What a joy to write again! It reminds her of laying out the washing. Untangling thoughts and placing them on a line, watching them take shape.

'I know!'

The pencil seems to have a life of its own now, dancing over the page.

'*Le pain ou la mort*,' she declares and then claps her hand over her mouth, realising she is shouting again.

Paul peers at the page. '*Le pain ou la mort*. Bread or death.'

'That's our slogan, Paul. Louise said they must force the big bakeries to give bread to the poor instead of hoarding it up. We need something simple and easy to remember. Most of the people can't read. And it'll be easy to chant. And easy to embroider on banners and that flag Louise wants to carry.'

'Yes, yes, Marie! You are a marvel!' Paul holds her cheeks in his warm, rough hands. A bolt of pure hope chases out her aching head, the numbness in her toes, even her worries about Gigi and Antoinette.

A chilly blast of air makes them both look up.

'Marie! Paul! What *au nom du bon dieu* are you doing here?'

Antoinette is standing right there in the doorway, hands on hips, red patches appearing on her neck.

Paul takes his hands off Marie's face and jumps up. He stands with his back to Marie, in front of the table as Antoinette storms towards him.

'Shut the bloody door!' shouts the man in the cap.

While Antoinette goes back to close the door, Paul grabs the piece of paper, screws it up and stuffs it in his pocket. Marie stuffs the pencil in hers. Antoinette is breathing hard. She ignores Marie and looks straight at Paul.

'You told me you were doing deliveries, Paul. You lied. You—'

Paul holds a finger to his lips to hush Antoinette because everyone in the café is staring now. The man in the cap shouts at them to shut up, gets up and stamps out, slamming the door as hard as he can.

The look on Antoinette's face makes Marie go cold inside. She can't bear to see the hurt and anger in her sister's eyes.

'It's not Paul's fault, Antoinette. It's not what it looks like. I... We... Please sit down and we'll explain.'

'*We* will, will *we*? And what exactly does *it* look like, dear sister?'

Marie can't move or think clearly.

Paul grabs Antoinette's arms. A drop of rain from her hat falls on the table. Paul tries to stroke Antoinette's cheek, but she pushes him off.

'I would never do anything to hurt you, Antoinette. Trust me. We just met in here by chance. I was coming back from my deliveries, and she was here having some dinner.'

'Liar! Fucking liar! Marie can't afford to eat here. It's hard enough for us to survive on the crumbs your stepfather throws for us. You're a terrible liar, Paul. I hate you! I fucking hate you!'

Antoinette is beating on Paul's chest now while he holds her shoulders. She looks just like Gigi with Papa trying to calm her down. Strands of red hair escape from her chignon and fall over her face.

'Stop it! Paul, let her go!' Marie knows that Antoinette will panic and fight like a feral cat if she is restrained like that. 'Let's all just sit down and talk about this,' she hisses. But Paul and Antoinette's eyes are locked. It's as if Marie is not there anymore. Antoinette spits a chunk of hair out of her mouth, kicks Paul's shins and breaks away.

'Come back, Antoinette. Come back!'

Marie catches hold of Antoinette's cold, bony hand.

'Let me go, Marie. This is none of your business.' Antoinette's voice is as cold as her hand. Marie drops it. For a moment Antoinette meets her gaze. Antoinette's amber eyes, so like Gigi's, are bloodshot and hazy. She is obviously drunk. What is becoming of them all? They used to feel so sorry for all those shabby, drunken families at the Moulin only a few years ago. And now they are nearly there themselves. All of them. The happiness and pride that was flowing through Marie a few minutes ago drains out of her. A shiver runs through her body. Marie moves to hug Antoinette, but she won't have it. She shoves Marie away.

'I will never forgive you for this, Marie. Never.'

Marie's head starts to spin. She stumbles and knocks the pan over. The café owner shouts at them all to get out and when Marie looks up from setting the pan right, she sees Antoinette's darned skirts disappearing out the door and Paul rushing after her, calling her name.

Marie slumps down onto her stool, elbows on the table, and cradles her head in her hands; she shuts her eyes to try and stop the dizziness. She hasn't got the strength to go after Antoinette and Paul, and it's probably best to leave them to it anyway. She'll explain, she'll make Antoinette understand. She knows how it must have looked: their faces close together, Paul looking into her eyes. The thought makes her blush despite herself. Didn't she put her head on his shoulder, didn't she enjoy the feel of his hand in hers? If he had leaned over and kissed her, would she have let him? Her head hurts too much to think anymore and the gravy is turning sour inside her. She wants to curl up right here in the café, fall asleep and never wake up again.

'We're closing, mademoiselle.'

'Yes, yes. I'm going.'

Marie drags herself up. Shutters are clattering down over the steamed-up windows, tables are being viciously scrubbed. The scrape of chairs tears at her skull. She stumbles out of the door and vomits into a pot plant.

When Marie reaches Rue Lepic, there's another shock in store. A 'final notice' pinned to the door, warning that the house will be repossessed on the 31st of March unless all rent arrears are paid. All rent arrears! That's a joke. Antoinette said last week they owed at least six months by now. There will be no more favours. Her mind starts to scrabble around for a solution but just hits walls. There is no way out this time.

Marie rips the notice off the front door, hoping the neighbours haven't seen it yet. She screws it into a ball and throws it on the floor, collapsing onto her bed. Antoinette is not there. Marie hopes she's made it up with Paul and is sleeping at the boulangerie, not somewhere worse.

She dreams they are all together in the middle of a tropical forest. Papa sits in his old chair. He is covered in paint. Gigi is ironing a turquoise waistcoat. She and Antoinette are hiding behind a tree, watching. Another woman is there, in the clearing, sitting on a bench.

'It is nearly time,' she says. 'It is nearly time.'

PART THREE

'I believe in violent revolution. Or nothing at all!'
Louise Michel

CHAPTER FOURTEEN

March 1880

The bakery where the demonstration is set to take place is on Rue des Cannettes in the sixth arrondissement. Reusteuffel et Fils is nothing like Emma Béranger's bakery on Rue Lepic. This bakery and patisserie is in a smartly painted three-storey building, has a brand-new shop sign hanging over the door and a wide shopfront with two huge plate glass windows, which look so clean it's hard to believe they are there at all. Behind the window on the left are sloping stands covered in red velvet adorned with cakes of every type, colour and size imaginable and displayed like jewels. Reusteuffel owns two bakeries in this arrondissement and has a reputation for hoarding his bread, exploiting his staff and sucking up to the police.

Marie and Paul are waiting in front of a building site on the street opposite the bakery with a pile of pamphlets on the ground next to them. Marie has butterflies in her stomach and notices that her hands are sweating despite the cold. She looks around anxiously for Louise. Louise is due to arrive at five o'clock on the dot. When she gives the signal the demonstration will start, a decoy will distract the baker and they will all rush in and take the bread.

Marie is just wondering if the unemployed workers will actually turn up when she feels a tap on her shoulder and turns to find the lady with the turban smiling at her along with six of the men they signed up at the last few meetings in tow.

'Welcome, thank you for coming,' Marie says awkwardly. Paul starts to give the men leaflets to hand out and tells them to wait for instructions. Two of the men are twins and have the most threadbare jackets she has ever seen, and the brightest blue eyes. An older man with no teeth smiles nervously and spits on the ground. Another mutters that he's changed his mind and rushes off.

Just as five o'clock is sounding Louise Michel comes around the corner of Rue Guisarde carrying a huge black flag with '*Le Pain ou La Mort*' embroidered on it in white. Marie exchanges a look of delight with Paul. She stole the black fabric from backstage at the opera and Louise's mother did the embroidery. Behind Louise are seven or eight others including Marceau, who breaks off to join Marie's group while Louise strides up to the front door of the bakery.

'Where's the fucking decoy got to?' pants Marceau as he arrives and pushes his way in next to Paul. The lady in the turban shrugs and waves at Louise. 'I knew that idiot of a decoy wasn't to be trusted,' he continues. 'He should be in place. I knew it. Louise has too much faith in people. Too much fucking faith.'

Louise is stationed outside the closed doorway of the bakery with a few faithful followers behind her, while Marie's group wait on the other side of the narrow street, hand out the odd pamphlet and watch out for the police.

'When the decoy has drawn the baker away, Louise Michel will wave the flag and we will all run into the bakery. Do you understand?' Marceau addresses the volunteers. 'If he ever fucking arrives at all,' he whispers behind his hand. One of the twins nods enthusiastically; the other one starts asking questions but Marceau waves them away and calls for silence. They wait a few minutes, but there's still no sign of the decoy. The manager of the bakery, a short barrel-like man with a bald head, appears in the doorway. He starts shouting at Louise Michel, gesticulating wildly. Louise is making placating motions at him with her free hand as if he's an overexcited horse.

'What's going on?' Marie asks Marceau.

'She's trying to reason with him, trying to get him out the way because she knows the decoy's not coming now. Start the chant, Marie. Otherwise we're going to lose everybody.' Marceau is right. The men behind her are shuffling and complaining and a couple behind Louise Michel seem to be having a row about what they should do. Somebody else pushes them; it looks like a brawl is breaking out.

'*Le pain ou la mort!* Bread or death! Bread or death!'

At first it's just Marie's voice but soon the lady in the turban joins her and then her whole group is chanting. Passers-by are gathering around now, some take pamphlets and stay to watch. Marie watches, her heart pounding as the woman from the arguing couple steps forward past Louise and pushes the baker in the chest.

'Serves him right!' Paul shouts above the chanting crowd. But Louise is pointing at the woman now, gesticulating at her to move back.

A few other people have joined the demonstrators behind Marie. They're all getting jittery now as time passes and the commotion outside the bakery gets worse and worse.

The baker is still blocking the doorway, refusing to move. Several men in overalls try to press forward again, to push the baker out of the way by force. But Louise Michel stops them with a look, and they move back behind her.

'No doubt she'll be calling that fat oaf of a baker "brother" and reasoning with him to let them in,' hisses Marceau in Marie's ear. 'She'll willingly blow up a fucking barracks but won't touch a worker. Fucking stupid if you ask me.'

Marie wipes Marceau's spittle off her cheek and says nothing; she's not sure if she agrees with him or not.

'Bread or death! Bread or death!' The chant grows louder and louder.

They are all squeezed together on the narrow pavement opposite the bakery.

Somebody shoves Paul from behind and he drops his pamphlets and stumbles forward into Marceau's back, making him drop his banner.

'Watch out! I spent all night making this fucking thing.'

Paul is distracted by a tall, thin man in a top hat outside Hotel La Perle up towards Place Saint-Sulpice. 'Who's that?' asks Marie.

'I don't know. Could be a police agent. We need to move, Marie, we need to get into the bakery right now. Or call it a day and leave.'

Marie sees the alarm in Paul's eyes and her stomach sinks. They can't give up now. They can't. Her heart starts to beat a march, Papa's face swims up into her mind, the way he was during Bloody Week, eyes wild, face covered in mud. She thinks of him running fearlessly towards Antoinette before he got shot. What would Papa do? She slips a sweaty finger into one of Papa's rings in her pocket. And suddenly she knows what must be done, she sees it happening in her head. Yes, that's it! The plate glass window is only, what, three or four steps away. Papa wouldn't have hesitated, not for a moment.

'*Le pain ou la mort, le pain ou la mort.*' The chanting is getting shriller now. Desperate. People press against her on all sides and spill out onto the street. A cart swerves to avoid them.

'Cover me,' she hisses.

'What?' shouts Marceau.

'Cover me!'

'Oh!' He steps in front of her, waves his banner around in the air.

This is it – this is the moment. Her moment. Marie ducks down and weaves her way back past the blue-eyed twins and fetches a brick from a pile at the building site behind them. It's rough in her hand, cold and wet at the edges. Heavy, but not as heavy as she'd expected. Before she knows what she's doing, she finds herself darting forward into the middle of the street. *Aim. Fire.* Time seems to stand still. Then a smash, glass flying. Silence. Even Louise Michel and the baker stop speaking. Then a cheer rises up, led by Marceau. The blue-eyed twins are jumping up and down with excitement and the lady in the turban beams at her, her gold tooth glinting. Did she do that? She, Marie van Goethem. She threw a fucking brick! What a beauty it was! It sailed through the air, across the narrow street and right into the middle of one of the mean baker's squeaky-clean windows. Her mind is suddenly clear, a mad giggle – or is it a scream? – lodged in the back of her mouth. Somebody is clapping her on the back. 'Bravo, Marie, bravo!'

Did Paul see her? Louise Michel? She hopes so. Her stomach contracts as a memory rushes in: the police checking for shot on men's hands before they were lined up and executed in Bloody Week, the search for water and soap, the desperate scrubbing. She spits on her palms, rubs hard at the brick dust on her hands, wipes them on her skirts. Too late now.

'Move, Marie, move!' shouts Marceau, pushing her forward. '*Allons-y, ma petite!* Let's go!'

A group of comrades has already pushed in through the broken window. The baker is running headlong down the street shouting, 'Police, police!' Not so smug now, Marie thinks to herself with relish.

Louise Michel is standing by the smashed window and encouraging looters through. She pokes at hanging shards with the point of her big flag as if she's pushing pigeons out of the way on Boulevard Haussmann.

'Come on! Hurry up, brothers and sisters. Let's liberate the bread – the steps to the cellar are there at the back.'

Marceau steps back at the window, kicks a hanging shard of glass off the star-shaped hole and ushers Marie through as if she were a duchess. She steps in and kicks a cake out of her path. Louise Michel squeezes Marie's shoulder and looks right into her.

'Bravo, *ma petite* Marie. You did well. I knew you had it in you. I knew you were your father's daughter.'

Louise's words feel like a benediction. Is it wrong to feel so excited, so happy, so full, so alive? Marie can't remember when she last felt like this.

'But now you must go, little one,' Louise says. 'In case you were seen. They'll arrest you on the spot. Run, Marie. Run! You have done enough for today. Leave the rest to your comrades.'

When Marie is a safe distance away, she slows to a walk. She hardly knows where she's going, feels like she's walking on air, like she's as tall as the buildings around her. She starts laughing for no good reason. The carapace of her old self is irrevocably broken. She smashed it herself when she threw that brick and there is no way back. She knows that now. She is reborn as a true anarchist, a true revolutionary – chin high, heart strong, spine defiant as a barricade.

'Marie! Marie!'

It's been a week since the looting at the bakery and Marie is on her way to a rehearsal at the opera. She turns and sees a woman in black waving at her through the tall windows of Café Balthazar. Oh yes, of course, Mary Cassatt. She should've known from the strange foreign accent, the imperious air.

'*Bonjour, ma belle,*' Mary chirps, standing up to kiss Marie on both cheeks. She smells of Provence soap. Mary is in layers of black as usual with a fur around her neck. A matching muffler lies on the table like a well-fed cat. Marie scrunches her toes in her damp boots. Mary's feet are no doubt toasty in her shiny black slippers.

Marie is caught between making a quick exit and trying to get hold of some of that freshly cut bread lying in a basket on the table.

'You look rather lovely with your cheeks all rosy like that, Marie.'

Marie manages a tight smile. Rosy? Her cheeks are flushed because she's in a total panic and rushing to get to the opera in time so that she doesn't get sacked. And because her old winter scarf was stolen from the dressing room, and she can't afford another one. I know your game; I won't fall for your charms. I will not sidle up to you to be stroked.

'You remember René, Edgar's brother?'

It's only then that Marie sees the man beside her. René has his chair precariously tipped back. He is tapping his foot and puffing on a cigar.

'*Bonjour, Monsieur René.*'

195

She expects him to get up and greet her with a kiss on her hand as he did the night of the circus. But he just nods at her and looks away.

'Excuse Monsieur René,' says Mary. 'He is not in the best of moods. Won't you take a seat, Marie?' She pats the chair next to her and moves the bread towards her.

Marie eyes the bread and sits down. How strange it must be to be able to sit at a table with a basket of bread on it and not just scoff the lot. Rich people live in another world. *We starve while they count their money and gorge themselves.* The words from one of Louise Michel's speeches come back to her and anger mingles with hunger in her belly. Louise is right. *They don't even notice until you set their world on fire.* She had thought René was kind that night. How could she have been so naive? He was just passing the time, toying with her. And now he has no further use for her he acts as if she doesn't exist. Oh well, just a few minutes here and she can just about make it to the opera on time, if she runs.

'How is the sculpture going, Marie, is it nearly finished? It's almost time. We have less than two weeks to go now, so please use your charms to encourage Edgar to the finish line. The reviewers can't write about nothing.'

'My charms, mademoiselle?'

'Yes, your feminine wiles, my dear.'

What is wrong with Monsieur René? Apart from the fact that he is a spoilt, greedy bourgeois. He looks ill. His forehead is covered in a film of sweat. But that's no excuse for him ignoring her and muttering under his breath.

'Are you perfectly well, monsieur?' says Marie pointedly, stuffing a second chunk of bread into her mouth. Mary has ordered her a hot chocolate. She fingers Papa's ring in her pocket and stares at Monsieur René, refuses to look away. There is ash all over his waistcoat. He rights his chair, looking flustered at her impertinent question, and stubs out his cigar in the ashtray. He looks at Mary, then at Marie. A muscle flickers on his cheek. He is obviously gritting his teeth. Just like Edgar does when he's frustrated.

'Well, as you ask, mademoiselle, I am not well at all,' René says, looking at Mary. He is leaning in now, gripping the table edge. 'I've spent my whole life trying to be a good son, trying to hold our family together and keep you women happy.' He wipes his brow with his handkerchief. Now he seems to be addressing himself to the entire café. 'And all I get is complaints. You're never satisfied, are you? Women! Puh! I come here to escape from the incessant demands of my wife and her two daughters and – and get an upbraiding from another tyrant in taffeta!' His voice rises as he speaks. People at other tables look over and tut. Mary Cassatt puts a hand on his arm.

'*Calme-toi, mon brave!* Control yourself. This is really not the time or the place to—'

René pushes her hand off. He tips back his chair again and calls out to a waiter to bring him a double brandy then crashes forward again. Marie takes the opportunity to reach for another piece of bread to stash in her pocket and offer to Antoinette as a peace offering. Oh, Antoinette. Please come to the opera today. Please let me explain.

'And as for your dear Edgar,' René leans over the table and grabs Marie's hand. 'He thinks he's so superior. Never wastes an opportunity to remind me of my failures. Do you think I want to go cap in hand to him again, like a common beggar? Do you?' He pulls himself taller. 'I tried my best. I've always tried my best. Haven't I, Mary?' He looks vaguely towards Mary for support, then stares into his glass as if looking for absolution. His face contorts and Marie is afraid he might start crying. She's seen so many other revolting men like René in the same state at the Martyrs Tavern: drunk, in debt and feeling sorry for themselves, lurching from rage to self-pitying tears and back again.

'Really, René,' says Mary, tightly. 'Please let's not rake over the same ground again. You might at least show some gratitude.'

A waiter comes to the table, forcing René to drop Marie's hand while he swings a huge round tray off his shoulder and deposits the brandy and hot chocolate on their table. Oh the smell of it! Marie grabs her drink as slowly as she is able, warms her hands on the cup before Monsieur René has a chance to knock it over. His breathing sounds like a steam train; he looks as if he might explode.

'So, Mary, any chance of Edgar actually making some proper money out of his daubings, his silly little obsession with dancing girls?'

'How dare you, René?' Mary cries out, then realises her voice is too high and leans towards him and hisses, 'How dare you, René. How dare you denigrate Edgar's art when it's the only thing keeping you out of a debtors' prison? If Edgar and I hadn't come to your rescue, God only knows what would have happened to you.'

René sinks into his chair and stares at the floor. He looks like a sullen child.

Mary's voice is gentler now. 'Look at me, René. It's not a *silly obsession*. We are gaining a reputation. The last exhibition was a moderate success. Admittedly some of the critics haven't been kind, but a few are starting to understand what we are doing. The next exhibition could be the making of Edgar, of all of us.'

René snorts, pulls his waistcoat down over his round belly and brushes the ash off it.

Marie is busy finishing her hot chocolate. She shrugs. She cannot imagine what rich people really care about. They don't have to even think about food or where they will sleep tomorrow. Who knows what fills their minds? René turns back to Mary.

'Listen, I'm sorry if I spoke out of turn, Mary. But I just can't understand why you and your merry band of… what is it you call yourselves?'

'Impressionists. Surely you know that by now,' Mary snaps.

'Yes, Impressionists. Whatever that means. What was I saying? Yes, I don't understand why Edgar insists on making things so difficult. Why can't he carry on with your group and paint some historical scenes for the Salon as well?'

'If you don't understand by now, René, I really can't explain it to you.'

'Perhaps my dear brother is too busy "entertaining" his dancing girls rather than doing any actual work, the lazy old scoundrel. Huh! I hadn't thought of that. That must be it – eh, Mary?'

'Of course not. Don't judge your brother by your standards, René,' says Mary.

Marie remembers when René told her about Edgar that night of the circus. Oh, that night seems like years ago. She felt sorry for René then. How easily seduced she was by a little attention and flattery! Since then, she's realised rich people only shed tears for themselves while watching people on the streets starve without a glimmer of compassion. And now she knows Edgar so well, her allegiance is with him. He does not lie on the floor smearing wax on old paintbrushes because he likes it.

199

It's more than that. He needs it. It mends him. It gives him life. And she's grown to love Edgar's mother too. It feels like the lonely-looking woman in the portrait is there with them in the studio, watching over her, Marie. They are three lonely people who are somehow less lonely, happier and more complete when they are together in the studio, with the strange wax figure forming between them.

'Edgar is not lazy!' Marie cries out. 'He works as hard as a stonemason.'

'I beg your pardon! Did she speak? Did the little monkey speak?'

Marie bites her lip and stares into her cup. She doesn't want to get sent away before she finishes her chocolate and can find out what's happening. It's true he's been very distracted the past few days. His bad eye was bothering him so much that he had to stop for a while yesterday. They sat on the divan together and she told him about rehearsals, the costumes they were going to wear, how the ballet master collapsed into tears when his dog Zou-Zou escaped. Edgar smiled and said she gave him hope, put his arm around her, then took it away as if he had done something wrong and went back to his work. Her heart nearly cracked open. She doesn't mind at all when he is distracted. But she certainly won't be telling René or Mary Cassatt that he ever takes a break.

Looking at René now, his red face, the hard look in his eyes, Marie sees a bitter, jealous man.

'You must be realistic, Mary,' René continues, ignoring Marie.

'No, René. Hear me out. Believe in your brother! Edgar is special. He has the makings of a great artist.'

René twiddles the ends of his moustache with a shaking hand.

'The only thing you care about is your career, Mary. And you know that without him you are nothing. If he had no work in the damned exhibition it would not even be happening. You are a woman. Unfortunately. Your name isn't even allowed on the poster. You are just riding on his coat-tails.'

'How dare you, monsieur!' Mary stuffs her hands into her muffler. Probably stopping herself from slapping him across his pudgy cheek, Marie thinks to herself.

'Please, René.' Mary's tone changes now. She is pleading. Marie resists the urge to feel sorry for her. She can see in her eyes that Mary is searching around in her mind for the right thing to say, the right tone to take, as it seems women always must when in conversation with men.

'You are an honourable man, René. I have agreed to help you out with your moving costs, so in return please stop haranguing Edgar and let him get on with his work. And if you need more money, please come to me, not him. I know you don't believe me but – and forgive me if I don't trust your judgement entirely on business matters – I really think this next exhibition, this new work he is doing, might enhance Edgar's reputation as well as his earning power considerably.'

René looks up at that and almost smiles, then shrugs and calls for the bill, slaps down a roll of fresh notes.

So that's why René is here with her, Marie realises. Mary Cassatt may be a woman, but she has money and therefore René begrudgingly accords her some respect.

'Fine, I agree. You win again, Mary.'

'Thank you, René.'

'Good. Then we have a deal. Now, excuse me, ladies, but my carriage is waiting.'

René obviously shares not only the twitching cheek but the ability to slam the door on his feelings and snap into his false self at the drop of a hat.

'Embrace me, Mireille!'

Marie doesn't bother correcting him. She has no choice but to get up and go to René. He bends to kiss her cheek, slides his hand down her back and grabs her behind. Marie grits her teeth and wills him to let her go.

At last, he releases her and strides off, shoving a little dog out the way with his jasper-topped cane as he goes.

Marie is left alone with Mary. The café is emptying, breakfast cups being carried away on shining silver trays, tables scrubbed, waiters heaving sighs of relief and counting their change.

Just as Marie is about to make her excuses and leave, Mary grabs her arm. She has tears in her eyes.

'I have to go, mademoiselle.'

'Would you like another hot chocolate, *ma petite*? Oh, please stay for a moment. I can't bear to be alone today.'

The waiter deposits another basket of bread on the table. Marie nods and gives in. It will be worth being late to stash some bread in her pocket and anyway there's something she needs to find out. She feels almost sorry for Mary Cassatt again. After all, they are both women, and must rely on men, just as Amélie relies on her Count. They are all desperate for some form of attention to make them feel their lives are worth something.

Marie turns Papa's ring around in her pocket, remembering the monkey comment. Remembering Louise Michel's warning about how the bourgeoisie seduce the working class to their own ends. Mary is just using her. Keeping her sweet. Look how she just twisted René around her little finger. These artists are as wily as fishmongers. She must stop selling herself for a cup of hot chocolate and a little loving attention. She's practically a whore already.

'Marie! Are you paying attention? Marie!'

'*Oui, mademoiselle.* I am listening,' she lies.

'If the finished sculpture is not in the exhibition we are all finished, Marie. It is going to be the centrepiece of the whole thing. Do you hear? Caillebotte won't let us go ahead without it; he will give up on our little group. Edgar won't let me see the sculpture. He's not himself at all. Will you try and persuade him, Marie? Just go to his studio and get him working. He's terribly fond of you, you know.'

Mary gives her a long look. Marie is unsure what that look is suggesting, uncomfortable at what she fears it implies. She manages a weak smile to cover her racing heart, looks to see if her hot chocolate is coming.

'I believe the sculpture is nearly finished, mademoiselle. Edgar – I mean Monsieur Degas – is very pleased with how she – it – has turned out.'

Marie says his first name on purpose, pretends to correct herself, to show they are close. For a moment she wonders if she could persuade Mary Cassatt to give her money to make sure the figure is finished. But she must not stoop that low. Spending time with these rich people is making her lower herself to their standards. But Mary's impression that Marie has power over Edgar is pleasing. It gives her hope. It might be this realisation that she has a scrap of power or the belly-warming effect of the hot chocolate, but she finds herself opening her mouth and asking a direct question.

'Does Monsieur Degas have a wife?'

It's something she's wondered about for a long time. He doesn't wear a ring and there is no sign of a wife, but you never know, she might be installed in a house in the countryside somewhere.

Mary Cassatt splutters on her cup at the impertinence of Marie's question and wipes it with her napkin. It's good to see her flustered for once. So what if Marie's late for the opera? It's worth the risk to find out more about Edgar and see Mademoiselle Cassatt suffer. And it's so lovely to be warm and safe, her belly full of bread and chocolate.

'A wife? Goodness, no. He believes that an artist must not have a private life. At least, that is what he says. And I must say that I tend to agree. Especially when I see how men like René become utterly engulfed by their marital problems.'

Mary smooths the muffler on the table with one of her long thin fingers. 'Edgar and I are married to our art,' she says to the muffler. Her voice is flat and sad.

Marie sees a blush on her face. She wonders if Mary is in love with Edgar, or perhaps she is just ashamed that she is a sad old spinster with no husband or children. And if they are lovers, why all this talk about Marie using her charms? Perhaps Marie doesn't count. After all, Amélie has told her that most wives don't mind their husbands having lovers as long as it doesn't become public and the courtesan is of a lower class.

'My view is that he is scared,' Mary burbles on. 'I pushed him on it once and he insisted that the only woman he could take as a lover would be a duchess or a chambermaid.'

She looks up from the muffler now and seems to emerge from her reverie. 'What a strange question, Marie, why do you ask?'

A chambermaid might mean she has a chance. After all, she could just about be a chambermaid. Or maybe she isn't even good enough for that. But she can't lose him again. And without the money he gives her, she'll be homeless, she'll be on the street outside this café taking gentlemen like René for 'trips'.

Mary Cassatt is staring at her now, eyes narrowed, spoon stopped in mid-stir, waiting.

'Why do you ask, Marie?'

'I – I don't know why I asked.' A flush is spreading up her neck. 'None of my business, I wasn't thinking. Anyway, I must go. I – I have to go.'

Marie slurps the rest of her hot chocolate and gets up. She must get to the opera, get through the rehearsal somehow, make things right with Antoinette. She looks up at Amélie's balcony through the windows of the café, remembers Amélie telling her not to come back until she has purloined a kiss on the lips from Degas and finds herself up for the challenge.

CHAPTER FIFTEEN

Marie runs from the café but is still twenty minutes late by the time she reaches the opera house. She's desperately hoping that the ballet master will be in a better mood than last week. Rumour has it that he's fighting with his superior regarding the proposed move to new premises, threatening to walk out if his job is not guaranteed and he's not offered a pay rise.

It's nearly two years since she first walked through the back door of the opera house, but it feels like much longer. Some of the flats from *La Source* and *Yedda* are still propped up against the walls of the dark labyrinth of corridors. She knows where to step to avoid holes and piles of rope almost without looking now. She swerves around a painter's bucket. The painter whistles at her and she can feel his eyes on her as she climbs the stairs up to the dressing room. Perhaps she is in possession of feminine charms after all. Her heart skips at the thought and she's smiling when she walks into the dressing room straight into the tall figure of the Crow.

'I'm sorry I'm late, I…'

The Crow looks behind her and then puts a cool, bony hand over Marie's mouth. Her face is even paler than usual.

'Hush, Marie. Hush. Come here, sit beside me.'

What on earth is going on? When she was late before, the Crow shouted at her in front of everybody.

'I won't be late again, I promise. I got stuck. I…'

The Crow pulls her down onto the bench.

'This is nothing to do with lateness, Marie. *Calme-toi.*'

Marie looks into the Crow's little black eyes. Tenderness. That's what she sees. An unmistakable warmth she has never seen there before.

'Listen carefully, Marie. The police are here. They are waiting for you.'

'The police?'

The Crow's breath smells of tobacco. She is shivering slightly in the cold. What are the police doing here? Has Antoinette been caught for thieving?

'Is Antoinette in there, is she with the police? I must go to her. Let me go to her!'

'No! Listen, Marie. Antoinette is not here. She didn't turn up again today. Thank *le bon dieu*. But you must leave now and never come back.'

'But why? I – I haven't done anything.'

'Madame Balnar saw you at a demonstration with Louise Michel outside a bakery on Rue des Cannettes and reported you. She's a troublemaker, that one. She'll do anything to advance her daughter.'

'She's lying. I don't know what you're talking—'

'Shh. I know it's true, Marie.'

'But surely if I just explain…?'

At least there's no mention of the brick. Damn Blanche Balnar and her ambitious mother to hell! And why is the Crow telling her this – is she lying? But why would she lie? It's impossible to know who to trust.

'I'm afraid it's worse than that, Marie. There's some plot to do with the Palais de Justice brewing. Probably just a story to frighten people, but it's all over the papers. Somehow, the police think you are involved. If they catch you, you'll be arrested immediately. Go, my little one. Take your things and go!'

'But – how…' She thinks back to that awful evening at the Veau à Deux Têtes, that man in the flat cap. It must be him. He must have heard Paul bragging about bombing the Palais de Justice and taken it seriously. He must have been one of the spies Louise Michel is always warning them about. Oh, how could she and Paul have been so fucking stupid?

She stares into the Crow's beady eyes. Is she to be trusted, this bony-faced old woman she has always hated? Piano music starts up, the introduction to her piece. She should be in there.

'Why are you helping me?'

'I am your friend, Marie. You must believe me. I fought with Louise Michel. I was there when thirty-two of our sisters were shot while we watched. I am too old to fight now, but I do what I can. I know you think I'm a mean old woman, that you all call me "the Crow".' A sad smile flickers on her thin lips. 'But I have to be like that, so I am above suspicion. Every day, I fear that somebody will remember me and what I did for the Commune.'

Marie tries to take in what the Crow is telling her. Then she remembers the way they let her in so easily, the little winks the Crow has given her, the fact it was she who delivered the first note from Edgar.

'Are you really a Communard, madame?'

'I know you find it hard to believe, Marie, but it's the truth.'

The introduction has stopped short now. She can hear the patter of Zou-Zou's claws on the parquet floor, the ballet master telling somebody off.

'Is that why I got a job here, because of you?'

'No. That was mostly Monsieur Degas. He helped Antoinette too. He's a good man.'

Edgar? Antoinette said he was a friend of the family, but she had not put two and two together. Of course! *We have friends in high places.* That's what Antoinette said. It was Edgar she was talking about!

'But, madame, how—'

'Hush, my dear. Go, Marie. You must go!'

Shouts from the rehearsal room, footsteps coming towards them. They both get up.

'Thank you, madame. Thank you so much.'

It's all she can think of to say. She kisses the Crow on her dry powdered cheeks. They both have tears in their eyes now.

'I will miss you, little one. I shall pray for you,' whispers the Crow, her voice breaking as she gets up and smooths her skirts. She raises her sharp chin, adjusts the bow at her neck as if she is going into battle. 'Fight for me, for the twenty thousand of our comrades who died.' Her eyes are sparkling through her tears now, little rivers cutting through the powder under her eyes. '*Vive la Commune!*'

Marie takes a last look around the dressing room, grabs her slippers and skirt.

She looks back at the Crow as she leaves, raises her fist and winks.

'*Vive la Commune!*'

CHAPTER SIXTEEN

Marie gasps when she sees the sculpture. Nearly all the wax is on, just one foot remains half uncovered. The wax is a fleshy orange-pink colour. The Creature is wearing a brand-new bodice (laced over her meagre chest) and a tarlatan skirt which looks much too big for her. The Creature is smaller than her, like a very large doll. Although nothing like a real doll. No little girl would want one like that, so skinny and ugly.

Her heart withers. How can she seduce Edgar when she looks like that statue? But she must try, for his protection is her only hope, her only way out of being left to scavenge on the streets. It's two weeks since she threw the brick and so far she has escaped the police, but it's surely only a matter of time. Two officers rapped on the door two nights after the looting and startled Marie out of deep sleep. She heard them muttering outside, then shouting at her to open up so loudly that the baby next door started screaming. One of them shoved the door so hard that a pan fell off the shelf in the kitchen, but luckily one of Gigi's old lovers had been a locksmith and installed two bolts on the door by way of courtship a few months ago so it held firm. Next time they will surely break the door down.

Marie tries to put the thought out of her head, looks around instead at the fireplace, the chaise longue where she and Edgar sit together sometimes, the jumble of canvases, and realises that this is her home now, the only place where she feels safe, where her heart and mind can rest. And Edgar could so easily give her shelter. She could curl up in the corner of the chaise longue when he didn't need her, he'd hardly notice she was here.

'What do you think of her, *ma petite*? I'm trying ideas for what she should wear. There will of course be ballet slippers, if I ever get that damned foot right, and perhaps a ribbon around her waist.'

Marie forces herself to speak. 'Please excuse me. I'm a little tired. It – she – she's nearly finished.' Marie looks at her mirror image and has to bite back tears. She looks so small and so alone. 'Will she have a name?'

'I'm going to call her *Little Dancer, aged fourteen years*.'

Marie tries to hide her disappointment that he will not use her name. She swallows and tries to force a smile. The fear in her rises that this is the end, that he will send her away. It seemed as though this was her world, that she would always come here. It has become the centre of her life. The backbone. She cannot imagine how she will manage without this. Without him.

Harden your heart, Marie. Emotions have no place on the battlefield. You have a goal, and you march towards it without looking back.

'Do you think she is beautiful, monsieur?'

'I think she is real. Reality is what interests me, Marie.'

Marie bites her lip, manages a tiny smile at the thought of how little reality he truly knows. While he's obsessing about the meaning of reality all she can think about is that her only income is from him, that he can send her away and ruin her on a whim if he so chooses. *That* is reality. He's totally and utterly protected from hunger and the need to pay the rent every month. If she's not arrested, she will soon be evicted and will have no home to go to. She's been trying not to think about it, hoping something will turn up, but has no idea what that something will be. All Degas has to worry about is the curve of a line and which waistcoat to wear. Look at that pile of logs by the fire, the box of half-used candles on his table.

'Do you find her real, Marie? Is she alive?'

She has to admit that the Little Dancer is disturbingly lifelike. It's as if she's about to move at any moment. Marie juts her chin out to mirror her. Yes, that is exactly what she does, or rather used to do, in the wings at the opera. She can almost hear the conductor coughing and tapping his stick on the music stand, feel that sense of expectation before the curtain goes up, smell the greenish gaslights at the front of the stage that blot out the audience. That's exactly how she was just before she stepped out onto the stage that time. Her body was aching all over and she took a moment to stretch, to raise her chin and force herself out onto the stage. And then she spotted Edgar in a box with Mary Cassatt. And her heart leapt. Hope returned. But not for long.

'Yes. She is very real.'

She and Edgar stand either side of the figure in silence. Sunlight knifes through a gap in dark heavy clouds and lights up the sculpted face. The pinky-orange stained wax glows like a church window. Marie feels so awkward next to this strange twin of herself. What would the Creature say if she could speak?

She puts out a hand to touch the Little Dancer's mouth, but there's no warmth there. Edgar seems totally at ease. He is smiling now as he walks around the figure, adjusting the skirt, bending to take a better look at a shinbone. A small intimate smile. A real smile. He runs a finger down the Little Dancer's forearm.

'See this body, Marie. This flesh is alive. It works for a living. That is what I mean by "real". It's not decorative, not milky and round and useless. In the past painters depicted heroes from Ancient Greece and Rome. But in our modern age, true nobility is with the people! The everyday struggles of working people are an epic battle. That is what interests me. See the sinews, the tension in the muscles as she stretches. Do you find her a good likeness of you, Marie?'

'I – I am not sure.' She takes a closer look at the face. 'I don't know what to feel about her, monsieur.'

'Good. That's good, Marie. Because to be honest, she is not just you. She is also me.'

'You? What do you mean, monsieur?'

'Not the outside, *ma petite*. I am not given to wearing tutus! I mean the inside, the essence. I am like her; I am always in the wings, watching. When you look at the sculpture, you are expecting her to burst out onto the stage. There is an air of expectation, of imminent action. But I, I am as frozen as this statue. I am paralysed, unable to step out. I am this little dancer!'

Edgar rubs at his bad eye, starts pacing around the figure. Marie frowns. What is he talking about, how can this little scrawny thing be anything like the strong gentleman before her?

'I'm sorry to speak like this, *ma petite*, but I want you to understand. You working people are the new nobility. You are the brave ones. Even when I was with your father, I did not fight. I watched, Marie. I watched. That is all I can do. Watch. My father and my brother wanted me to take over the family business and I refused. My brother thinks I am lazy, that I avoided joining him in any of his catastrophic business ventures because I like to be idle.'

'I know you are not lazy. I told your brother so myself.'

'Yes, yes. Thank you, Marie. I was very touched by that. Mary told me how you defended me so valiantly. People see me disappearing into my studio for months and emerging with nothing but a couple of half-finished canvases. Of course they question what I'm doing. But you know, Marie, don't you?'

Marie nods but Degas' attention has wandered away from her; he seems to be addressing himself to an invisible audience.

'They have no idea what torment I subject myself to, how hard I toil over every brushstroke. Oh, René has intimated many times that my refusal to step in and help save the business made our father ill.' He tears at his hair now, looks up at his mother on the wall. 'I will not accept that, Marie. I will not! I am not idle, I am… incapable. I am an artist, or I am nothing.'

Marie has never seen Edgar like this before. So agitated and breathless.

'You, monsieur… you never stop working. And I see you come alive when you are here in your studio. You remind me of Papa. When he used to speak from the stage outside the Palais de Justice.'

'I must rework that foot, it just isn't working. But the head is perfect now.' Edgar isn't really listening. He puts a shaking hand on the statue's head, his long fingers curving right around its bald, knobbly skull.

'So much depends on the success of this exhibition.'

He's speaking to the sculpture. Marie stares at his profile. His long straight nose, which flares like a horse's when he is angry, the slight pulse at his temple, the crinkles under his eyes that come and go constantly as he studies things. He's very smartly dressed today, must be going somewhere. No scraps of paint in his hair, yellow pinstriped trousers freshly pressed. She can't bear the thought that she might not see him again.

Marie knows she must *act*. Most gentlemen have a liking for young girls, everybody knows that. Mary Cassatt herself said that Edgar has an eye for a chambermaid, so seducing him should not be beyond her. Amélie says all men are the same. They want sex like Marie wants bread. And the longer they are without it, the more they hunger for it. All you need to do is remind them of their hunger. *Wait. Wait like a cat for the right moment. Then pounce without fear.*

A flickering silence, like sitting beside a fire in the dark. Edgar is crouched on the floor now with a small bowl in one hand and a palette knife in the other. He's applying wax to the top of the Creature's foot, smoothing it with his thumb. She longs to just stay here and listen to the sound of his breathing for a bit longer. There's that feeling again. Descending on her like morning sunlight. As if they are at church. That feeling she often gets in his presence when he is working. As if they are summoning up something from another world, another dimension. As if she is dissolving and re-forming around the sculpture under his gaze. As if the edges between her, Edgar and the Creature are blurred. And there is peace.

Degas gets up and sets the bowl and palette knife on the table, rubs his hands together.

'There! She's finished.' He walks around the statue very slowly, nodding to himself. 'Perfect. She's perfect.' His voice is soft and clear as he comes over towards Marie and takes her hands.

Wake up, Marie. Stop daydreaming. This is the moment. You must be bold. Act, Marie.

She smiles the brightest smile she can muster. He smiles back and lets out a deep sigh. Oh, and now his warm hands are cupping her head, just as he cupped the head of the statue a moment ago. He strokes her hair, tucks a stray strand behind one ear, bends towards her. She holds her breath but can't stop her heart galloping. He tips her chin up towards him. As he bends, his hair falls over his eyes so that they are in shadow and she can't see his expression. She shuts her eyes. His breath is warm on her eyelids and his hair oil has a bittersweet smell. He kisses her slowly on the forehead, then straightens up again and looks into her.

'You are perfect too, Marie. Just perfect.'

Act, Marie! Step out from the wings! She forces herself to put her hands around his neck, to draw his mouth towards hers. *Sometimes they need some encouragement, Marie. Gentlemen can be incredibly stupid; you have to show them that they want you.* She pulls harder at his head, but he doesn't budge.

'No – no! What on earth are you doing, Marie?'

He lets out an awkward laugh, pushes her off. She darts forward, tries to kiss his mouth but ends up grazing his shoulder as he pushes her away again. She stumbles back, grabs onto the chaise longue to stop herself falling.

'I thought you – I...'

'What on earth were you thinking of, Marie?'

'I thought you cared about me. I thought...'

'Don't cry, *ma petite*. Please don't cry.'

He comes towards her and hands her a handkerchief. She stares at the fine lace and embroidered initials. The same handkerchief that covered Papa's face when his body was brought in. Edgar must have lots of them.

'You are beautiful, my Marie. And I do. I do care about you. But – I...'

He seems terribly agitated again now. He's walking about in circles like a mad man, raking at his hair. He stops suddenly, stares up at the portrait of his mother. Marie follows his gaze. As she and Edgar stand there staring up into Madame Degas' strange forest landscape, it's almost as if they are there with her. She's sure Edgar is thinking the same thing. And in that moment, she realises that Madame Degas is the woman in her dream. The one who said, 'It is nearly time.'

'It's nearly time, Marie.'

Edgar's voice breaks the spell. She can't be sure if it was him or the portrait who said those words. She rubs her head; it feels very hot and sweaty. She must be delirious.

'For the exhibition, I mean. Only a few days to go. You can go if you want, Marie, I don't really need you.'

Marie bites her lip. Damn the fucking exhibition. He's right back in his shell now, his voice has gone hard and shiny. He smooths his waistcoat, tucks his shirt back in and flashes her that awful false smile he always uses in public.

Never surrender! She *must* try again. She can't just let him send her away like this. She must break through that shell, it's her last chance. She threw that brick and turned things around and she can do it again. She imagines the window breaking, the thrill of it. *Just one more push, Marie.* She closes her fist around her papa's ring in her pocket. Papa strode willingly into battle. Again and again. He risked his life. The least she can do is cross this room and try again. Not give up like a deserter. She marches over to Edgar, reaches out her arms, closes her eyes. Please, *au nom du bon dieu*, bring him to me.

'Kiss me, Edgar. Please kiss me.'

She waits. But nothing happens. When she opens her eyes, Edgar is staring at her with such a strange look in his eyes. His temples are pulsing; she can tell he's trying to keep control. In his eyes she expects to see anger or disgust. But there's just confusion and hurt. Exactly what she herself is feeling.

'I'm so sorry, Marie. I should never have invited you here in the first place. It was wrong. I see it is wrong now. I thought I could manage. I thought I could keep the two things apart. I just wanted a part of you – I didn't know it would be like this. I...'

'But I don't understand. You said I was beautiful. Am I really that ugly that you can't bear to even touch me?'

The sound of her own voice pleading is revolting. She sounds like Maman begging the landlord for another month's reprieve. A rumble of anger warms her belly. Anger that she should have been so stupid as to fall for his bourgeois charm. Rich people think nothing of veering from flattery to contempt in one sentence. You can't believe a word they say. For all their soft words and warm smiles, underneath they are as cold as undertakers. She must face reality. She digs a broken nail into her palm. For all his fancy talk about nobility and working people, it's obvious he's just using her, like those gentlemen complimenting the prostitutes on Boulevard Haussmann before they drag them off to a dark room somewhere, drop them a few sous and forget they ever existed. He doesn't care and she's a fool to ever have thought he did. He's a bourgeois, like all the others. He'll never betray his class. She's just a creature to him. A dog to be petted one moment and kicked the next.

She tries to leave, to retain some small scrap of dignity. But she's pinned to the spot.

Look at that monstrous sculpted creature! Standing over there all safe and sound. Free from the burden of being alive, immune to hunger and cold and pain. *She* will be here when

Marie is long gone. Edgar will keep *her* forever; he will never reject *her*. Marie finds herself marching up to the sculpture and kicking her on the shin. The figure wobbles but remains impassive. Everything is lost. Edgar doesn't love her. He doesn't love her. Neither do Maman or Antoinette. Nobody is left. She has nothing else to lose. Nothing. She stamps on the statue's foot.

'*She* feels no pain! See, Edgar! How lucky she is. *Saloppe! My* feet are covered in blisters; they fill my old boots with blood, no matter how much newspaper I stuff them with.'

The sun from the window is blinding now, it makes her dizzy. She pinches the Creature's shoulder as hard as she can, then scrapes some wax off with a nail and flicks it on the floor.

'*Calme-toi, ma petite.* What on earth are you doing?'

She yanks at the tutu.

'Do you think I wanted to be a little rat doing stupid dances for you and the other lecherous old *abonnés*? Do you think any of us do it for pleasure? You look at us in our pink tulle and ribbons and think how pretty we are. But all we feel is pain. It's a choice between that and prostitution, monsieur. There's not much difference. All we have is our bodies. There is nothing left for us to sell. And when nobody will buy our bodies, then what?'

She pushes the Creature, knocking it off centre. Edgar springs forward to catch it. He rights the statue carefully, with tenderness. Such awful tenderness. Of course he does. He goes to the statue first. Not her, the living Marie. Not her, even though her legs are shaking and only the force of her own rage is keeping her upright. His statue is more important than her. She doesn't matter. She doesn't matter to anybody. Oh, now the tears are coming. Wretched female tears. She grits her teeth, stares at the statue to stifle the tears with hate.

Edgar grabs her by the shoulders.

'Calm yourself, Marie. What has got into you today? You'll make yourself ill.'

What does she care if she gets ill? It would be easier if she got ill and died. Easier for everybody. She kicks out at him. She can't stop now, the force of everything she has kept inside is flooding out. She sees herself from the outside, crying and lashing out like an animal in a cage. Edgar is speaking to her softly but she can't take in what he says. She collapses onto his chest. Buries her face in his waistcoat so she can't see the damned Creature. Bangs her head against him. 'I hate you. I hate you.'

Her own sobs sound as if they don't belong to her.

There's nothing left to live for. Let the panic come and drown me.

'There, there, *ma petite*. All will be well. Just you wait and see. Just you wait and see.'

Let the tide of life take me. I'm sick of fighting it.

He smells of lemons and paint. The satin of his striped waistcoat is cool and soft against her face. It's the one he wore when she first came to the studio. She admired the impeccable stitching as he strode up the stairs, two at a time. That seems like a lifetime ago. Back when hope still flickered in her heart. She stares at the fine fabric through her tears. Papa! Papa made the waistcoat. Of course. How could she not have guessed before?

She bangs her head on the exquisitely covered buttons. Why is Papa dead, while Edgar is strutting around in the waistcoat he made? Why is she crying against this stranger's silk-covered chest, listening to the steady beat of his heart, while Papa lies in the cold earth? Everything is so unfair, so cruel, so senseless. Better to smash everything up than live in such a world. Edgar is not her friend; he is her enemy. It's people like him with their grand ideas and selfish obsession with beauty who walk past starving people on the streets and curse them for their ugliness.

She pushes against Edgar's chest, makes herself straighten up and face him squarely. She feels cold inside now under the hot tears.

'You love that thing, don't you, Edgar. You care about her more than me.'

'You are right, Marie. I admit it. I do love this statue.'

She follows his gaze to the Creature.

'But she's not real, Edgar! How can you love something that's not real?'

'That's exactly why I love her. I'm not proud of it. I can't help it. I – I am incapable of real love, Marie. That is what I was trying to explain to you. It's nothing to do with you, it's just the way I am.'

He points to the portrait of his mother. 'I am like her. I have always denied it, but it's true.'

Marie gazes up at Madame Degas, sitting awkwardly on her bench, hands tightly clutched around her hairbrush, all alone in that strange forest.

'Do you see, Marie? I have to dissect life and pin it down so that I am not destroyed by it. I make things out of the glare of life so that I can survive its brightness.'

He's looking right into her now, his head on one side, as if he's pleading with her for something, but she can't understand what it is he wants from her.

'Do you understand anything of what I am saying, Marie? I need you to understand. 'If you love me, please leave me. To my art. Please, Marie.'

In that moment, she realises that Edgar is scared too. His art is what he needs to stop himself going mad. To stop him getting that feeling she gets when she remembers Papa and the red wall. When the feelings all join up together inside her and flood her senses. The only time she feels strong and ordered now, apart from her time with Edgar in the studio, is when she's with Louise Michel, when she writes a leaflet or throws a brick through a window. Then she is moving forward, then she is alive. Then her life has meaning.

The sobs have mangled her mind now, scrubbed it clean, and now she feels nothing. Even the pain in her shoulder has gone.

'I – I think I understand.'

Edgar lets out a shuddering sigh. He looks from Madame Degas to Marie and back again a few times.

'I wish you'd been able to meet her. My mother, I mean. She would have liked you.'

He cups her face in his hands. There are tears in his eyes. Marie is so startled to see the tears that she can't move. Being with him is like watching the light change on the Seine. Always different, yet always the same.

'But I want to stay here. With you.'

'Oh, Marie. My Marie.'

He's studying her now, looking at her the way he looks at the sculpture. As if she's something he has created. Something he can love.

'Edgar! Edgar!'

A man's voice. Heavy footsteps on the stairs outside the door. They jump away from each other.

René storms in, waving his cane. His face is bright red, he stumbles over a wonky floorboard and charges up to Edgar. She can smell the drink on him.

'I might have known you'd be buried here, Edgar.'

René bangs his cane on the floor. He's huffing and puffing

like a train. Edgar's hands are fists. Marie hopes Edgar will punch René. Punch him hard.

He rocks back and forth on his polished shoes, stares at his brother. He's stuck there, chomping at the bit, reined in by his bourgeois education. Watching.

René waves his cane at the sculpture.

'So, this is your little monkey girl, eh, *mon brave*? This little monster of a dancing girl? And you seriously wish me to believe that *this* – this revolting creation – will be the making of your artistic reputation?'

Marie can still hear the two brothers squabbling from the doorstep. She pauses on Place Blanche, feeling lost in the middle of the city she loves. Oh, that climb up to Montmartre, the thought of going home to find the house repossessed or the police waiting for her. Or, even worse, Antoinette screaming at her. She can't face it. There's nowhere to go. Nobody to turn to.

She finds herself sitting outside a café on the square. She picks a scrap of wax from under a broken nail and flicks it on the pavement.

Brandy! Just one glass to take the edge off. Then she'll go up the hill and face her fate. She props herself up on her elbows, holds her aching head in her hands. The metal chair is cold beneath her worn-out dress, but her head is boiling hot. She downs the brandy in one gulp. The bitterness is good. A pleasant numbness blooms up from her empty belly, fogs up her head. Until she feels as blank as a clean sheet.

'Mademoiselle! Wake up, mademoiselle. You can't sleep here.'

She jolts awake, knocks over her glass with an elbow, apologises. Ouch, her head is throbbing.

'You are too young for this. Go home, *ma petite*. Things will get better.'

The proprietor is hugely fat with tiny eyes. He looks at her kindly, shakes his big head while he clears the shattered glass away.

CHAPTER SEVENTEEN

The streets are both familiar and strange. Marie finds it hard to walk straight. The flapping sole on her boot keeps making her trip over, people curse her when she bumps into them. She can't summon up the energy to care. A homeless man wearing a sign saying 'help me' grabs at her skirt and it is so tempting to slump down on the wall beside him and fall asleep. She's sure to be living on the street herself soon. Occasionally she stops at a street sign, tries to make a map in her head. Just to check that her mind is still working.

She can smell chocolate! She must be in the Passage des Panoramas. The door opens at Chocolatier Basquier et Fils. She darts in, grabs a handful of chocolates, and runs out, closely followed by the owner.

'Stop, thief!'

His shouts die out as she stuffs the chocolates in her mouth, dodging carriages as she crosses Boulevard Haussmann. Up a few stairs, and she flattens herself against the wall by Amélie's door, waits for her heart to stop trying to escape from her chest.

'What are you doing here, Marie? I was out feeding the parrots, heard a right old commotion on the street. Thought it was another drunk looking for a quick trip to eternity. Then I looked down and realised it was you. You almost got yourself killed, *petite saloppe*!'

Amélie is in her white silk dressing gown. She looks like an angel at the pearly gates, ready to hear Marie's confession. Marie clears her throat, wipes chocolate off her mouth with the back of her hand, tries to concentrate on Amélie's face.

'I failed.'

'What are you talking about, *ma petite*?'

'I failed. But I'm about to be evicted – or arrested – and… and I have nowhere to go.'

Amélie puts a hand on Marie's forehead. Her hand feels cold as ice.

'You are boiling hot, Marie. You look terrible. Have you been drinking? Hmm, well, you'd better come inside. Hang on a moment.'

Amélie bites her lip, leans out from the doorway, looks out into the street, up and down. She seems anxious. Her hair is in curling papers with grey roots showing.

'I failed. I failed to get a kiss, Amélie. From my artist. You said I couldn't come back until I got a kiss. But I didn't know where to go, so I came here.'

Amélie puts a finger to her lips.

'Keep the noise down. The whole boulevard's swarming with police.'

'I tried everything you said,' she whispers. 'But it didn't work. He – he pushed me away. Twice. I tried. But I'm no good at it. I'm too ugly. And now…'

The sound of her own pitiful voice makes Marie start to cry.

'And I've lost my job – and I didn't mean to hurt Antoinette, but I did. And now she's disappeared. I thought I was brave. But

I'm not. I'm a coward. A deserter. I can't march on anymore – I just can't do any more, I can't go on – I…'

'You're not making any sense, little one. Hush, hush.'

Amélie's arm is around Marie now, drawing her inside.

'Come up. The Count is away for a couple of weeks. You can stay tonight and tell me everything in the morning.'

Marie dreams she's buried underground in a glass coffin. She's banging on the sides, screaming to be let out. But nobody can hear her.

She wakes in a cold sweat. Amélie's bed is so soft. Marie is lying curled up on her side, her dress still on and twisted around her body. She can feel Papa's rings in her pocket pressing into her hip. *I'm still alive.* She rubs a blistered foot against smooth, freshly ironed cotton, pushes up with her big toe against a thick, heavy blanket. The smell of expensive soap *de Provence*. It's not heaven, but it certainly feels like it. She's surprised to find that she's glad to be alive, despite the banging in her head and a rumble of nasty thoughts coming nearer, like the soldiers coming up Rue Lepic the day Papa died. She pushes them back, and cracks open one eye. Light cuts in, falling in stripes from the huge white shutters. There are two boxes on the floor, half-full of shoes and trinkets. She sees Amélie lying next to her across the huge expanse of white cotton. The bed must be three times as wide as her bed on Rue Lepic. Amélie has one arm flung out over the covers, pudgy hand palm up, perfectly manicured nails gleaming like pearls. There's a big yellow and purple bruise on her upper arm. Many of the poorer, skinnier girls come into the opera like that. Not difficult to guess who is responsible for it.

The whinny of a horse from out on the boulevard, followed by loud squawks from the parrots outside. Amélie snorts and half opens her eyes.

'Amélie! Are you awake?'

'I'm awake, Marie.' Amélie lets out a huge yawn, rolls onto her back and pulls the sleeve of her nightdress sharply over the bruise. 'How are you feeling?'

'Is the Count violent with you?'

Amélie doesn't answer. She props herself on an elbow and smooths back her hair. There's mascara smudged around her eyes, powder pooled in the lines around her mouth. She puts a hand on Marie's forehead.

'You've cooled down, *ma petite*. That's good. I was worried about you. You've been asleep nearly two days, little sleepyhead!'

'Really? Two days!'

Marie rolls over to face Amélie, pulls the covers up around her neck. They both yawn at the same time.

'He's violent with you, isn't he?'

'Yes.'

'Oh, Amélie, I'm so sorry.'

'I really thought he was different. Pff! You'd think I'd know by now! Anyway, at first, he just pushed me around and shouted a bit – when he was drunk or had lost at Bezique. Or had a row with his wife. The usual stuff. But in the last few weeks it's got worse, much worse. Now he seems to enjoy it. A new thrill for him – the rest of it is just a prelude.' Amélie picks at one of her nails and bites her lip.

'I'm thinking of leaving him. Should I leave him, Marie?'

'I – I...'

'Sorry, I shouldn't have asked you. Ignore me, *ma petite*. I probably won't have the guts in the end, anyway. And the next one will probably be the same. Fucking bastards. All of them.'

Amélie lets out a long sigh and smooths a strand of Marie's hair off her cheek.

'Anyway, *ma petite*. Let's not talk about that. Tell me about your artist.'

As soon as he's mentioned, Marie feels her heart contract.

'He's not my artist anymore, Amélie. Or even Edgar. He's just Monsieur Degas. And I'll probably never see him again.'

'Monsieur who?'

'Degas. Monsieur Degas. That's his name. I thought I told you before. Although it doesn't matter now, does it? What's the matter, Amélie? You look like you've seen a ghost!'

'You didn't tell me before, Marie. I've never known his name.' Amélie's voice is flat. She's sitting up now, eyes wide, a strange faraway expression on her face. She scratches her head, looks around the room as if searching for something.

Marie sits up too. Ouch, the ache in her head spreads into her neck, but the pillow at her back is lovely to lean against.

'Well, he's doing an exhibition. With some other artists. It's opening in three days' time. There are posters all over the boulevard. So you've probably seen his name on that.'

Amélie gets up and pulls on a red satin dressing gown with elaborate embroidery on the back, exotic flowers and leaves. Like Madame Degas' forest in the picture in Edgar's studio. Marie shudders at the thought, it's too much to take in. She tries to turn away in her head from all that happened at the studio, the image of Edgar standing there next to the statue and smiling into her, Marie, as if he loved her.

Bright sunlight washes in from the windows and makes Marie blink. The sound of horses' hooves is a constant rhythm now, interspersed with the sound of awnings being rolled out outside Café Balthazar, stiff brooms on clean, new paving stones, whistling workmen rushing by. The workmen in Montmartre are too tired to whistle.

Amélie is coming towards her. Something in her silhouette frightens Marie.

'What is it, Amélie?'

Amélie climbs onto the bed, takes Marie's rough hands in her smooth ones, and rubs them gently.

'I have to tell you something, Marie. I thought you knew. But it's obvious to me now that you don't.'

'I don't understand. What are you talking about?'

'So, your artist is called Degas? Monsieur Edgar Degas? Tall, dark hair, moody-looking?'

Marie nods.

'I know Monsieur Degas, Marie. Or I should say I knew him. He used to come to the bar where your mother and I worked fifteen years ago. Your mother sang and he sketched her and some of the old drunks at the bar. He used to stay late some nights and drink with us.'

'Why are you telling me this, Amélie? I know he was a friend of my family. But I don't want to think about him anymore. It's all over. Let's talk about something else.'

Marie can feel the tears coming. She tries to free her hands, but Amélie holds them harder.

'Look at me, Marie. You remember when we met at the boulangerie, and I said you looked like your father?'

'Yes. Why?'

'Oh, I don't know if I should tell you – I...'

'What on earth are you saying? Amélie, *nom de dieu*! I am so sick of secrets. If you have something to tell me, say it. I've grown up all my life with people trying to cover up what happened. Tell me the truth. I have to know the truth.'

'You're sure?'

Marie looks into Amélie's eyes. There's nothing to fear. Edgar told her all about her past. There can't be anything she doesn't know.

'Yes, I'm sure.'

'So, we worked at a bar in Pigalle together, Gigi and I – didn't she ever tell you about it? No, I suppose she wouldn't have done, in the circumstances. Anyway, she was fresh in from the country and I was teaching her how to survive in the city. We became friends very quickly. Your *maman* was very beautiful then, and she made me laugh so much with her Provençal accent. I served and she sang. Gigi had such a wonderful voice, I can hear it now. Everyone said she would become a star. She used to stand like this...' Amélie jumps off the bed and stands with her arms in front of her as if conducting an orchestra and her chest thrust out. She lets out a screeching high sharp note and then bends over laughing. Marie laughs too; it's wonderful to think of Gigi commanding an audience like that.

'Oh, Marie. You should have seen her! That red hair shining out in the dark. She looked like Joan of Arc, Marie. There was something about her.'

Marie sits up on the bed and hugs her knees to her chest.

'Tell me more, Amélie. Please tell me more.'

'Very well. It was different in those days, Marie.' Amélie starts to pick discarded necklaces and ribbons off the floor and put them away as she speaks. 'People had more money then and things were easier. The bars were full of all sorts of people on the make who were happy to give big tips. And there were always a few students and artists hanging about.'

Amélie comes to sit on the bed beside Marie now. She lowers her voice and swallows hard.

'We were both a bit in love with one of them. One of the artists, I mean. He stood out from the crowd with his fancy clothes and graceful ways. A real gentleman. Mostly he was bent over a big sketchbook, scribbling away like a madman. But sometimes he'd leave the sketchbook on the bar and drink with us after closing. Gigi and I both dreamed about becoming his mistress. Do you want me to carry on, Marie? Are you sure you want to hear all this?'

Marie thinks of Gigi's bitterness about losing her career as a singer. Poor Maman, all those auditions she went to, all those awful men. She isn't sure she does want to hear more. She's not sure of anything anymore. But she finds herself speaking anyway.

'Yes, yes, please go on.'

Amélie sighs deeply and swallows. She pats Marie's legs under the covers. 'You are a brave girl, Marie.

'*Et alors*, Serge and Gigi weren't on good terms by then, I'm afraid. She was sick of his politics, had no patience with the Garde Nationale. He was always off planning demonstrations and supporting strikes. Gigi said he wasn't the man she'd married. Serge went away to Belgium for two months to be with his sick mother and that's when it happened.'

'When what happened, Amélie?'

Panic is rising up in her now.

'I'll get to that in a minute, Marie. What was I saying? Yes, so Gigi and Serge weren't getting on – she was always talking about leaving him. She used to say Serge was in love with Louise Michel but that the Red She-Wolf wasn't interested in him, or any man.'

'Really?' asks Marie. She's having trouble making sense of everything that Amélie is saying.

'I'm sorry, *ma petite*. I'll try and slow down a bit.' Amélie smooths the covers on the bed and sighs, then turns back to Marie.

'Right, where was I? Serge and Gigi. Yes. It wasn't true. What Gigi said wasn't true, Marie. It wasn't true at all. Serge was obviously devoted to her. He used to bring your sister in some nights. She was such a sweet little thing. I used to take care of her while Serge watched Gigi sing and applauded her loudly after every song. He always watched her with such tenderness, Marie, such love. No man has ever looked at me like that, I can tell you!'

Amélie lets out a dry laugh, but Marie finds herself just staring blankly at her, trying to take it all in, to imagine Papa watching Gigi like that.

'Gigi wanted flowers and fine jewellery, Marie. But Serge wasn't that kind of man – he just wasn't.'

Amélie starts picking at a nail again, lost in her reminiscences, but then seems to draw herself up again and see Marie sitting there open-mouthed. She takes Marie's hands in hers.

'Anyway, that's how Serge got to know Edgar. Soon they were huddled together most evenings talking about politics and justice – or whatever those people talk about – while I looked out for Antoinette and Gigi sang. I think Gigi was jealous, if I'm honest.'

Marie feels completely lost in Amélie's story and is starting to feel sick again.

'But what happened, Amélie? You said something happened. I don't understand why you're telling me this.'

'Sorry, *ma puce*. I'm rushing ahead. Anyway, when Serge came back from Belgium, the two of them seemed happier for a while. But then Gigi started missing work and rushing off in the middle of her act. Serge was really worried about her,

233

thought she'd got the pox or something. But I knew, Marie. I knew before she even told me.'

Amélie stops again and looks towards the window. 'I'd better feed the parrots soon. The poor loves must be starving.'

Marie pokes Amélie's thigh.

'What happened, Amélie? Tell me. You must tell me.'

Amélie swallows hard; she seems to be forcing herself on. The look of fear in her eyes is making Marie scared now.

'Well, one night I made Gigi tell me. I sat her down and told her I knew. She broke down and confessed that she was pregnant.'

'Pregnant?'

Marie fingers the satin edging on the blanket. She can't look at Amélie. Her mind panics like a horse before a huge jump, rears up, is being driven on but shrinks away at the same time.

'Yes, Marie. Pregnant. The next day Gigi left the bar. And Edgar never came back. That day we met in the boulangerie was the first time I'd seen Gigi in years. We carried on seeing each other every few weeks after you were born until you were four or five and then we... we drifted apart, what with the Commune and your dear father being killed. She wasn't the same after that, hid herself away. Emma and I tried to get her to come out to the Martyrs Tavern sometimes with the other survivors of the Vigilance Committee, but she wouldn't have anything to do with us anymore. Can't really blame her. Anyway, I had no idea you didn't know. I'm so sorry, Marie. Oh, you look shocked, *ma petite*. You've been through so much, I'm so sorry.'

Amélie puts her arms around Marie. Marie puts her head on Amélie's shoulder. She can't feel anything now. It's as if she is watching the scene from outside herself.

'Listen, don't try and work it all out now. I know it's a shock. I'll draw you a nice hot bath. You can take a clean chemise from the wardrobe and my red dress, it's the smallest I've got. Then I'll go and get us some breakfast and we'll talk some more.'

CHAPTER EIGHTEEN

Marie stays in the bath until it gets cold. She sinks deep down into the water until her nose is just above it. Amélie has gone out and all is quiet. No sound from the parrots. Amélie fed them before she went out; they've probably fallen asleep on their perches. Amélie's bath is huge with a rolled top and clawed legs. Nothing like the chipped little troughs at the bathhouse, where you are only allowed in for two minutes at a time and the water is four fingers deep. Amélie's bath is deep as a grave.

She takes a breath and slides down deeper until her nose is under the water and she can't breathe. Her hair lifts and spreads over the surface of the water above her head. She's never been fully underwater before. Her legs lift up, she feels her knees breaking through the surface and lets her arms float in the water like weeds. Her whole body feels as weightless and blank as her mind. Yes, yes. This is like sleep. This is like another world. Better than the world she's in. That world doesn't make sense anymore, doesn't belong to her anymore. Why bother ever going out into it ever again? Nobody cares if she does or if she doesn't. Better to just stay here in Amélie's white apartment, to sink under the water and let it all fade away. She opens her eyes underwater, stares at one of her hands. It looks like the hands in one of Edgar's watercolour studies. Not hers at all. In her mind she sees Edgar, then Papa. Edgar with Papa's head, Papa with Edgar's head. The pressure is building in her own head now. One of her heels jabs into the enamel and sets off a strange juddering sound. Blood beats in her ears. No, she will stay under. Enough. Enough of truth. Of reality. Of everything. She tries to breathe the water in; only a few moments then it will all be over.

She jolts out of the water, spluttering and coughing, heart galloping. A high-pitched wail comes out of her. And then the tears come. Hot against the cold bathwater on her cheeks. The struggle to continue marching on is too much and she can no longer see why she must. Damn this force that pushes her on! She wishes she could be as dead and impassive as the Little Dancer in Edgar's studio. Frozen forever. Safe and hopeful. If she could change places with her, she would. But instead, her obstinate heart beats on.

Amélie comes in some time later. Marie looks into her kind face and apologises.

'You are shivering, *ma puce*. Here, let me help you.'

Amélie drops her shopping, fusses around Marie, helps her out of the bath and into clean clothes and makes her eat.

Marie sits and says nothing, while Amélie talks and tidies up. Amélie says she's leaving the Count, she's had enough. She's going to go and see her old friends later, see if she can find some work and a place to live. She'll go back on the streets, if necessary, until she finds something better. Would Marie like more to eat?

Marie feels as if she's still underwater. She manages to shake her head, asks if she can stay a couple more nights and lies back down on the bed, shuts her eyes, and falls asleep.

*

She dreams that Madame Degas is on her seat in the forest playing with a little wax doll. Bright green parrots fly about. 'It's time,' they squawk. 'It's time.'

Madame Degas gets off her seat and points at the sky. She's wearing Louise Michel's old army coat.

'It's time,' she says. 'You must go.'

Marie feels wings sprouting under her shoulder blades. She raises her chin and feels herself taking off. Up, up, up into the sky.

When Marie wakes up, her mind feels strangely calm and clear. And now when she stands up, she feels a bit dizzy but strong again. Solid. Her spine straight and proud as a flagpole. The pain in her shoulder has gone. All her body parts are in the right place and connected. Nothing floating off.

She opens the shutters slightly so the early morning light will come in but not wake Amélie and sits down at Amélie's dressing table. It's littered with hairpins and tiny glass bottles of all colours, which scatter the morning light around the room like jewels. The white lace cloth which covers the dressing table is stained with rouge and hair powder. Marie looks at her head in the three-way mirror. The line of her nose is edged in morning light from the window behind her.

Of course. She looks again, traces her nose with a shaking finger. The steep downward slope, the fleshy tip she's always hated. Yes – yes. His nose. His horsey nose, the nose she has stared at and wanted to touch when he's mixing paint or spreading wax. As she turns her head, her hair shines purple and blue, just like his. How could she not have noticed before? How stupid she has been. She holds onto the edge of the dressing table, closes her eyes for a moment.

No wonder Maman didn't know whether that grandmother of hers was Italian or Spanish. Puh! She must have been making it up, to cover up her dirty little secret. And what about Antoinette talking about Papa calling Maman a whore the night before he was killed? The way they both froze as if a shared secret was coming out. Now it's all starting to make sense! Does Antoinette know? Has she been hiding it all these years?

She forces herself to open her eyes and look at herself in the mirror the way Louise Michel looks at her.

'But my courage comes from Papa,' she says to her reflection as she picks up a pair of scissors and starts to chop off her hair. *He brought me up, he taught me everything. He made me who I am.*

Snip! She'll never see Edgar again. She'll never have to endure an injured shoulder from clasping her hands behind her back for hours at a time, or the anger of the ballet master because she couldn't raise her arms high enough.

Snip! No more shivering while she stands naked and Edgar fiddles with the fucking Creature. No more being pushed away and ignored. No more begging for love.

Snip! He lied to her. She trusted him and he lied. Over and over again. He sat her down on the chaise longue and said he'd tell her the whole story about Papa, about how Papa died. But he lied. He held back the truth. There was that moment when he hesitated. He sat back and took a deep breath, the coal shifted in the grate. She should have known then. But she pushed her doubts away because she trusted him. What a fool! He was hiding the truth from her all along. While she stood there naked, showed her whole self to him, cried and humiliated herself in front of him.

Marie's hands are shaking now. They've all been lying to her. All of them.

She takes a deep breath, grabs a long thick strand from the nape of her neck. Snip! She holds it up to the light. It's exactly the same colour as Edgar's and Madame Degas' too, in the picture. Her grandmother. Madame Degas is her grandmother! So perhaps she really was watching over Marie all along. Poor Madame Degas – all alone on that bench, without her books. Shut in her bourgeois cage.

Marie lays the hair carefully on top of the pile. She wonders what will happen to the Little Dancer, whether the people who come to the exhibition will love her or hate her, whether they'll touch her.

Snip! Who will buy her? And where will she live? Marie shouldn't care. But she finds that she does. Edgar said he would keep the Little Dancer with him always. He said that. The thought of the Little Dancer standing alone in the echoing hallway of some grand house next to a Chinese vase makes her feel sick. Edgar must not sell her. He can't.

Snip! *The Little Dancer is not me anymore. Now I am somebody new. But without her I might still be her, waiting in the wings, half-formed, not knowing the truth.* She lets out a shuddering sigh.

Snip! Somehow that mess of wood and wax and paint has made her feel complete, more grown-up, less unformed, more defiantly real. So that's something.

Snip! And Edgar said she, the Little Dancer, was *him* in some way too. Marie didn't understand what the hell he was talking about then. But now it makes sense. Now she knows she and Edgar are joined by blood. She is part of him and he will live on through her. She must be brave and go out into the world. Because he can't and neither could Madame Degas. They are both stuck, pinned on green felt. Madame Degas on her bench, he in his studio. And, come to think about it, maybe she wouldn't be happy stuck in Edgar's apartment all day, living like a rich girl. She loves the street too much.

Snip! *I am free. I have nothing to lose. Nothing. And nobody cares if I'm like Edgar or Madame Degas. Nobody would even notice.*

She holds up the last chunk of hair from the crown of her head and twists it around her fingers. Edgar has given her the gift of freedom; he has pushed her out of the wings and into the world. Maybe that's all he could give her. A good shove. And that look he gave her. Maybe she's lying to herself, but it felt like love. No, it *was* love. She's as sure of it as she is of her own name. Her heart warms to think of it now. It was love. Not the love she thought she wanted. But love, nonetheless.

Louise says that saying vows in a church, working yourself to death as a domestic slave for your husband, signing your body away for nothing to be the possession and plaything of a man is not love.

Snip!

'*L'amour c'est la liberté, et la liberté, c'est l'amour!* Love is liberty. And liberty is love!'

It's only when the parrots jump and squawk in alarm that Marie realises she's said the words out loud. A chuckle rises up from her belly as she looks at herself in the mirror. What a funny-looking creature! Oh dear, Amélie is stirring in her sleep. *Calme-toi!*

She folds the lengths of silky dark hair in four and ties them up in one of Amélie's big silk scarves. Then she goes over to the Count's writing desk and looks in the heavy drawers for paper.

Dear Edgar – no. *Dear Monsieur Degas* – too formal. *Dear Papa* – no. Impossible. She screws the heavy sheet of cream-coloured paper into a ball and starts a new sheet.

241

Dear Edgar,

You said to me that if I loved you, I should leave you to your art. You said you wanted a part of me. So I am leaving you this package of my hair for the Little Dancer. It should be tied with a ribbon, dark green if possible. Please keep her safe.

I am leaving Paris very soon with Louise Michel but will always remember the time we spent together. I wish you well with the exhibition.

Thank you for setting me free,

Your daughter,

Marie van Goethem

Marie folds the note into an envelope and puts the envelope on top of the package of her hair. She stuffs the whole lot into her bag and stares at herself in Amélie's full-length mirror. *The old Marie is dead, I am somebody new.* The thought pleases her and scares her at the same time. She smiles at this new self, dressed in Amélie's expensive low-cut red dress and bright white, lace-edged chemise showing underneath. Her hair is a fuzzy halo in the morning light slicing through the shutters behind her. Oh, her head feels so wonderfully light without the big heavy plait dragging her down. Better not go out like this, though, or she'll be mistaken for somebody who's escaped from the asylum. She takes a few hatboxes down from the wardrobe, finds a maroon-coloured turban topped with red feathers the exact shade of her dress. Perfect. And now for the shoes. Amélie's feet are a bit smaller than Marie's, but the pain will be nothing compared to cramming her blistered toes into her damned ballet shoes, which she will never – never – have to wear again.

She picks a pair of red slippers with satin rose-buds at the toes. Then she slips Papa's rings into the deep soft pocket of the dress, slips the package of hair and the note into her bag and creeps out of the apartment.

On Boulevard Haussmann, the spring sunlight is blinding. Two ladies walking arm in arm nod at her in greeting. She looks behind her to see who they are looking at and then realises it's *her* they are greeting. Normally she scurries around and nobody notices that she even exists. She's part of the street, like the lampposts or the drains. But in her expensive clothes and hat she must look like one of them. Impossible not to be a little pleased by the attention. She smiles and apologises to Papa in her head for betraying her class.

She starts to feel sick when she finds herself at Edgar's door. She must leave the strange-looking package on the doorstep and walk away. He will know what it's for. Any wigmaker would be happy to have such thick, healthy hair and will be able to make it fit the sculpture perfectly. Her hand almost goes up to pull on the bell. If only she could see him once more. No. The most loving thing she can do now is to leave him alone. *Don't look back, Marie, don't look back.* A flash of her grandmother gesticulating at her from the bench in the jungle. *March on, Marie.* In honour of Madame Degas, and Edgar. And in Papa's honour too.

As she drags herself away, she forces herself not to look back and see if she can see his tall figure in his studio. On Place Blanche, she stops at the café and sits down to steady herself. The owner with the tiny kind eyes comes over.

'Is that you, mademoiselle? I hardly recognised you.' He rubs his eyes with one hand, while balancing a big round tray on the other. 'Wonders will never cease! Would you like a drink on me to celebrate your transformation, my little *papillon?* Not brandy perhaps.' He winks at her. 'But something more sophisticated. Maybe a *citron pressé*?'

Marie nods. She pulls the turban down to cover the stubble behind her ears, feels the feathers rippling in the breeze above her head.

'Marie! Is that you?'

Antoinette appears in front of her, bends down and kisses her on both cheeks.

'I've been looking for you everywhere. You're lucky I recognised you in that getup. It was only the way you were sitting that made me know it was you. What on earth are you wearing? Did you steal it from the costume cupboard? I heard you were sacked. When I go in, I expect I'll be sacked too! The police are crawling all over Montmartre and—'

'Listen, Antoinette. About that night at the Veau à Deux Têtes. There's nothing between me and Paul. I promise. We are just—'

'Oh, I know that. I've forgotten all about it. And anyway, who would go for a raggedy thing like you?'

Antoinette laughs wildly and stumbles against a chair, leans forward to touch the silk of Marie's turban, pulls at a tuft of hair that has escaped at the back. They haven't seen each other for ages and already Antoinette is making Marie angry. But at least it seems Antoinette is not angry about her and Paul anymore; she must have realised she'd read the situation wrong.

Antoinette draws up a chair and sits down. Her gaze is never still, it flickers to Marie's face then off again to look into the street. Her mouth twitches as if she doesn't know whether to smile or cry.

'What have you done to your hair, Marie? Were the lice that bad?'

Marie nods. She doesn't feel like explaining, and Antoinette is not listening anyway, obviously lost in her own world as usual. She's picking at one of her nails, biting her lip and frowning. She looks just like Papa when she frowns like that. And the freckles over her nose are like his. A sinking in Marie's stomach. Papa is not her papa. She has none of his blood. None. No freckles, no redness in her hair. When Amélie said she looked like her father, when they met at the bakery, Marie had been so thrilled. But Amélie meant Edgar, not Papa. That's why Gigi rushed them away, so she could keep her secret. She and Antoinette aren't even proper sisters.

Marie heaves a big sigh. Her head is itching under the turban. A lame pigeon hobbles around under the table pecking last night's crumbs out from gaps in paving stones. A war veteran with one leg hobbles past and half-heartedly asks for spare change. The café owner plonks the *citron pressé* down on the table and Antoinette takes a sip. There's so much to say. Too much. It's as if they're playing a game to see who will give in and speak first. In the end, Antoinette breaks the silence.

'Paul has been taken in by the police for questioning,' she says blankly, staring at the table.

'What? How come, what happened?'

'I was furious that night when I found you two together in the café. You looked so happy and close, laughing like that, like lovers. Anybody would have got the wrong idea.'

'But we were just—'

'Shut the fuck up and listen!' Antoinette slams her hand on the table. Her voice is so loud that the pigeon under the table flies off in panic; the proprietor stops polishing the glasses and looks over.

'Keep your fucking voice down then!' Marie hisses.

Antoinette's temper is out of control. She didn't get that from Papa. He was always calm.

'Paul explained everything the day after. But by then it was too late.'

'What, Antoinette? What do you mean? Too late?'

Antoinette takes in a deep breath. It's obvious she's trying to steady herself. She's even thinner than before. Her collar bone sticks out above her old dress when she breathes in. Her head with the mass of auburn hair piled on top looks too big for the rest of her.

'Paul refused to talk to me that night. I was so angry, I said things to him I shouldn't have said. He told me I'd lost my mind. He got undressed and fell asleep as soon as we got back to the shop. I couldn't sleep at all. I ended up looking through all his things. I looked in his trouser pocket and found that note with your writing on.

'The leaflet for the demonstration?'

'Yes. I was in such a rage, Marie. I can't explain it now. I heard old Fumble Fingers pacing about downstairs; he'd been groping me even more than usual that day. Before I could stop myself and think it through, I went down and handed him the note, told him Paul was involved with Louise Michel. I knew he'd be angry, I wanted him to be angry, wanted to wipe the smirk off his face. I thought he'd just tell Paul off, or maybe give him a beating. I never imagined he'd go to the fucking police.'

'Did you tell him about me too?'

'No, no, of course not. Oh, don't look at me like that, Marie. I just wanted to stop him going to meetings and getting poisoned by that witch, Louise Michel.'

'She's not a witch—'

246

'Oh, shut up, Marie. She's nothing but trouble. She got Papa killed. And now she's after you and Paul.'

Marie bites her lips together to hold the words back. It strikes her that Antoinette is angry because she has to be. If she calmed down, she might sink like a stone.

They both fall into that deep well of silence again. The one where secrets are kept. Marie thinks of Antoinette embracing Papa for the last time, them both falling to the ground.

I know you blame yourself for Papa's death, Antoinette. But it wasn't your fault. You were so young, you shouldn't have been there at all. Those are the words Marie really wants to say, the ones she means, the ones she's about to say. But before she can lay them out, Antoinette is off again.

'You're as bad as Paul. In fact, I blame *you*. You got him into it. And you could have stopped him. You covered up for him, you lied.'

It's impossible to make peace with Antoinette when she never stops sniping.

'I didn't. He got *me* into it if you must know.' Marie takes a sip of her drink; her hands are shaking too. 'And if you're so keen on honesty, how come you didn't tell him about your thieving?'

'You know nothing of the real world, Marie. You've always been protected.'

'Well, at least I dare to look at what's really going on, instead of getting drunk every night. And – and…'

'And what, Marie?'

'Nothing! What's the point in talking to you? You never listen, Antoinette. You never listen.'

She grabs her glass and takes a sip to stop the tears coming again. Her hands are shaking. She knocks the teaspoon off the table and onto the floor. The café owner comes to pick it up and gives her a little wink, which calms her slightly. At that moment she decides she will never tell Antoinette what she knows, the truth about Papa and Edgar. Antoinette doesn't want to know the truth and it's not up to her, Marie, to force it down her neck. There's no point. They sit in silence for what seems like hours.

'So what are you going to do? What will happen to Paul?'

'I'm going to meet Maman outside St Pierre, see if she can help.'

'Maman?' Saying the word sets off a howl inside Marie. She thought she'd hardened her heart to Gigi, but she's wrong. 'What has Maman got to do with it?'

'She has a regular client who's high up in the police.' Antoinette sits back in her chair and crosses her ankles. Her boots are covered in mud and full of holes. She jiggles her feet up and down – why can't she stay still for once? 'I'm going to ask her if she can get her policeman to get Paul off with a warning.' She crosses her feet the other way and yawns loudly. 'Anyway, the good news is that Madame Béranger is so disgusted that her bastard of a husband went to the police that she's finally seen sense and thrown him out.'

'Good. I'm glad.'

'So that means we can get married and Paul will take over the bakery.'

'Really? Oh, that's wonderful, Antoinette.'

Marie had meant to go back and hide at Amélie's straight after delivering her hair at Edgar's studio, but the pull of spending more time with Antoinette and trying to make peace, the prospect of seeing Maman once more, however painful it will be, is too strong.

'Can I walk with you for a bit?'

Antoinette rolls her eyes at Marie. 'Come on then.'

It feels so good to be walking arm in arm along the streets of Montmartre with Antoinette again. They start to hum a song together and walk in time to the tune.

'Marie, tell me the truth. Even if I manage to get Paul out, do you think he'll ever forgive me?'

'He loves you, Antoinette. He is completely devoted to you. He always has been.'

That seems to comfort Antoinette. She squeezes Marie's arm and kisses her on the cheek.

As they get to the steep part of the hill, Antoinette stops to cough. That cough hasn't gone away since she got it last autumn.

'You are as tall as me now, Marie. Have those fancy slippers got hidden heels?'

Marie laughs. Amazing that she can feel so angry with Antoinette one moment and adore her the next. It's always been like that.

'I can hardly walk in these fucking things. I have to scrunch my toes to keep them on. They're meant for the boulevards, not the muddy streets of Montmartre.'

'Unlike you and me then, Marie. We are pure Montmartre!'

'Yes, we are, and always will be!'

Marie takes off her slippers and continues in bare feet. Bits of cherry blossom stick to her blisters. She has to duck to stop the feathers in her turban getting stuck in the branches that hang over the path, which makes Antoinette break into peals of laughter.

'Hang on a minute, Marie! I forgot I've got something for you.'

Antoinette digs in her bag. 'Here! I saved these things for you yesterday. I thought you might want them.'

'Ah, *Fantine*! And Papa's old shoes. So you got there before the bailiffs? I saw the notice, but I couldn't face going back.'

'Yes. I thought you might have seen it, and that you'd probably gone to Amélie's. I made sure I got there before the bastards arrived to board up the door.'

Marie shrugs. She's surprised to find she doesn't feel sad at all. In fact, it's a relief to know that after all that struggle to keep the house, it's over. She has no home to cling to now. No going back.

'Why don't you wear Papa's shoes now?' asks Antoinette. 'You always had big feet to go with your knobbly knees. A bit of newspaper in the toes and they'll do you fine.'

Marie stares at the shoes. They are curled by use and hardened by time. There are still creases just above the toe line where Papa used to rise up and down when he was making an important point. Which was most of the time. Antoinette has obviously shined them up and replaced the laces.

'Go on then, Marie. Take them!'

But he's not my real father. How can I wear his shoes? She bites her lip to stop the words spilling out. Then something Edgar said about the sculpture comes into her mind: Reality is what interests me. Well, Edgar is her blood father, her true father. But Papa was her real father, wasn't he? It was he who tucked her into bed at night, who held her on his knee when he sewed, who roared at anybody who tried to put her down.

Something in Antoinette's look commands her. It's almost as if Papa is there with them under a cherry tree heavy with blossom, urging her to march on. To carry the flag. For the family. For the Commune.

Marie brushes dried mud and petals off her feet. She leans on Antoinette to get her balance, slips her feet into Papa's shoes and laces them up tightly.

'Here, you take Amélie's slippers. She won't notice. You should get a good price for them.'

Papa's shoes fit Marie quite well, just a slight rub on the blister on her heel when she starts to walk. 'What do you think?'

Antoinette looks Marie up and down from her fancy turban to her low-cut red dress and battered men's shoes and breaks into laughter. Marie shrugs and does a mock salute, links her arm back through Antoinette's and drags her forward. A new resolve seems to rise like sap through the worn soles of Papa's shoes. The echo of a thousand marching feet beats time with her heart. They walk on.

Antoinette asks Marie to tell her something interesting, so she describes Amélie's apartment, her make-up and clothes, the black velvet chair, but not the nasty Count. Then Antoinette describes the wedding dress she wants and how she will redecorate the bedrooms above the boulangerie. Marie knows that as long as she doesn't drag up the past or go too deep or ask too many questions, as long as she holds Antoinette's interest and doesn't frighten her, she and Antoinette can carry on chatting and laughing like this until they part. Then she can remember this time they had together forever.

And that will have to be enough.

CHAPTER NINETEEN

As they reach the gate of the churchyard of St Pierre, Marie recognises Gigi from her posture; one hand on her hip, the other hand fiddling with her hair. That was always the way she stood when she was nervous about something. When the bailiff came, or somebody complained about their laundry. Marie hasn't seen her mother for six months and the sight of her makes Marie's stomach lurch and her heart beat faster. She curses herself for coming here with Antoinette; it will only make it more difficult to leave.

Gigi is standing just outside the railings of the cemetery where Papa and his division are buried, in unmarked graves. By law, the graveyard is locked; memorials to those killed during the Commune are not allowed for fear of inciting civil unrest.

'What *are* you wearing, *ma puce*?' Gigi kisses Marie awkwardly on both cheeks. 'I love your turban, *ma chérie*. You look like a waitress at the Café des Indes!'

She smells clean. A slight whiff of alcohol on her breath maybe, but no sign of bruises on her neck or arms. Gigi and Antoinette exchange smiles. Competing for jokes and attention, as usual, with Marie left on the sidelines.

'*Bonjour, Maman.*' Her voice sounds cold, even though she doesn't mean it to. She'd stupidly hoped Gigi would cry and sweep her up in her arms. 'Are you well?'

'I am, Marie. Yes, I am. Work is going well – oh, and remember that friend from Aix I told you about, Violette? Well, I bumped into her in Pigalle the other day and we talked about opening a laundry together, maybe even moving back down to Provence.'

Marie is pleased. Gigi certainly looks well, slightly plumper than before, her complexion clear, her hair freshly washed.

'And you, Marie? Are you well? Are you still dancing at the opera?'

Her words sound more like a plea than a question.

'Yes, yes. I'm fine,' Marie lies.

'Emma told me you were staying with Amélie Reine. Landed on your feet there, eh, Marie.'

Say you're well, say I'm not guilty, let me have my happiness. That's what Gigi's tone is asking of her. That's what she has always wanted from her. And, as usual, for all Marie's talk of being honest and facing the truth, she chooses to give Maman what she wants. To cheer her up, to make her feel better, just as she has always done. For all her talk of courage, when it comes to her mother, she's a coward.

Antoinette draws Gigi aside and starts to talk about Paul. Gigi seems unsure about involving her policeman. Marie gazes into the graveyard and wonders what she is doing here, why she bothered coming at all. She closes her eyes, lifts her head to the spring sun. A warm breeze plays on her bare neck, a robin sings insistently in an old cypress tree.

She should tell them both that she knows the truth, make them face it. She could blurt it out right now. But she doesn't. She can't. The words will not form. It would be like firing a cannon at her own family, destroying this fragile peace. Even if it's false, it's better than ruining everything. Maman and Antoinette don't want to know. They never have. She must carry it alone.

Antoinette's voice starts to rise with anger.

'But why, Maman? If your damned policeman cares so much about you, he'd help you. Just offer him extra favours, threaten to tell his wife. Actually, maybe I'll tell his wife!'

Here comes a row. Just as Marie is about to step in, the sound of footsteps approaching makes them all stop and look around.

Louise Michel is marching towards them, her old army boots crunching on the gravel. She's carrying a huge bunch of red chrysanthemums. Gigi and Antoinette look open-mouthed at each other and then at Marie. She shrugs; she has no idea what Louise is doing here.

'Well, well. What a lovely surprise! Is that really you, Gigi? And Antoinette!'

Louise Michel embraces Marie and goes to embrace Gigi and Antoinette but they both shun her. Louise doesn't seem to mind.

'Glad you are in disguise, Marie. Very wise. The police are everywhere at the moment. It seems there is an informant in our midst.'

A deep silence. Antoinette's face turns a dark red, her mouth twitches.

'Don't you ever feel the need to hide, Mademoiselle Michel?' Antoinette spits out her question.

'Oh, the police won't bother with me again, my dear. Not for a while anyway. Every time I'm arrested our movement gets stronger. I begged them to incarcerate me after the bakers' demonstration and they refused. Damned cowards!'

'It's fine for you, Mademoiselle Michel. But not so easy for your disciples who take the bullets for you,' Antoinette mutters under her breath.

Louise waves Antoinette's comment aside.

'Perhaps you would all like to join me in paying your respects to our fallen soldiers? I always come here before I go away, in case I never return. To remember their sacrifice. It's important to honour the dead, don't you think?'

Marie looks into Maman's and Antoinette's blank faces and back at Louise Michel.

'I have a key to the graveyard,' Louise says. 'The gravedigger is a comrade. But we must be quick. Montmartre is swarming with police these days. Entering a proscribed graveyard carries a heavy sentence so let's hurry.'

Antoinette's face goes from dark red to white. She looks like she might faint.

'Is this where... where Papa is buried?' Antoinette starts coughing loudly.

'Well, yes of course,' says Louise Michel, inserting a huge key into the rusty lock.

'But surely you all knew?'

Antoinette makes a strange whimpering sound. She looks at Gigi for confirmation, grabs her arm. Gigi shrugs it off and stares at Louise. Marie can feel the panic rising in both of them.

'I have to go, I'm on shift soon – I...' Gigi's voice is high and shrill.

No. No. They must stay. They must all stay.

'No, don't go, please don't go, Maman! Antoinette! Please stay.'

Marie's voice seems to halt Gigi for a moment. The three of them stand in a triangle, looking at each other, paralysed. Waiting for something. For somebody to do something. It strikes Marie that this is how they've been since Papa died. Inside themselves they've been frozen like this. Unable to break away, unable to move forwards.

The robin above Marie's head falls silent. All she can hear now is the faraway rumbling of carts and the shifting of marble at the new Basilica of the Sacré-Coeur. Soon the 'marble monstrosity' will be finished and the old church of St Pierre will be demolished. What will happen to the bodies then?

Louise strides up to Gigi, shakes her by the shoulders, just as she did the night Papa died. 'Come, come, Gigi! It'll only take a few minutes. Courage!' Her voice is low as thunder, her gaze a bolt of lightning pinning each of them to the spot in turn.

And suddenly, Marie is back there. On Rue Lepic, nine years ago. She and Maman. The smell of burning. Papa's body on the table, shards of dusty light through the barricaded windows. Edgar's pale hand in the grainy dark. Louise's face up close to hers. 'Courage.' The cool weight of Papa's rings in her palm. She feels them now, in the pocket of Amélie's dress. *One for the family, one for the Commune.*

'*Allons-y!*' Louise holds the cemetery gate open, beckons with a bony, commanding arm. The brass buttons on her old army coat gleam in the spring sunshine. Two are hanging off, one has been sewn back on with crimson thread.

'Come, come, Gigi. Lead your girls in. It's been nearly a decade. It's time, Gigi, it's time.'

The graveyard is a narrow strip of ground with just a few old gravestones at one end, covered in moss. In the back corner is a long, low unmarked mound. Louise leads them there.

'This is the place. One day we will have a proper memorial for our brave comrades. Every name shall be etched in stone.

We shall sing and fire live ammunition into the air! Stand there. Yes, there, at the foot of the mound.'

They line up awkwardly opposite Louise. Gigi in the middle, Marie and Antoinette either side, hands clasped, heads down. Marie tries not to faint. She feels as if she can't breathe, as if she has rope coiled tightly around her stomach like Degas' sculpture. She looks down at her feet. This must be the mound of earth where Papa lies with his comrades, buried in a makeshift wooden coffin. She wiggles her feet in Papa's shoes, nudges a patch of daisies, tries not to imagine Papa's decaying body beneath her feet.

'On the 23rd of May 1871, here at the church of St Pierre, we fought and lost the battle for Montmartre and buried our dead. May all the soldiers of the third battalion of Montmartre, who gave their blood for the people of Paris, rest in peace.'

Marie glances to the side at Antoinette and Gigi. But they both have their eyes closed. She looks into Louise's eyes to steady herself.

'May Serge van Goethem, father to Antoinette and Marie, husband to Gigi, rest in peace.'

Louise makes the sign of the cross, looks up to the sky.

'He fought valiantly.' Louise pauses here. She fixes her eyes on Antoinette, but Antoinette doesn't look up.

'Would you like to say a few words, Antoinette?' Antoinette keeps her head down and shakes it slightly.

'May Serge's spirit live on in his family and in the struggle for the liberty of working people all over the world. *Vive la Commune!*'

Marie looks up and raises her fist to the sky. All her tiredness, her doubt, her hesitation falls away. It feels to her as if her very bones are humming with new life.

'*Vive la Commune!*'

But Antoinette and Gigi stay silent. She can hear Antoinette breathing heavily. Gigi doesn't seem to be breathing at all.

Louise unties the string around her bunch of chrysanthemums, hands one to each of them. She lays a single flower on the grave and makes the sign of the cross, gestures to Marie to do the same.

The stem is still wet in Marie's hand. She steps forward, lays the stem gently on the grave. As she touches her hand to the right and left side of her chest, to her forehead and then her heart, she feels that something broken is being mended inside her. When she looks up, Louise is smiling at her. Or as near a smile as Louise is capable of.

Now, it's the turn of Gigi and Antoinette.

Gigi steps forward quickly and drags Antoinette with her. She lays her stem on the grave so tenderly that Marie feels tears welling up.

'Come on, *ma puce*,' Gigi whispers to Antoinette.

Antoinette opens her eyes, looks from Gigi to Marie. Her mouth is twitching. The terror in her eyes makes Marie gasp.

'Go on, Antoinette,' whispers Marie. 'You can do it!'

Antoinette makes the strange whimpering sound again. She throws herself on the ground face first and starts crying.

'Papa! No, no! Papa, no. Papa, Papa.'

Marie's never heard Antoinette sob like that. She starts to choke on her tears and cough at the same time. Marie squats down by Antoinette and strokes her hair. If only she could have been there nine years ago. Marie looks up at Gigi. But Gigi is staring at Louise with pure hatred.

'Police! Police!'

Marie recognises the booming voice of Marceau.

'Run, comrades, run!' cries Louise. 'If any of you are caught in here, you'll be blacklisted forever. I'll stay here and distract them.'

Marie wipes Antoinette's tears with the skirts of Amélie's dress and helps her onto her feet.

'*Je t'adore*, Antoinette.'

'I love you too, Marie,' Antoinette shouts over her shoulder and starts to run. Gigi follows Antoinette, as if she's in a daze.

'I'll see you soon, Marie.'

'Yes, yes. *Au revoir, Maman.*'

Louise winks at Marie.

'Go, Marie. Go! Take Rue Saint-Rustique. The train leaves at noon the day after tomorrow. Make sure you are not followed.'

'Thank you, Louise. Thank you.'

Marie dashes out onto the street. She can see two policemen standing a bit further down. One of them points at her, blows his whistle and starts running headlong towards her. A strange elation grips Marie as she gathers speed and darts into a side alley. She finds herself laughing like a madwoman. She knows what she must do now. She knows the way forward.

As she picks her way down over the steep cobbles of Rue Saint-Rustique in Papa's shoes, holding her turban on with one hand, she feels she might take off and fly.

CHAPTER TWENTY

1 April 1880

Hiss, thump, hiss. Pfsh, hiss, thump. Pfffft. Pscht. The sound of hot metal on water takes Marie back to the laundry. So much noise, so much life. It's frightening and thrilling at the same time. People are streaming in, looking right and left, trying to find their bearings. Suitcases everywhere, railway workers weaving in and out in their blue uniforms.

Marie remembers again that trip to St Lazare station with Papa and Antoinette so long ago, when he was determined to show them 'the meaning of modernity'. Papa had the most rapturous expression on his face, as if he was taking communion at Chartres. He made a speech about how technology would bring freedom to the workers, promised he would let them ride on one of the sleek black engines one day. So much for modernity! All it's done so far is to put Gigi's laundry out of business and push up rents.

'Excuse me, sir!'

Marie turns to find a porter with a cart piled high with luggage frowning at her.

'Excuse me, sir!'

She moves out the way but can't stop herself laughing out loud. Marie cannot believe that their trick has worked, that people really do mistake her for a boy. It was Amélie's idea to disguise herself like this when they realised the police would be watching out for a small young woman in a turban. Amélie told Marie that many of the women on the Vigilance Committee dressed as men during the Commune, that some of them regretted ever having to go back to corsets and bulky skirts after wearing shirts and trousers. Marie hid at the apartment while Amélie went out and bought her a tweed suit and an English cap, then they spent yesterday dressing her up and getting her ready. Amélie taught her how to walk, sit and stand like a man. It was much easier than when she'd tried to teach Marie how to flirt. Amélie declared her a natural and set about polishing Papa's shoes to a high shine.

Marie tugs her cap lower over her forehead, adjusts her waistcoat, puts her bag on the floor between her legs so it doesn't get stolen, plants her feet wide apart like a man. *Fantine* is stashed at the bottom of the bag along with her old dress and a couple of Amélie's chemises. Marie sighs and wonders how she will ever manage without Amélie.

An excited-looking couple rush past Marie towards the ticket office. They are speaking some foreign language, which Marie thinks might be English. She tries to say *Dieppe* to herself in the mangled way they do and to imagine what it will be like in England.

Louise Michel had talked about the trip when they were all gathered in the Martyrs Tavern. At the time, Marie had had no wish to ever leave Paris. Somehow, she doesn't feel sad at all to be leaving now – perhaps she has run out of tears. She remembers Louise saying she'd arranged lodgings in the stables of a huge house in London belonging to a grand lady called Madame Pankhurst, who apparently wears strange silk dresses with no corset at all. That made Marie's ears prick up – the lady sounded fascinating, a bit like Amélie. Louise added that the lady was very kind, could speak good French and was very much to be trusted, an honorary Communard. 'And you will have hot running water in the stables. And your own beds and as much to eat as you like.' That sounded tempting but Marie had thought to herself at the time that wild horses couldn't drag her away from Montmartre and Degas. How quickly things have changed. Louise Michel was a little vague about what exactly they would be doing. But she did say there would be plenty of work sewing and washing banners and sashes. Well, very soon she will find out.

A whistle sounds and Marie is suddenly besieged by fears that she will drown in *La Manche* or get abducted by highwaymen. She makes herself jut out her chin like the Little Dancer and summon her courage. Louise Michel will protect her. And at least she'll see the sea and find out if it really is salty.

The slow tick of the huge station clock above her head is grinding on Marie's nerves. She taps Papa's shoe on the tiled floor in time with it. No sign of Louise Michel. No wonder really since the train doesn't go for over an hour. Her mind is racing again now, making her feel dizzy. The smoke is sticking in her throat and her head itches. A lock of pomaded hair falls onto her forehead, and she tries to smooth it back with the heel of her hand, the way men do.

Today is the first day of Edgar's exhibition. She promised herself she'd stay away. It would do no good to go. The gallery will be open right now. It's only a brisk fifteen-minute walk away. Easily enough time to get back before the train goes. Where will *Little Dancer* be? Her stomach flutters to think of it. In pride of place in the middle or stuck in a corner somewhere? Will Edgar be there? A quick peek in the window can't hurt. She's already halfway out of the station before she realises that she's forgotten her bag and rushes back to grab it.

Marie is out of breath by the time she reaches Rue des Pyramides. She stares at an exhibition poster on a wall outside a café to check she is indeed in the right place. This seems to be a quiet residential street, no sign of the kind of place where an exhibition might be held. She was imagining a grand building or at least a large shopfront. The screeching sound of a carpenter's plane from the building site opposite makes Marie jump. A door opens behind scaffolding and a striking-looking woman carrying a canvas with hair piled very high on her head rushes out and starts shouting at the carpenter to be quiet. This must be the place. A man in a top hat comes out and starts talking to the lady. Is it him? Is it Edgar? Her heart starts to gallop. No time for hesitation. She crosses the road and enters the building. There's a sign saying the exhibition is on the second floor.

'*Excusez-moi, monsieur!*' A boy clutching a notebook is thundering down the staircase pursued by a red-faced doorman. 'I told you earlier. No sketching, you scallywag.' Marie takes the opportunity while the doorman is distracted to run up the remaining stairs and slip into the gallery. It's a dusty room the size of Edgar's studio. There's no sign of Edgar. Or the Little Dancer. Just some pictures of fields on the walls and an angry-looking man in steel-rimmed glasses, standing in the middle of the room, jabbing a pencil into a notebook.

Raise your chin, Marie, act as if you own the place. That's what Papa used to say when they walked into the museum. Yes. She is dressed smartly enough, she could easily be a visitor, interested in the art.

She walks around the room, affecting the leisurely, lilting walk of the bourgeoisie, remembering to look around with her chin up, and not smile too much. No sign of the Little Dancer anywhere. She must go soon, or she'll miss the train. But she cannot leave without seeing the Little Dancer. She must see her before she leaves. She must.

The gallery is starting to fill up now. Several ladies in huge hats are chatting next to a small canvas showing some tired-looking flowers in a blue vase.

From the other end of the gallery, Marie's eye is caught by the man in the steel-rimmed glasses. He is walking around in circles, the metal heels of his shoes tapping the tiled floor like a metronome. As she gets closer, she realises he's walking around an empty glass case. It reminds her of one of the display cabinets at the museum where they used to house dusty monkeys and ancient pottery. It's a little taller than her and quite narrow. The size of a small coffin. An image of Papa's body crammed into a wooden box flashes through her mind.

She follows the man's gaze to a small label on the top right-hand corner of the case:

Little Dancer, aged fourteen years.

Marie swallows hard. Where is she? There's nothing there. The glass casket is completely empty.

The man with the pencil and pad catches Marie's eye. 'Have you ever seen anything like it? This whole exhibition is an obscenity!' He twiddles his pencil around in his perfectly manicured fingers, pushes his spectacles down his nose and stares into the case.

'You look confused, monsieur. Can I help you at all?'

Marie turns around to see a handsome gentleman with the penetrating gaze of a bailiff and the warm smile of a priest. It must be Caillebotte. Edgar has always said he has the kind of charm that cheats American ladies out of their inheritances.

'I – I'm just looking. *Merci, monsieur.*'

'Do I know you, monsieur? You look very familiar.'

Caillebotte is staring at her now. He will certainly have seen the Little Dancer.

She must get out now, before he realises who she is. What if he calls the police on her? You never know who might be a spy, that's what Louise Michel always warns. Trust nobody. Nobody.

Out on the street she is dazzled once again by the sunlight reflecting off the zinc-topped tables in the café. How can she leave without knowing what's happened to the Little Dancer? Just one more look. She shields her eyes with her hands and looks up at the second-floor window. There's the man in the top hat again. She can't see the details of his face, but it must be him. It must be Edgar. She can make out the white cuffs of his shirt under his jacket and his big pale hands clasped in front of him. Has he seen her? He seems to straighten up. He turns towards the window. Surely he's seen her?

The sun is beating down on Marie's neck as she squints up at the window.

'Marie, Marie! Is that really you?'

Marie turns around and finds herself face to face with the unmistakable figure of Mary Cassatt. Mary is dressed in a black taffeta dress with lace sleeves and a miniature top hat, with veil to match, perched on her neat little head. Mary tilts up the peak of Marie's cap and stares at her. Marie notices powdery beads of sweat on Mary's top lip.

'What on earth have you done with your hair, and why are you dressed like a boy?'

'I'm – it's – it's a costume. I'm on my way to – to a rehearsal and…'

'Never mind, I haven't got time for all that now. Have you seen Edgar at all in the past few days, *ma petite*?'

The endearment is so irritating coming from Mary Cassatt. And there's a hint of accusation in her question.

'No, mademoiselle.'

Marie can feel herself blushing at the lie. But Mary is too flustered to notice, she keeps looking over towards the door and tapping her manicured fingers against her fan.

Marie must get back before she misses the train. But she can't help herself staying to find out more.

'Why? Is there a problem, mademoiselle?'

'More like *une catastrophe*, my dear. My paintings are receiving a good reception so far, despite this awful, squalid exhibition space, thank God. What on earth was Gustave thinking? I should have taken charge of it myself. Excuse me babbling on, my dear, I'm a little overwrought. Anyway, the thing is that Edgar's beloved *Little Dancer* was supposed to be the star of the show. And instead, we have an empty glass case. At the soirée for the press last night, it was all the critics could talk about and Edgar was nowhere to be seen. It was embarrassing. I just don't understand it. He was totally obsessed with his damned sculpture and now he won't even talk about it.'

Mary snaps open her fan, starts waving it furiously. Then she snaps it shut and leans in towards Marie.

'Are you sure nothing has happened between you and Edgar?'

How delicious it is to have a secret that she and Edgar share, that Mary won't ever know anything about.

'No. Nothing's happened. Nothing at all.'

Mary Cassatt is frowning at her now, narrowing her eyes like she did at the hat shop, whenever Edgar spoke to her.

Jealousy! That's what it is. Mademoiselle Cassatt is jealous of her! How delicious! Marie bites her lip to stop herself smiling.

'Did he say anything else, mademoiselle? When you talked to him about it, I mean?'

'Oh, he just got very angry. You know how he is, gritting his teeth and flaring those nostrils.'

So, Mary watches him too. Perhaps they are lovers, after all. Well, it's none of Marie's business now, she really mustn't think about it.

'But what exactly did he say?' She tries not to sound too desperate, but she must know. She must.

'Well, he did say something rather strange,' Mary mutters. 'But that's not unusual for him and I didn't really pay any attention.'

'What was it he said?'

Marie's heart is thumping so loudly now, she's surprised Mademoiselle Cassatt can't hear it.

'He said he wanted to keep her close for a while. Keep her safe. Sometimes I fear his mind will collapse like his poor mother's. I tried to talk sense into him; I reminded him that we needed to make this exhibition a success and that I wouldn't bail him out forever. But he just got that faraway look he sometimes gets and started mumbling something about reality or freedom, I can't remember which. I must admit I was so furious by then that I wasn't in the mood for listening to one of his lectures.'

Marie makes an excuse and leaves. She asked Edgar to keep *Little Dancer* safe in the letter she left at his house, and he has done just that. So he must have read it, and he's done what she asked. Perhaps he even guessed she was in trouble with the police and wanted to keep her image hidden until she had left, hence the empty vitrine. Well, that thought really is something to warm her when she's tucked in her English bed. She stashes the thought close to her heart and weaves her way in and out of the morning crowd humming '*Le Temps des Cerises*' to herself with a definite masculine swagger in her step.

It's lovely and cool back in the station, but there's still no sign of Louise Michel. Only five minutes until the train departs! Maybe she won't turn up. She might have changed her mind. Or she could easily have been arrested again. The station is filling up now. Marie steps to the side to see if she can see Louise Michel and a maid carrying a stack of hat boxes swerves around her, muttering something about young men with their heads in the clouds.

Ah, there's Louise Michel now. Up on the Pont de l'Europe. Through the iron latticework of the bridge, Marie can see her striding through the crowds, holding a red handkerchief high in the air and trailed by the usual crowd of loyal followers.

A burst of whistles, men shouting things Marie can't understand, a tide of people surging towards the train in front of them from every direction.

'*Allons-y!*' Louise Michel shouts, raising her long bony arm in the air like a railway signal. They all follow in Louise Michel's wake along to the far end of the platform, up two metal steps into a carriage at the front end of the train. She leads them along an endless corridor, with tarnished brass fittings and dirty windows, into a small, stuffy compartment. It's made for eight people, with plush red velvet banquettes on either side, stained with pomade. Louise Michel declares that twelve will easily fit, that they must stay together in case of trouble. Marie finds herself sitting next to the lady from New Caledonia with the turban, who tells her she looks very handsome and giggles. The lady smells of church. Louise Michel sits bolt upright by the window, still as a church spire. A few cursory introductions are issued, and Louise congratulates Marie on her disguise. Marceau sits next to Louise Michel, dressed in his best Sunday suit. Opposite Marie there's a tiny, very wrinkled lady she recognises from the Martyrs Tavern, who sits with her feet resting on a stack of crumpled pamphlets, looking absolutely miserable.

A burst of whistles and shouts, the train coughs and lurches. Marie falls against the turbaned lady, who is still chuckling to herself and offers Marie a cherry from a paper bag. Marceau is beaming like a child on a *jour de fête*. Even the tiny lady is smiling now.

As the train starts to move, Marie feels an unstoppable excitement rising inside her, like a flag. The platform slides by, like a remembered dream. A cloud of steam from the engine up ahead seems to take on the shape of Papa's face.

The astonishing machine takes up a rhythmic canter over the huge flat fields Marie used to stare at from the roof of the house on Rue Lepic. *Rat-a-tat-tat, rat-a-tat tat.* Brass candle holders rattle, the whole carriage shakes. As Marie watches the last dregs of Paris slide by, the train settles into a smooth low gallop. *Da-da-dm, da-da-dm.* She smiles as the giant iron horse clatters over the sleepers laid out beneath her feet like bar stops on the conductor's sheet music at the opera house. She sniffs the air and catches a whiff of salt. Soon she will see the sea.

'*Au futur, les filles. Au futur!*' the train seems to sing. Over and over again.

AFTERWORD

Degas' *Little Dancer* was absent for the duration of the exhibition in 1880. An empty vitrine took centre stage for four weeks, much to the consternation of critics and public alike.

The actual sculpture appeared one year later, at the Sixth Impressionist Exhibition in 1881. She shook the art world, was greeted with shock, anger and disgust by the public and most critics, and was never seen again in Degas' lifetime.

She was, however, never forgotten. By her absence she gained almost legendary status and influenced, among others, the poet Mallarmé and the artist Walter Sickert.

Degas kept the sculpture in his studio until he died. He resolutely refused to exhibit her, and in 1903 he doggedly fought off two attempts to buy her by Louisine Havemeyer, a prominent benefactor, suffragist and friend of Mary Cassatt. Degas was always passionately disinterested in money.

When *Little Dancer* was found after Degas' death, she was in a miserable state. His family set about making bronze replicas and selling them to galleries, museums and collectors all over the world for very large sums. They allowed the original to be bought for a pittance and taken to America, where she resides to this day at the National Gallery of Art in Washington, D.C.

Marie van Goethem was sacked from the opera. No records of her later life or death have ever been found.

ACKNOWLEDGEMENTS

I'd like to thank Umi Sinha for her early work on shaping the book, Fiona Lensvelt for championing it, Rachael Kerr for being the best editor I could have dreamt of and DeAndra Lupu for bringing the project together so artfully, as well as the excellent design team and all the other wonderful people at Unbound.

Thanks, as ever, must also go to my husband, Craig Melvin, for always believing in me, shamelessly promoting my work and cheering me on and up.

A NOTE ON THE AUTHOR

Melanie Leschallas is a writer, performer, therapist and yoga teacher who danced and modelled in Paris in her twenties.

She holds a BA from Bristol University in French and Italian and two MAs – one in Drama and Movement Therapy from Central School in London and one in Creative Writing and Authorship from Sussex University.

Melanie divides her time between the UK and Spain, where she leads yoga and creativity retreats from her house in the magical mountains behind Málaga.

Unbound is the world's first crowdfunding publisher, established in 2011.

We believe that wonderful things can happen when you clear a path for people who share a passion. That's why we've built a platform that brings together readers and authors to crowdfund books they believe in – and give fresh ideas that don't fit the traditional mould the chance they deserve.

This book is in your hands because readers made it possible. Everyone who pledged their support is listed below. Join them by visiting unbound.com and supporting a book today.

Louisa Ackland
Geoff Adams
Ali Ali
Iain Anderson
Moose Azim
Lee Baker
Grace Barnes
Shelley Barnes
Tim Barton
Jacob Bartynski
Adam Bates
Helen Beard
Ramesh Bhayani
Pete Blunt
Suzy Bolt

Thaisa Box
Eleni Calligas
Livia Carlini Schmidt
Peter Carr
Jane Carter
Sarah Chiappini
Andrea Childs
David Michael Clarke
Toni Clarke
Martin Cole
Clara Cornaro
Jenny Crabbe
Daisy Cresswell
Tayler Cresswell
Jessica Duchen

Breeda Duggan
Tom Ellett
Teresa Elliott
Darvish Fakhr
Eimear Flynn
Claire Ford
Janet Freeman
Zoe Freeman
Nigel Gilderson
Mike Grenville
Damien Griffin
Beverley Hamilton
Julie Harding
Flo Hardy
Gail Hewitt
Rebecca Hindle
Sue Hirschler
Helen Hubert
Tom Hulley
Gabrielle James
Mary Jordan-Smith
Vincent and Caroline Kamp
Fozia Khanam
Dan Kieran
Hayley Knight
Cicely Knowles
Susan Lansdell
Fiona Lensvelt
Anna Liversidge
Julia Marshall
Marie McGinley

Alan Meggs
Craig Melvin
David Melvin
Mel Melvin
Lucy Miller
John Mitchinson
Fiona Moncur
Ellie Monks
Paula Moorhouse
Bernard Moxham
Sean Murphy
Carlo Navato
Niels Aagaard Nielsen
Lorraine O'Mahoney
Steph Parker
Cassie Parkes
Rebecca Partridge
Esme Pears
Bianca Pellet
Sharon Lee Perkins
Belinda Peters
Alessandra Pino
Justin Pollard
Ali Prosser
Mark Pruce
Micha Ramsay
Barbara Richards
Joe Roberts
Andreas Robichaux
Carla Rollins
Beverley Ross

Janet Rutter
Paul Savage
David Shrigley
Milly Sinclair
Greg Spiro
Lucinda Sporle
Jonty Summers
June Swindell
Karen Turner
Clive Upton
Alex Vernon

Tamsin Walker
Shirley Walton
Stanley Watson
Lucy Wilkes
James Wingfield
Pete Wingfield
R Wingfield
Ceri Womack
Leigh Woolf
Timothy Wright